Node.js for Beginners

A comprehensive guide to building efficient, full-featured web applications with Node.js

Ulises Gascón

Node.js for Beginners

Group Product Manager: Rohit Rajkumar

Publishing Product Manager: Vaideeshwari Roshan

Senior Content Development Editor: Feza Shaikh

Technical Editor: K Bimala Singha

Copy Editor: Safis Editing

Project Coordinator: Shagun Saini

Indexer: Subalakshmi Govindhan

Production Designer: Joshua Misquitta

Marketing Coordinators: Anamika Singh and Nivedita Pandey

First published: May 2024

Production reference: 2230424

Published by Packt Publishing Ltd.

Grosvenor House

11 St Paul's Square

Birmingham

B3 1RB, UK

ISBN 978-1-80324-517-1

www.packtpub.com

To all the maintainers who are thanklessly keeping the modern world turning.

– Ulises Gascón

Contributors

About the author

Ulises Gascón is a member of the **Express Technical Committee (TC)**, as well as a **Node.js core collaborator** and releaser. With over 10 years of experience as a software engineer, he has worked for prominent companies such as Google and IBM, as well as various consultancy firms and start-ups. Additionally, he is a leading contributor to numerous open-source organizations and projects, with several packages ranking in the top 25 on the npm registry.

He has earned recognition as a **Docker Captain**, **Microsoft Most Valuable Professional** (MVP), and **Google Developer Expert** (GDE) for his noteworthy contributions to the Node.js community. With extensive experience, he specializes in building IoT solutions with open hardware, developing SaaS products, creating developer tools, managing microservices, migrating legacy systems, and designing distributed systems.

I want to thank the people who have been close to me and supported me, especially my family.

About the reviewers

Abhijeet De Sarkar is a senior engineer with experience in designing and building scalable systems in the fraud detection, Fintech, and Edtech domains. His expertise is in Node.js, TypeScript, Golang, MongoDB, PostgreSQL, and Kafka. He is the founder of Hyperlearn.

Jon Wexler, senior engineer and leader of Hacky Apps, combines his vast experience in tech with deep Node.js expertise. Known for turning complex concepts into accessible projects, Jon's work spans from leading innovative app development to educating at coding bootcamps. His practical approach has earned him accolades, making him a guiding force in the industry. As the author of *Get Programming with Node.js*, he empowers developers to elevate their skills through real-world applications, reflecting his commitment to tech excellence and leadership.

Pranshu Jain is a dynamic software engineer renowned for his innovative approach and user-centric solutions. With a strong background in open source development, he has revolutionized user experiences with creations such as the Sunbird ED-Search widget. Pranshu's talent lies in translating complex business requirements into practical solutions, showcased through his successful roles at Parentheses Labs and DigiLocker. Proficient in cloud technologies, full stack, and API development, Pranshu is committed to driving noble initiatives forward. His collaborative spirit and unwavering commitment to excellence make him a valuable asset in any project. Follow Pranshu's journey on LinkedIn at @ pranshu32 to stay updated on his impactful contributions.

Table of Contents

3

JavaScript Fundamentals   25

4

Asynchronous Programming   67

Part 2: Node.js Ecosystem and Architecture

5

Node.js Core Libraries   87

6

External Modules and npm   103

7

Event-Driven Architecture   129

Part 3: Web Application Fundamentals

9

Handling HTTP and REST APIs   159

10

Building Web Applications with Express   181

Part 4: Building Solid Web Applications with Node.js

11

Building a Web Application Project from Scratch   209

12

Data Persistence with MongoDB   235

13

User Authentication and Authorization with Passport.js   257

14

Error Handling in Node.js   279

15

Securing Web Applications   289

Part 5: Mastering Node.js Deployment and Portability

16

Deploying Node.js Applications   307

17

Dockerizing a Node.js Application   325

Preface

Hello world! *Node.js for Beginners* is a book designed with a specific goal in mind: to take you from zero to deployment as quickly as possible while building a real application that reinforces the lessons from every chapter.

Node.js has been a leading technology for many years, and while there are numerous resources available to learn from, this book takes a unique approach. The knowledge you gain here will remain relevant even if you decide to change parts of your tech stack. Let me illustrate this now with an example.

Throughout the book, we use MongoDB, a non-relational database, to build our project. You might wonder how to adapt the project if you prefer using PostgreSQL, for instance. The approach I've taken in writing this book will make such transitions smoother. You'll have unit tests and a clear interface to manage these changes seamlessly. I wrote a dedicated chapter to introduce testing with the Node. js API and using third party libraries such as *Jest* or *supertest* and we integrate tests as a security net that allows us to refactor the code without fear.

I've written this book from the perspective of 2024, thinking about what I wish I had been taught when I was new to Node.js.

The book covers the wide range of challenges you'll encounter while building a web application, from REST API design principles to security and proper application distribution with Docker, continuous integration, and much more.

It's a consolidation of what I've been teaching my students and sharing with the community for the last decade. I hope you'll find it as enjoyable to read as I found it to write.

Also, at the end of every chapter, you will find additional resources that will help you explore more deeply and learn the concepts that are most relevant to you.

Who this book is for

Node.js for Beginners is a comprehensive introduction for those who are new to Node.js and/or web application development that will have you up to speed in no time. It will also help more experienced hands if you just want to refresh or extend your knowledge.

The three main personas who are the target audience of this content are as follows:

- Any developer who is interested in learning Node.js quickly or wants to use Node.js to develop a web application

- Frontend developers who want to learn more about backend development or become full stack developers with Node.js

- Developers who already use Node.js on a daily basis and want to expand or refresh their knowledge in certain areas

What this book covers

Chapter 1, Introduction to Node.js, provides an introduction to Node.js as a runtime and also explains the core architecture behind the single thread. It will also cover the versioning of Node.js and its release schedule.

Chapter 2, Setting Up the Development Environment, covers how to install Node.js on the most popular operating systems and you will learn how to manage multiple versions of Node.js on the same machine. It will also cover how to use the Node.js REPL and the web browser console to debug Node.js and JavaScript applications.

Chapter 3, JavaScript Fundamentals, helps you to refresh your knowledge of JavaScript basics such as operators and loops. You will also learn how to use specific JavaScript features such as closures, hoisiting, and prototype inherit.

Chapter 4, Asynchronous Programming, teaches you how to implement the callback pattern, handle promises, and use Async/Await syntax, and you will also learn how to properly combine all the patterns, including error handling

Chapter 5, Node.js Core Libraries, covers the core libraries' structure including the stability index and command-line options for the Node.js binary. Also, you will learn how to modularize any code using ESM and CJS and how to combine them.

Chapter 6, External Modules and npm, covers how to use the NPM CLI to manage dependencies, and use npx to use CLI tools without adding them to your project. You will learn how to build isomorphic code that can be executed in Node.js and in the browser and you will publish your first package to npm. We will also discuss npm alternatives such as Yarn or PnPM.

Chapter 7, Event-Driven Architecture, explores how the event-driven architecture is included in many core libraries such as `fs` and `http`. You will create applications that react to changes in files or receive HTTP requests, and will learn how to include an event API in your own modules as an API layer.

Chapter 8, Testing in Node.js, explores how testing is done in Node.js and all the possible approaches. We will use the Core testing library and Jest to build unit tests, and will use the coverage report to understand where to improve our testing strategy. Additionally, we will explore how the **Test-Driven Development** (**TDD**) approach in practical terms.

Chapter 9, Handling HTTP and REST APIs, teaches different strategies to build a web application (such as SPAs and server-side rendering) and how HTTP is structured in a way that allows us to build modern and solid APIs (with HTTP headers, status codes, payloads, and versions). We also learn how to use te URLs to build powerful interfaces while transferring data using JSON format.

Chapter 10, Building Web Applications with Express, shows how to use Express in depth (request, response, redirections, status codes, and header management) and also covers how to use middleware libraries and built your own ones.

Chapter 11, Building a Web Application Project from Scratch, We will begin our work on our project and will build a REST API covered by tests using the supertest library. This project will evolve, so we will iterate over the project adding new features and new tests, so you can experience the full development cycle of a real world application using Node.js.

Chapter 12, Data Persistence with MongoDB, demonstrates how to set up MongoDB and how to handle secrets in Node.js (.env files and environmental variables). We will explore the ORM universe with Mongoose and will evolve the project to use MongoDB as the database solution, including tests and coverage reports.

Chapter 13, User Authentication and Authorization with Passport.js, teaches the differences between authentication and authorization, as well exploring how modern web security is built based on cryptography by covering in detail how **JSON Web Tokens (JWT)** work. We will also implement this with our middleware in the project, and will learn how Passport.js can be used to handle social login strategies.

Chapter 14, Error Handling in Node.js, covers how to make our applications more resilient by properly defining and handling errors of any kind. We also see how to gracefully shut down the application and avoid generating zombie processes.

Chapter 15, Securing Web Applications, explores social the impact and attack vectors for your projects. We will explore how the OWASP Top 10, **Common Weakness Enumeration (CWE)**, and **Common Vulnerabilities and Exposures (CVE)** work together to evaluate risks and mitigate them in our applications. We also cover the offical Node.js security best practices and the thread model. You will have the opportunity to put all of this into practice with the project that we build together, along with exploring other ways to grow in this area by exploring the ethical hacker universe.

Chapter 16, Deploying Node.js Applications, sees us deploy our application to the public internet, emphasizing clear requirements and solution choices. We will use GitHub Actions for CI, and DigitalOcean, PM2 and MongoDB Atlas for the database

Chapter 17, Dockerizing a Node.js Application, we deploy our application to the public internet using Docker and DigitalOcean. Also we will use GitHub Actions for Continous Integration (CI). We will explore domain setup, Cloudflare SSL, and the twelve-factor app principles.

The author acknowledges the use of cutting-edge AI, such as ChatGPT, with the sole aim of enhancing the language and clarity within the book, thereby ensuring a smooth reading experience for readers. It's important to note that the content itself has been crafted by the author and edited by a professional publishing team.

To get the most out of this book

Software/hardware covered in the book	Operating system requirements
JavaScript	Windows, macOS, or Linux
Node.js and Node.js core libraries	Docker
Docker	Node.js 20.x
npm packages (Express, Mongoose, Passportjs, etc.)	

If you are using the digital version of this book, we advise you to type the code yourself or access the code from the book's GitHub repository (a link is available in the next section). Doing so will help you avoid any potential errors related to the copying and pasting of code.

Download the example code files

You can download the example code files for this book from GitHub at `https://github.com/PacktPublishing/NodeJS-for-Beginners`. If there's an update to the code, it will be updated in the GitHub repository.

We also have other code bundles from our rich catalog of books and videos available at `https://github.com/PacktPublishing/`. Check them out!

Code in Action

The Code in Action videos for this book can be viewed at `https://packt.link/FDJvJ`.

Conventions used

There are a number of text conventions used throughout this book.

`Code in text`: Indicates code words in text, database table names, folder names, filenames, file extensions, pathnames, dummy URLs, user input, and Twitter handles. Here is an example: "To use a `.nvmrc` file, you will need to create a file called `.nvmrc` in the root of your project with the Node.js version that you want to use."

A block of code is set as follows:

```
userSchema.pre('save', async function (next) {
  const user = this
  if (user.isModified('password')) {
    const salt = await bcrypt.genSalt()
    user.password = await bcrypt.hash(user.password, salt)
  }
  next()
})
```

When we wish to draw your attention to a particular part of a code block, the relevant lines or items are set in bold:

```
userSchema.pre('save', async function (next) {
  const user = this
  if (user.isModified('password')) {
    const salt = await bcrypt.genSalt()
    user.password = await bcrypt.hash(user.password, salt)
  }
  next()
})
```

Any command-line input or output is written as follows:

```
encodeURIComponent('P@ssword') // P%40ssword
```

Bold: Indicates a new term, an important word, or words that you see onscreen. For instance, words in menus or dialog boxes appear in **bold**. Here is an example: "Open DevTools by right-clicking on the page and clicking **Inspect**."

Tips or important notes
Appear like this.

Get in touch

Feedback from our readers is always welcome.

General feedback: If you have questions about any aspect of this book, email us at customercare@packtpub.com and mention the book title in the subject of your message.

Errata: Although we have taken every care to ensure the accuracy of our content, mistakes do happen. If you have found a mistake in this book, we would be grateful if you would report this to us. Please visit www.packtpub.com/support/errata and fill in the form.

Piracy: If you come across any illegal copies of our works in any form on the internet, we would be grateful if you would provide us with the location address or website name. Please contact us at copyright@packt.com with a link to the material.

If you are interested in becoming an author: If there is a topic that you have expertise in and you are interested in either writing or contributing to a book, please visit authors.packtpub.com.

Share your thoughts

Once you've read *Node.js for Beginners,* we'd love to hear your thoughts! Scan the QR code below to go straight to the Amazon review page for this book and share your feedback.

https://packt.link/r/1803245174

Your review is important to us and the tech community and will help us make sure we're delivering excellent quality content.

Download a free PDF copy of this book

Thanks for purchasing this book!

Do you like to read on the go but are unable to carry your print books everywhere?

Is your eBook purchase not compatible with the device of your choice?

Don't worry, now with every Packt book you get a DRM-free PDF version of that book at no cost.

Read anywhere, any place, on any device. Search, copy, and paste code from your favorite technical books directly into your application.

The perks don't stop there, you can get exclusive access to discounts, newsletters, and great free content in your inbox daily

Follow these simple steps to get the benefits:

1. Scan the QR code or visit the link below

https://packt.link/free-ebook/9781803245171

2. Submit your proof of purchase
3. That's it! We'll send your free PDF and other benefits to your email directly

Part 1:
Node.js Overview and
JavaScript Language

In *Part 1*, you will learn how Node.js works and why it is one of the most popular tools used to build web projects today. Together, we will set up the development environment and you will learn the details of the JavaScript language and how you can take advantage of its asynchronous programming.

This part includes the following chapters:

- *Chapter 1, Introduction to Node.js*
- *Chapter 2, Setting Up the Development Environment*
- *Chapter 3, JavaScript Fundamentals*
- *Chapter 4, Asynchronous Programming*

1
Introduction to Node.js

Welcome to the first chapter of the book! Node.js is one of the most relevant technologies available and allows you to build any kind of project (web, desktop, CLI tools, microservices, IoT, and so on) within the same stack. The community around the project is very powerful and innovative.

In this chapter, we will explore the main features of Node.js and why it became so popular over time. Then, we will explore the Node.js architecture and how it works. Finally, we will explore the different versions of Node.js available to us.

In this chapter, we're going to cover the following main topics:

- What makes Node.js so special and why it is a revolutionary technology
- The Node.js architecture and how it works
- How to identify the right Node.js version for your projects

This knowledge will help you to decide when it is a good fit for your projects and will guide you around the complex ecosystem.

Technical requirements

The code files for the chapter can be found at `https://github.com/PacktPublishing/NodeJS-for-Beginners`.

Why is Node.js so popular?

The official definition of Node.js is very simple, but it doesn't explain why Node.js has become so popular over time:

> *"Node.js® is an open-source, cross-platform JavaScript runtime environment."*

In *Figure 1.1*, we can see how the popularity of Node.js has been increasing over time, and even today, it is still growing fast.

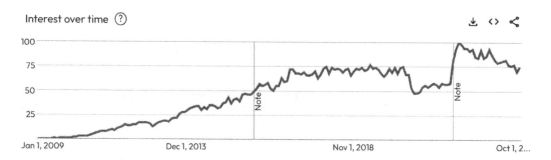

Figure 1.1 – The interest in Node.js, generated using Google Trends

Next, let's explore the main reasons why Node.js is so popular.

Lightweight and fast

Node.js is a lightweight and fast runtime based on the V8 JavaScript engine, which is the same engine that powers Google Chrome and Microsoft Edge, among others. It is based on a single-thread architecture and event-driven model, which means that it doesn't need to create a new thread for each request, as in other popular tools such as PHP. This is a huge advantage because the memory consumption is very low and the performance is very high.

We will explore the single-thread architecture in detail in the upcoming sections.

Cross-platform and multi-purpose

Node.js is cross-platform, which means that we can run it on any operating system and architecture available in the modern market.

Node.js is not only used to build web applications but it can also be used to build any kind of application, from a simple command-line tool to a complex desktop application such as Slack or Visual Studio Code.

Easy learning curve

Node.js is based on JavaScript, which is one of the most popular programming languages in the world. This means that millions of developers already know the language and they can easily start using Node.js.

Any application that can be written in JavaScript, will eventually be written in JavaScript.

– Jeff Atwood (Atwood's Law)

Also, the Node.js **application programming interface** (**API**) – the methods, libraries, and utilities that Node.js provides for us to use – is very simple and easy to use, so the learning curve is very small. You don't need to master the Node.js API to start building web applications; you can progressively learn while you are building your application.

There are a lot of resources available to learn Node.js, from official documentation to online courses and tutorials in many languages and oriented to different profiles.

Ecosystem

Node.js has a huge ecosystem of packages, JavaScript libraries, and resources developed by the community that can be used to build any kind of application. There are more than two and a half million packages available in the npm Registry (`https://www.npmjs.com/`), which is the official package manager for Node.js.

Also, Node.js has huge support from cloud providers, which means that you can easily deploy your application to the cloud and scale it as much as you need.

Most of the emerging technologies provide **software development kits** (**SDKs**) for Node.js, so you can easily integrate your application with them. Many companies are using Node.js in production, so you can easily find support and resources to solve any problem that you may have.

Also, many popular libraries are isomorphic, which means that they can be used in the browser and in the server, so you can reuse your code and avoid duplications.

Community-powered

For me, the most important reason why Node.js is so popular is the community. Node.js has a huge community of developers that are constantly contributing to the project. This means that you can easily find support and resources to solve any problem that you may have and also to include new features or solve specific bugs.

The Node.js Foundation merged with the JS Foundation in 2019 to create the OpenJS Foundation `https://openjsf.org/`, which is the current organization that governs the Node.js project and other key projects in the JavaScript ecosystem, such as Appium, jQuery, Electron, Express, and webpack.

> **Important information**
> You can find the governance model of the OpenJS Foundation at `https://openjsf.org/about/governance/` and the Node.js project at `https://nodejs.org/en/about/governance`.

Many companies are members of the OpenJS Foundation, such as Google, IBM, Microsoft, Netflix, Red Hat, GitHub, and many others (https://openjsf.org/about/members/). These provide a lot of support and resources to keep the project alive.

As you can see, many factors are helping Node.js to become so popular, from a proven community-powered model to a solid ecosystem that brings many capabilities to Node.js. It appears that Node.js will remain popular in the future!

In the next section, we will explore how the architecture works under the hood.

The Node.js single-thread architecture

When Node.js came out in 2009, it was a revolution in the web development world, as Ryan Dahl, the creator of Node.js, decided to use a very unusual approach at that time: a single-thread architecture.

In his presentation about Node.js at the JSConf (https://www.youtube.com/watch?v=EeYvFl7li9E), Ryan Dahl said he wanted to achieve two key things when building Node.js: server-side JavaScript and non-blocking I/O.

I/O needs to be done differently

The common approach for I/O operations in web applications is to create a new thread for each request. This is a very expensive operation because the memory consumption is very high and the performance is very low.

The idea behind this approach is to split the system resources and assign them to each thread. This is a very inefficient approach because, most of the time, the CPUs are idle, just waiting for the resources.

The other problem is that we are limited in the amount of memory that we can use because each thread needs to have its own memory space.

Overall, this process was very inefficient, and it was not scalable.

Non-blocking I/O

With Node.js, we use a different approach. We won't split the resources; we keep a single thread and use a non-blocking I/O model that allows us to free the resources while waiting, so we can continue processing requests.

To make this possible, Node.js has two key dependencies: libuv (https://libuv.org/) and V8 (https://v8.dev/).

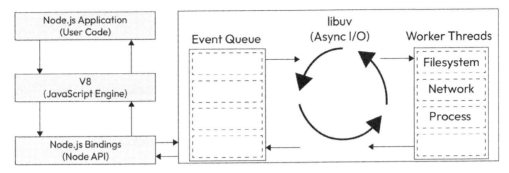

Figure 1.2 – Diagram that showcase the relationship between the user
code, v8, Node API and libuv (event queue and worker threads)

As you can see, the architecture has many pieces and it can be a bit overwhelming at first. This diagram is not the full picture but it is a good starting point to understand how Node.js works in the context of this chapter. There are many pieces to understand from this figure, so let's go step by step.

Node.js application

This is the code that we write to build our application. It will be done in JavaScript and it can use Node.js APIs and third-party libraries.

V8

This is the engine encapsulated in Node.js that will execute our JavaScript code. V8 is the same engine that is used in the Chrome browser under the hood.

Node.js bindings

It is surprising for many developers to see that Node.js is written mostly in C/C++, but this is one of the reasons why Node.js is so fast. The Node.js bindings are the C/C++ code that will be executed when we use the Node.js APIs under the hood.

libuv

This is the C library that will handle the I/O operations with multi-platform support. It will use the thread pool to execute the blocking operations and it will notify the Node.js bindings when the operation is completed. We will program Node.js defining functions that will be executed when certain async operations are completed. For example, when we try to read the content from a file, we will execute certain code when the content is available. libuv handles the low-level logic for this coordination to happen.

Going deeper into the event loop

The event loop is the most critical part of the Node.js architecture. Keeping this in mind will help you to understand how Node.js works.

As we have seen before, the new I/O operations approach is not magic, just a very smart way to handle and abstract using an asynchronous layer that is easily handled with JavaScript. This introduces the need for us to know how to do asynchronous programming. We will cover this topic in more detail in *Chapter 4*, but for now, we need to understand how the event loop works.

One fantastic resource to understand the event loop in more depth is this talk from Philip Roberts at JSConf EU 2014: *What the heck is the event loop anyway?* (`https://www.youtube.com/watch?v=8aGhZQkoFbQ`). It also includes a tool called Loupe (`http://latentflip.com/loupe`) to experiment with the event loop architecture yourself.

As you can see, Node.js is the product of combining several technologies. The event loop is quite an advanced topic that you will require some time to digest and understand fully, but don't worry, as you can start working with Node.js even if you are not yet 100% clear on how the event loop and all the pieces work together. You will be able to learn about it better in practice with the exercises from the book. Now, let's explore how Node.js organizes the versions.

Node.js versions

Node.js follows **semantic versioning (SemVer)** (`https://semver.org/`) and it is important to understand how this versioning works in order to choose the best version for the project.

Semantic versioning (SemVer)

When considering semantic versioning, it helps to determine what changes to anticipate as a user, especially whether they might cause disruptions or not. This understanding assists our end users in preparing for potential updates.

Semantic versioning is one of the most popular ways to version software. In the following figure, we can differentiate the elements used to build the release version.

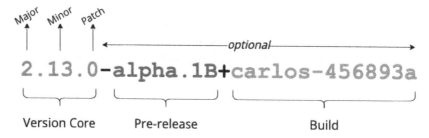

Figure 1.3 – Parts of a semantic version number (source: Devopedia 2020, https://devopedia.org/images/article/279/2766.1593275997.svg)

When a new version is released, the version number is incremented following the SemVer rules:

- **Major** versions add incompatible API changes

- **Minor** versions add functionality in a backward-compatible manner

- **Patch** versions add backward-compatible bug fixes

Following these rules, we can easily upgrade the Node.js version in any project without breaking the code when the changes are cataloged as minor or a patch.

If we want to upgrade to a new major version, we will need to check whether there are any breaking changes that we need to address before upgrading. In most cases, the breaking changes are not related to our own code but to the dependencies that we are using in the project.

> **Important note**
> **Metadata** is optional, and it is not used to define the version of the software but provides additional information. In general, we will try to avoid using versions with metadata as they are not stable versions but they can be used for testing purposes.

Release details

Before we move on to the release schedule, it is important to understand how we can check the details of any release. This is very important if we plan to upgrade to a major version, as it contains breaking changes.

In this case, we will analyze the Node.js 20.0.0 release, so we can see the details of the latest LTS version through the blog details: `https://nodejs.org/en/blog/release/v20.0.0/`.

Every release has a structured blog post with the following information:

- **Summary**: Here, we can find a brief description of the release.

- **Notable Changes**: Here, we can find the most important changes in the release, including examples and a lot of contexts behind the new features or deprecations. We can also see the more relevant changes in the dependencies that may affect the Node.js APIs.

- **Semver-(*) Commits**: Here, we can find the commits that are related to the SemVer changes (**Semver-Major Commits**, **Semver-Minor Commits**, and **Semver-Patch Commits**) and access the code changes directly using the *commits* reference.

> **Information**
>
> The release information is available directly in the changelog. The changelog version includes references to all the commits and pull requests included in the release, so it is a great source of information when you need to migrate from another Node.js version. You can find the changelog version at `https://github.com/nodejs/node/blob/main/doc/changelogs/CHANGELOG_V20.md#2023-04-18-version-2000-current-rafaelgss`.

One of the best ways to explore the change in a release in more detail is to directly use the Node.js documentation – for example, `https://nodejs.org/dist/latest-v20.x/docs/api/`. The website offers the option to navigate through the different versions so we can check the changes in the APIs between versions more easily.

Figure 1.4 – Node.js official documentation screenshot

Release schedule

The Node.js project has a release schedule that is published on the official website (`https://nodejs.org/en/about/releases/`) and it is updated by the Node.js Release Working Group.

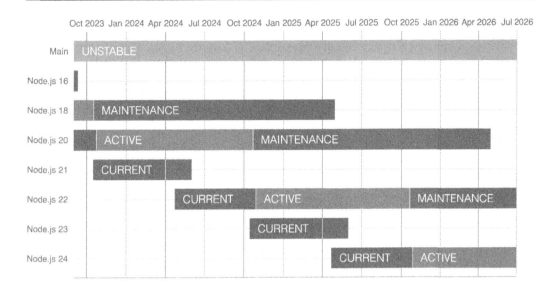

Figure 1.5 – Official release schedule from the Node.js website

In Node.js, releases have three different phases:

- **Current** is the phase where new features (non-major changes) are added to the project. This phase is very active, and it is not always recommended to use it in production as it is not a stable version.

- **Active Long-Term Support (LTS)** is the phase where the version is stable and has been updated by the LTS team. This phase still includes new features, bug fixes, and updates. This phase is stable, so it is recommended to use it in production.

- **Maintenance** is the phase where the version is not receiving any new features, only critical bug fixes and security updates. This phase is recommended for projects that are not able to upgrade yet to the latest active LTS version.

> **Important note**
> Odd-numbered release lines are not promoted to active LTS, so they are not recommended for production use.

As of today, for any new project, I will recommend using the latest LTS version, which is 20.11.0. This version will be supported until April 2026, so it is a good choice for any new project.

For any existing project using Node.js v18, it is recommended to start migrating to Node.js 20 as v18 is entering the *maintenance* phase.

> **Important note**
>
> While releasing a new version seems like an easy task, it is not. The Release Working Group has defined the complete process, which includes more than 20 steps. You can find all the relevant information in the official documentation (`https://github.com/nodejs/node/blob/main/doc/contributing/releases.md`) or this talk: *The Life and Times of a Node.js Release*, by Danielle Adams at NodeConf EU 2022 (`https://www.youtube.com/watch?v=OiSBodpU174`).

Summary

In this chapter, we explored what makes Node.js so special and how it differs from other backend systems. We also covered the history of Node.js and how it has evolved over the years.

Additionally, we covered the Node.js architecture and how it works under the hood. We learned about the event loop and how it allows Node.js to handle many concurrent requests efficiently.

In the next chapter, we will learn how to set up the development environment and start using Node.js.

Further reading

- Node.js governance: `https://nodejs.org/en/about/governance`

- OpenJS Foundation governance: `https://openjsf.org/about/governance/`

- *The Life and Times of a Node.js Release*, by Danielle Adams at NodeConf EU 2022: `https://www.youtube.com/watch?v=OiSBodpU174`

- Node.js dependencies: `https://github.com/nodejs/node/blob/main/doc/contributing/maintaining/maintaining-dependencies.md`

- Node.js event loop architecture: `https://medium.com/preezma/node-js-event-loop-architecture-go-deeper-node-core-c96b4cec7aa4`

- *How Node.js Bootstraps Itself*, 2019 edition, Joyee Cheung, Igalia: `https://www.youtube.com/watch?v=bwiLlcGvFEk`

- *Node.js 12: A Decade of Node.js*, Beth Griggs, IBM: `https://www.youtube.com/watch?v=HP4N0u_dEgI`

- *Node.js 2023 Year in An Article*: `https://blog.rafaelgss.dev/nodejs-2023-year-in-review`

2

Setting Up the Development Environment

To use Node.js, we first need to prepare our development environment. In this chapter, we will cover the details of how to install Node.js and check that everything is working as expected, so we can execute JavaScript and Node.js.

Node.js is one of the most simple and easy-to-install software, so we will not spend too much time on this topic. However, we will cover some important details that you need to know in order to be able to work with Node.js in any environment.

To sum up, here are the main topics that we will explore in this chapter:

- Installing Node.js in any environment
- Managing Node.js versions
- Using Chrome DevTools and the Node.js REPL to interact with JavaScript and Node.js.

In this chapter, you will learn how to properly set up Node.js in any environment, such as Windows, Linux, or macOS. This knowledge will also be applicable when you deploy your projects to the cloud or a specific device.

Additionally, you will learn how to debug any issues using the debugging tools included in your web browsers and the Node.js REPL.

Finally, you will learn how to manage multiple versions of Node.js running on the same machine. This skill will be very useful when you need to migrate a project between different Node.js versions.

Technical requirements

The code files for the chapter can be found at `https://github.com/PacktPublishing/NodeJS-for-Beginners`.

Check out the code in action video for this chapter on `https://youtu.be/xElsOS9Pz4k`

Installing Node.js on macOS, Windows, and Linux

Node.js can be installed in three different ways:

- **Downloading the binaries from the official website**: This is the recommended option for beginners, as it is the easiest way to install Node.js. You just need to download the binaries from the official website and execute the installer.

- **Using a package manager**: This is the most common way to install Node.js in Linux, FreeBSD, IBM i, Android, and similar environments. You just need to use your system's package manager and install Node.js from there.

- **Build from source**: This is the most advanced way to install Node.js and opens the door to many customizations, and it is only recommended for advanced users. You need to download the source code from the official repository and compile it on your machine.

> **Important note**
>
> As part of Node.js continuous integration, there are many different environments and architectures where Node.js is tested, which means that Node.js maintains solid cross-platform support over time.
>
> While writing this book, the latest Node.js version is 20.11.0, so we will use this version as a reference. However, you can use the last LTS version available, as the installation process is the same for all versions.

The upcoming sections will explain how to install Node.js on various operating systems, beginning with macOS.

macOS

The easiest way to install Node.js on macOS is by downloading the binaries from the official website. You just need to go to the Node.js download page at `https://nodejs.org/en/download/`, download the macOS installer, and follow the installation wizard.

You can also install Node.js using a package manager, but this is not recommended for beginners. If you want to install Node.js using a package manager, you can use Homebrew (`https://brew.sh/`) or MacPorts (`https://www.macports.org/`).

To use Homebrew, open your Terminal and type the following command, which will manage the installation process for you:

```
brew install node
```

To use MacPorts, open the Terminal and type the following command to start the installation process:

```
port install nodejs20
```

Next, we'll see how to install it on Windows.

Windows

The easiest way to install Node.js on Windows is by downloading the binaries from the official website.

You just need to go to the Node.js download page at `https://nodejs.org/en/download/`, download the Windows installer, and follow the installation wizard.

Let's see how to install it on Linux next.

Linux

The best way is to install Node.js using your package manager, but you can also use the binaries distributed by NodeSource (`https://github.com/nodesource/distributions/blob/master/README.md`). This will cover Debian and Ubuntu-based distributions (deb) as well as Enterprise Linux-based distributions (rpm).

Let's look at an example using Ubuntu.

First, download the setup script from NodeSource using `curl`:

```
curl -sL https://deb.nodesource.com/setup_20.x -o /tmp/nodesource_
setup.sh
```

Then, review the content of the script (optional):

```
cat /tmp/nodesource_setup.sh
```

Finally, execute the script as `root` and install Node.js:

```
sudo bash /tmp/nodesource_setup.sh
sudo apt install nodejs
```

Other environments

The Node.js Build Working Group provides an official platform list that includes all the supported platforms and architectures with their different tiers of support. You can find it at `https://github.com/nodejs/node/blob/main/BUILDING.md#platform-list`.

Additionally, Node.js has an initiative called the unofficial-builds project that provides support for other platforms and architectures, including `loong64`, `riscv64`, `linux-armv6l`, `linux-x86`, `linux-x64-glibc-217`, and `linux-x64-musl`. You can find more information at `https://github.com/nodejs/unofficial-builds`.

If you have solid skills with Docker, you can also use the official Docker images provided by Node.js to avoid installing the Node.js binaries on your machine (`https://hub.docker.com/_/node`).

Verifying the installation

Node.js is shipped with npm. We will now check that both Node.js and npm are installed correctly. The installed versions can be different depending on the Node.js version that you have installed, but if it is not throwing an error, the installation was correct.

We will use the terminal to check that the installation was done properly for both (Node.js and npm).

To verify the Node.js installation, open your terminal and type the following command:

```
node -v
```

The expected output is the Node.js version installed:

```
v20.11.0
```

To verify that npm is installed, type the following command:

```
npm -v
```

The expected output is the npm version installed:

```
10.2.4
```

Congratulations! You just installed Node.js on your machine! In the next section, we will get familiarized with the Node.js versions so we will have a better understanding of which Node.js version we should use for our next project.

Managing Node.js versions

Node.js is a fast-moving project, so new versions are released every few months. To manage the Node.js versions on your machine, you will need to use a Node.js version manager.

There are several Node.js version managers available, but the most popular are as follows:

- **Node Version Manager** (**nvm**): `https://github.com/nvm-sh/nvm`
- **n**: `https://github.com/tj/n`

- **Fast Node Manager** (**fnm**): `https://github.com/Schniz/fnm`
- **Volta**: `https://github.com/volta-cli/volta`

In this book, we will use nvm as the Node.js version manager, but you can use any other version manager that you prefer.

> **Important info**
>
> In production environments, you should use the latest LTS version available, as this version is the most stable and is supported for a longer time. In most cases, there is no need to install a version manager on your production machine, as you will use a specific version.

Now that we are familiar with how the Node.js versions are organized, we will need some tools to help us handle several Node.js versions in the same environment. We will start in the next section with nvm.

Managing Node.js by using nvm

nvm is the most popular and beginner-friendly way to manage multiple Node.js versions on your machine.

I use nvm to manage my Node.js versions, as it is a great tool, but nvm can be tricky to install so you will need to follow the installation instructions carefully. There is a troubleshooting guide with common issues and solutions at `https://github.com/nvm-sh/nvm#installing-and-updating`.

This is my preferred way to install nvm in macOS, as it is the easiest way to install it:

```
brew install nvm
```

For Linux and macOS, download and execute the installation script from the official repository:

```
curl -o- https://raw.githubusercontent.com/nvm-sh/nvm/v0.39.3/
install.sh | bash
```

nvm doesn't work in Windows, so if you are using Windows, you will need to use another version manager or **Windows Subsystem for Linux** (**WSL**).

Alternatives to nvm for Windows are as follows:

- nodist: `https://github.com/nullivex/nodist`
- nvm-windows: `https://github.com/coreybutler/nvm-windows`
- **Node Version Switcher** (**NVS**): `https://github.com/jasongin/nvs`

Once you have installed nvm, you can use it to install and manage Node.js versions.

Installing and using versions

In order to use a specific Node.js version, you will need to install it first:

```
nvm install 20.11.0
```

Then, you can use it:

```
nvm use 20.11.0
# Now using node v20.11.0 (npm v10.2.4)
```

You can check the Node.js version in use with the following:

```
node -v
# v20.11.0
```

You can also set a default Node.js version for your machine:

```
nvm alias default 20.11.0
```

You can list the installed Node.js versions with the `ls` command:

```
nvm ls
```

The output will be a list of all the installed Node.js versions.

We can list the available Node.js versions with the `ls-remote` command:

```
nvm ls-remote
```

The output will be a list of all the available Node.js versions, and it is a very long list!

We tend to accumulate Node.js versions over time, so it is a good practice to uninstall the Node.js versions that you are not using anymore.

To uninstall a Node.js version, you will need to use the `uninstall` command:

```
nvm uninstall 20.11.0
```

Using a .nvmrc file

You can also use a `.nvmrc` file to specify the Node.js version that you want to use in a project. This is useful when you are working on a project with other developers and you want to make sure that everyone is using the same Node.js version.

To use a `.nvmrc` file, you will need to create a file called `.nvmrc` in the root of your project with the Node.js version that you want to use:

```
20.11.0
```

Then, nvm can use the Node.js version specified in the `.nvmrc` file when you enter the project directory and run the following command:

```
nvm use
# Now using node v20.11.0 (npm v10.2.4)
```

If the Node.js version specified in the `.nvmrc` file is not installed, nvm will throw an error and will not change the Node.js version in use:

```
Found '/<full path>/.nvmrc' with version <20.11.0>
N/A: version "20.11.0 -> N/A" is not yet installed.
You need to run "nvm install 20.11.0" to install it before using it.
```

If you run the command and the file is not found, nvm will throw an error:

```
No .nvmrc file found
Please see `nvm --help` or https://github.com/nvm-sh/nvm#nvmrc for
more information.
```

Now that we are familiar with nvm usage, it is time to start using Node.js in our terminal, so in the next section, we will explore how to use Node.js in an interactive environment with the Node.js REPL.

Node.js REPL

Yes, Node.js has a REPL, and it is very useful to test code and try new things.

REPL stands for **Read-Evaluate-Print Loop**, and it is a simple interactive computer programming environment that takes single user inputs, executes them, and returns the result to the user.

To start the Node.js REPL, you will need to run the `node` command without any arguments. The output will be something like this:

```
Welcome to Node.js v20.11.0.
Type ".help" for more information.
>
```

Now, you can start writing JavaScript code and it will be executed immediately:

```
> console.log("The Node.js REPL is awesome!")
"The Node.js REPL is awesome!"
undefined
```

```
> 1 + 1
2
>
```

To exit the REPL, you can use the .exit command:

```
> .exit
```

You can also use the .help command to get a list of all the available commands:

```
> .help
.break    Sometimes you get stuck, this gets you out
.clear    Alias for .break
.editor   Enter editor mode
.exit     Exit the REPL
.help     Print this help message
.load     Load JS from a file into the REPL session
.save     Save all evaluated commands in this REPL session to a file
Press Ctrl+C to abort current expression, Ctrl+D to exit the REPL
```

As you can see, the Node.js REPL is very simple, but it is useful to test code and try new things. You can learn more about the Node.js REPL in the official documentation at `https://nodejs.org/en/learn/command-line/how-to-use-the-nodejs-repl`.

As well as the Node.js REPL, we can use web browsers to debug and test our JavaScript code. In the next section, we will see this in action using Google Chrome.

Interacting with JavaScript using Chrome DevTools

There is a set of utilities included in the Chrome browser (`https://developer.chrome.com/docs/devtools/overview/`) defined as follows:

> *"Chrome DevTools is a set of web developer tools built directly into the Google Chrome browser. DevTools can help you edit pages on-the-fly and diagnose problems quickly, which ultimately helps you build better websites, faster."*

All Chrome-based browsers have Chrome DevTools, so you can use it with any browser based on Chromium, such as Google Chrome, Microsoft Edge, Brave, and so on.

The Node.js REPL is very useful, but in order to build web applications with Node.js, we can use Chrome DevTools for debug purposes. This debugging will be limited to client-side JavaScript as the Node.js code is not executed directly in the browser.

Chrome DevTools is a very complete tool, so this can be quite overwhelming at first, but we will focus on the most important features for this book: the **Console** and **Network** panels.

The Console panel

The Console panel is the primary way to interact with the JavaScript on the website. The console is interactive so we can write JavaScript code and it will be executed immediately; we can also read the console output.

The following video provides a great overview of the tool: `https://www.youtube.com/watch?v=76U0gtuV9AY`.

You can read the official documentation here: `https://developer.chrome.com/docs/devtools/console/`.

The Network panel

The Network panel is very powerful. It allows us to inspect HTTP requests and responses so we can see the headers, body, status code, and so on. This will be very useful when we need to debug any kind of web application. You can find a great tutorial at `https://www.youtube.com/watch?v=e1gAyQuIFQo`.

You can read the official documentation here: `https://developer.chrome.com/docs/devtools/network/`.

Using Chrome DevTools

In our case, we will start from an empty website. We will use the Console panel to write JavaScript code that will change the page, and then we will inspect the HTTP requests. Follow these steps:

1. In your browser, go to `about:blank`; by default, this will show a blank page.

2. Open DevTools by right-clicking on the page and clicking **Inspect**.

3. Go to the **Console** tab and type `document.body.innerHTML = '<h1>Hello World!</h1>'` and press *Enter*.

Figure 2.1 – Web browser screenshot

4. Now, you should see the **Hello World!** text on the page.

Figure 2.2 – Web browser screenshot with Hello World! text

5.   Go to the **Network** tab and navigate to `https://packt.com`. You should see a lot of activity.

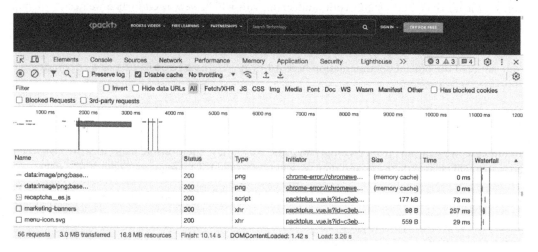

Figure 2.3 – Web browser activity

This was a simple example for you to get familiar with the Chrome DevTools, but you can do much more with it. I recommend you read the official documentation to learn more.

Summary

Congratulations! Your environment is ready to start developing new projects with Node.js!

In this chapter, we explored the process of installing Node.js on various operating systems. Node.js is compatible with Windows, macOS, and Linux, but we also looked at the installation process for other operating systems, including non-officially-supported ones.

Additionally, we delved into the usage of nvm to manage multiple Node.js versions. nvm allows you to switch between different versions of Node.js effortlessly. This can be particularly useful when working on projects that require specific Node.js versions or when testing compatibility across different versions.

Furthermore, the chapter covered the usage of the Node.js REPL and Chrome DevTools. The Node.js REPL is an interactive shell that allows developers to experiment with JavaScript code, execute commands, and see immediate output. It provides a convenient environment for quickly testing code and debugging issues. Chrome DevTools is a set of web development tools built into the Google Chrome browser. It allows developers to inspect and debug JavaScript code and debug the network request among other things.

In the next chapter, we will learn about JavaScript fundamentals. You will use Chrome DevTools and the Node.js REPL to run the examples and practice.

Further reading

- How to install Node.js: `https://nodejs.org/en/learn/getting-started/how-to-install-nodejs`

- Building Node.js from source: `https://github.com/nodejs/node/blob/main/BUILDING.md`

- Node.js unofficial-builds project: `https://github.com/nodejs/unofficial-builds`

- The official platform list supported by Node.js: `https://github.com/nodejs/node/blob/main/BUILDING.md#platform-list`

- The Node.js binaries distributed by NodeSource: `https://github.com/nodesource/distributions/blob/master/README.md`

- Official Node.js Docker images: `https://hub.docker.com/_/node`

- How to use the Node.js REPL: `https://nodejs.org/en/learn/command-line/how-to-use-the-nodejs-repl`

- Chrome DevTools – Console: `https://developer.chrome.com/docs/devtools/console/`

- Chrome DevTools – Network: `https://developer.chrome.com/docs/devtools/network/`

3

JavaScript Fundamentals

In this chapter, we will review all the aspects of JavaScript that are relevant to this book. While this topic could be a book in itself, this chapter synthesizes the most basic parts (arrays, objects, strings, and data types) in order to do a deeper analysis of the most complex parts, such as functions and closures.

Even if you are already familiar with JavaScript, this chapter will help you to refresh your knowledge of certain areas. Also, you will learn about the latest changes in JavaScript introduced by the latest specification.

We will also learn how JavaScript has become a standard on how decisions are made when a request change is made for the language.

Additionally, we will review some tools that will help us to write better JavaScript by using linters, debugging tools, and proper documentation for our code.

To sum up, here are the main topics that we will explore in this chapter:

- Refresh or acquire JavaScript knowledge, including about many of its features
- Understand JavaScript versioning and the TC39 committee
- Get familiar with the JavaScript documentation and linting
- Understand the most commonly used parts of JavaScript (comments, data types, operators, conditionals, loops, functions, objects, arrays, classes, and so on)
- Understand advanced JavaScript concepts such as closures and prototypes

Technical requirements

The code files for the chapter can be found at `https://github.com/PacktPublishing/NodeJS-for-Beginners`.

Check out the code in action video for this chapter on `https://youtu.be/BxM8XZzINmg`

JavaScript is a powerful language

JavaScript is a very powerful language. It is used in the frontend, backend, mobile, desktop, IoT, and so on. It is very flexible, and it is very easy to get started, but it is also very hard to master in depth.

There is a very famous quote (https://www.crockford.com/javascript/javascript.html) by Douglas Crockford that says:

JavaScript is the world's most misunderstood programming language.

JavaScript is a multi-paradigm language, which means that you can use different programming styles, such as object-oriented programming, functional programming, or declarative programming. This is very useful because you can use the programming style that best fits your needs. But on the other hand, it can be very confusing for beginners, and not all the programming styles are equally supported by the language.

JavaScript is a very dynamic language, which means that you can change the behavior of the language at runtime. Thanks to JavaScript, you can learn complex concepts, such as closures and prototypes, and use them to create very powerful and complex applications. But you can also use them to create very confusing and hard-to-maintain applications.

In the next chapters, we will learn how to use JavaScript to create powerful applications, but we will also learn how to use it in a way that is easy to understand and maintain.

> **Important note**
>
> Don't worry if you're not deeply familiar with any of the mentioned paradigms. Throughout this book, we'll gradually incorporate elements from each paradigm, introducing them as needed.

In the next section, we will explore the role of the TC39 in JavaScript and how the specification works.

Understanding versioning – TC39

JavaScript is getting old; it was created in 1995 by Brendan Eich at Netscape Communications Corporation. It was originally called Mocha, but it was renamed LiveScript and finally JavaScript.

The first version of JavaScript was released in 1996. It was called **ECMAScript 1 (ES1)** and was standardized by the **European Computer Manufacturers Association (ECMA)** in 1997.

Understanding versioning – ECMAScript

Over the years, many new features were added to the language, such as classes, modules, and arrow functions. The new features were added to the language through a submission proposal process called ECMAScript proposals (`https://github.com/tc39/proposals`) that are managed directly by the TC39 (`https://tc39.es/process-document/`), which refers to a committee of ECMA that is responsible for the evolution of the language.

From 1997 until 2015, new features were added to the language every few years, but in 2015, the TC39 decided to release a new version of the language every year, which means that the language is evolving faster than ever. This also helps us with the adoption of the new features because we don't need to wait many years to use them in production environments.

Currently, the latest version of the language is ECMA-262 2023 (`https://tc39.es/ecma262/`), which was released in June 2023.

What is included in the next version of JavaScript?

In order to add new features to the language, the TC39 committee has a process that is divided into stages. Anybody can submit a proposal to the TC39 committee, but it is not an easy task, because the proposal needs to be approved by the committee before it is implemented.

You can find all the proposals in the TC39 GitHub repository (`https://github.com/tc39/proposals`). You can participate in the discussions and get involved in the community.

What is not included in the JavaScript specification?

The JavaScript specification is very big, but it does not include many APIs that are commonly used in JavaScript applications, such as browser APIs and Node.js APIs.

If you are using JavaScript in the browser, you can use browser APIs, such as the **Document Object Model** (**DOM**). If you are using JavaScript in Node.js, you can use Node.js APIs, such as the filesystem or HTTP.

At the end of the day, JavaScript is just a programming language. If you are used to building JavaScript applications in the browser, you might be familiar with many APIs that are not included in the JavaScript specification and are not available in Node.js. For example, the window object (`https://developer.mozilla.org/en-US/docs/Web/API/Window`) is available in the browser, but it is not available in Node.js.

Now that we know how the specification works, it is time to explore the JavaScript documentation in the next section.

Exploring JavaScript documentation

While ECMA-262 (`https://262.ecma-international.org/14.0/`) is a great source of information, it is not very beginner-friendly.

The most complete source of information is the MDN Web Docs (`https://developer.mozilla.org/en-US/docs/Web/JavaScript`), which is a community-driven documentation. It is very comprehensive, and it is updated regularly and even translated into other languages.

If you are familiar with frontend development, you might have used the MDN Web Docs before, because it is the main source of information for browser APIs, such as the DOM (`https://developer.mozilla.org/en-US/docs/Web/API/Document_Object_Model/Introduction`) and the Fetch API (`https://developer.mozilla.org/en-US/docs/Web/API/Fetch_API`).

If are looking for more concise documentation, you can use W3Schools (`https://www.w3schools.com/js/default.asp`), which is a great source of information for beginners, with a lot of examples.

Finally, if you are looking for a specific answer to a question, you can use Stack Overflow (`https://stackoverflow.com/questions/tagged/javascript`), which is a community-driven Q&A website.

In the next section, we will learn how we can use linting tools to improve our JavaScript code easily.

Linting JavaScript code

Linting is the process of running a program that will analyze your code for potential errors. It is very useful in catching errors before running your code, so you can fix them before they cause any issues.

JavaScript is a very flexible language, which means that it is very easy to make mistakes. As you get more used to it, you will make fewer mistakes, but it is always good to have a linter to help you.

In the next chapters, we will use ESLint (`https://eslint.org/`) to lint our code, but there are other options available, such as JSLint (`https://www.jslint.com/`) and JSHint (`https://jshint.com/`).

Configuring a linter is not a trivial task, but it is worth the effort. There are many rules available, and it is not easy to know which ones to use. I highly recommend that you use the standard rules (`https://standardjs.com/`), which are one of the most popular and used by many open source projects (including Node.js, Express, and MongoDB) and companies. You can find all the rules available on the JavaScript Standard Style page (`https://standardjs.com/rules.html`).

In *Figure 3.1*, you can see how the standard is used to review the source code of the project. It will recommend what to do in order to follow the configured rules.

Figure 3.1 – Screenshot from GitHub Codespaces

In the next section, we will learn how to document our own code, so it becomes easier to maintain.

Commenting JavaScript code

You have multiple options to include comments in your code:

```
// Single line comment
/*
Multiline
comment
*/
```

If you are new to JavaScript, I recommend you use a lot of comments to help you understand what is going on in your code. As you become more experienced, you will need fewer comments. Comments also help other developers to read and understand your code.

Using JSDoc

If you need guidance on how to write good comments, you can use the JSDoc (`https://jsdoc.app/`) syntax. Another additional benefit of using JSDoc is that you can use it to autogenerate documentation for your code.

This is quite a popular solution. For example, Lodash uses this approach. Use the following links to check out how the _.chunk method is documented:

- JSDoc in practice: `https://github.com/lodash/lodash/blob/4.17.15/lodash.js#L6818`

- Documentation automatically generated by JSDocs: `https://lodash.com/docs/4.17.15#chunk`

In the next section, we will learn how to use console to speed up our debugging process.

Printing values and debugging

The console object is non-standard; it is not part of the JavaScript language, but it is provided by the browser and Node.js. You can use it to print messages to the console, which is very useful for debugging purposes and for the purposes of this book, to follow along with the examples. It is quite common to use it to print the value of a variable. Take the following example:

```
const name = "Ulises";
console.log(name); // Ulises
```

Yes, you can use console.log to print multiple values at the same time, separated by commas, and even include additional information to explain what you are printing. You don't have to worry about the type of the variable as in other languages; console.log will do it for you.

In some cases, you will need to help console.log print the value of a variable; for example, if you want to print an object, sometimes you end up getting [object, object] or similar as the output message. In this case, you will need to use console.log(JSON.stringify(object)) to print the object as a string:

```
const data = {
  nestedData: {
    moreNestedData: {
      value: 1
    }
  }
};

console.log(data); // [object, object]
console.log(JSON.stringify(data)); //
{"nestedData":{"moreNestedData":{"value":1}}}
```

Over time, the JavaScript engines improve the console output, so this simple example might be printed as expected in your browser; but certain complex objects might still need to be stringified, for example, the response from a long HTTP request.

> **Important note**
>
> The `console` object offers many methods to print the information in different formats, which will improve your developer experience a lot. Documentation is available for web browsers (`https://developer.mozilla.org/en-US/docs/Web/API/console`) and for Node.js (`https://nodejs.org/api/console.html`).

In the next section, we will learn how JavaScript uses constants and variables to store the information that we need when building applications.

Variables and constants

We use variables to store values, and we use constants to store values that will not change. In JavaScript, we can use the `let` keyword to declare a variable and the `const` keyword to declare a constant. Before ES6, we could only use the `var` keyword to declare variables, but it is not recommended to use it anymore.

Naming conventions

In JavaScript, it is very common to use *camelCase* to name variables and constants, but other conventions are supported too, such as *snake_case* and *PascalCase*. It is also possible to start variables with symbols, but it is not recommended.

There are a few limitations that we need to consider when naming variables and constants:

- Avoid starting with a symbol, such as `$resource`
- Don't start with a number, such as `1variable`
- Don't use spaces, such as `const my variable = 1`
- Don't use reserved words, such as `const const = "constant"`

let versus const

We use `let` to declare variables and `const` to declare constants. The main difference is that we can reassign a value to a variable, but we cannot reassign a value to a constant. Here is an example of reassigning a value to a variable:

```
let userName = "Joe Doe";
console.log(userName); // Joe Doe
userName = "Jane Doe";
console.log(userName); // Jane Doe
```

As we can see here, we cannot reassign a value to a constant:

```
const userName = "Joe Doe";
console.log(userName); // Joe Doe
userName = "mary"; // TypeError: Assignment to constant variable.
```

It is important to notice that we can change the value of a constant if the value is an object, but we cannot reassign a new value to the constant:

```
const user = {
  name: "Joe Doe"
}
console.log(user.name); // Joe Doe
user.name = "Jane Doe";
console.log(user.name); // Jane Doe
user = "Mr. Joe"; // TypeError: Assignment to constant variable.
```

Later in this chapter, we will explore objects in more detail, and we will understand these mutations deeper.

In JavaScript, there is another mechanism that you need to understand. Hoisting is a behavior in JavaScript where variable and function declarations are moved to the top of their containing scope during the compilation phase. This is done to optimize the code, but it can have some side effects. You can find a great guide at `https://www.freecodecamp.org/news/what-is-hoisting-in-javascript-3`.

Now that we are clear on how variables and constants work, it is time to explore the different data types available in JavaScript in the next section.

Understanding data types

In JavaScript, there are several primitive types. We can group them into two groups: before ES6 (`undefined`, `object`, `boolean`, `number`, `string`, and `function`) and after ES6 (`bigint` and `symbol`). In order to check the type of a variable, we can use the `typeof` operator.

undefined

Not all languages have an `undefined` type, but JavaScript does. It is used to represent the absence of a value. It is also used as the default value for uninitialized variables.

object

The `object` type is used to represent a collection of data. It is a very generic type, and it is used to represent many different things, such as arrays (lists), objects (dictionaries), class instances, and `null`.

boolean

The `boolean` type is used to represent a logical value. It can be either `true` or `false`. This type can be generated by using the `Boolean` function too, as everything in JavaScript can be converted to a `boolean` value.

number

The `number` type is used to represent a numeric value. It can be either an integer or a floating-point number. It is also used to represent special numeric values such as `Infinity`, `-Infinity`, and `NaN` (which stands for Not a Number).

string

The `string` type is used to represent a sequence of characters. It can be created explicitly by using single quotes (`'`), double quotes (`"`), or backticks (`` ` ``) or implicitly by using the `String` function or expressions.

function

The `function` type is used to represent a function. Functions in JavaScript are very powerful. We will explore them in detail in this chapter. There are two ways to create a function, by using the `function` keyword or by using the arrow function syntax.

bigint

`bigint` was introduced in ES6 in order to work with large numbers. `number` is limited to values between $-(2^{53} - 1)$ and $2^{53} - 1$

symbol

The `symbol` type is used to represent a unique identifier. It is a new type that was introduced in ES6; you won't really need to be familiar with it to follow along with this book.

In the next section, we will explore numbers in depth, including the Math built-in library, common operators used for comparison, and useful methods for converting numbers and strings.

Exploring numbers

JavaScript has good support for mathematical operations and dates, but sometimes it can be tricker and more limited than other programming languages, so many developers use specialized libraries when the application requires advanced math. For example, if you need to work with vectors, matrices, or complex numbers, you should use a library such as Math.js (`https://mathjs.org/`).

Here is a typical example of the floating-point precision problem:

```
console.log(0.1 + 0.2); // 0.30000000000000004
console.log(0.1 + 0.2 === 0.3); // false
```

As you can see, the result of 0.1 + 0.2 is not 0.3, but 0.30000000000000004. This is because JavaScript uses the IEEE 754 standard (https://en.wikipedia.org/wiki/IEEE_754) to represent numbers, and it is not possible to represent all decimal numbers in binary. This is a common problem in many programming languages; it is not an exclusively JavaScript problem. But you can solve it by using the Number and toPrecision functions as you will implicitly convert from number to string and then back to number:

```
let impreciseOperation = 0.1 + 0.2;
Number(impreciseOperation.toPrecision(1)) === 0.3; // true
```

As you can see, there are some edge cases that are not easy to understand or solve intuitively. Most of the time, you will not need to worry about this, but it is important to know that this problem exists and you can use libraries if you are not experienced enough with numbers in JavaScript.

Arithmetic operators

JavaScript has the expected arithmetic operators, +, -, *, /, %, and **, and indicates priority with brackets as in any modern language.

Assignment operators

JavaScript has the expected assignment operators, =, +=, -=, *=, /=, %=, and **=, as in other languages.

Also, you can use ++ and -- to increment and decrement a variable. This operator can be added before or after the variable, and it will change the value of the variable before or after the operation:

```
let a = 5;
console.log(a++); // 5
console.log(a);   // 6
console.log(++a); // 7
console.log(a);   // 7
```

> **Additional info**
>
> JavaScript also supports bitwise operations, so you can work with a set of 32 bits (zeros and ones), rather than decimal, hexadecimal, or octal numbers. You can check out the full documentation here: https://developer.mozilla.org/en-US/docs/Web/JavaScript/Guide/Expressions_and_operators#bitwise_operators.

Useful methods

There are methods that are key to performing mathematical operations or transformations in daily work:

- `Number.prototype.toFixed():https://developer.mozilla.org/es/docs/Web/JavaScript/Reference/Global_Objects/Number/toFixed`

- `Number.prototype.toPrecision():https://developer.mozilla.org/es/docs/Web/JavaScript/Reference/Global_Objects/Number/toPrecision`

- `Number.parseInt():https://developer.mozilla.org/es/docs/Web/JavaScript/Reference/Global_Objects/Number/parseInt`

- `Number.parseFloat():https://developer.mozilla.org/es/docs/Web/JavaScript/Reference/Global_Objects/Number/parseFloat`

The Math object

JavaScript has a built-in `Math` object that provides a lot of useful methods to perform mathematical operations. I will list some of them here, but you can find the full list in the MDN documentation (`https://developer.mozilla.org/en-US/docs/Web/JavaScript/Reference/Global_Objects/Math`).

Useful methods

There are methods that are key to performing mathematical operations or transformations in daily work:

- `Math.random()`: Returns a pseudo-random floating-point number between 0 (inclusive) and 1 (exclusive) `https://developer.mozilla.org/es/docs/Web/JavaScript/Reference/Global_Objects/Math/random`

- `Math.max()`: Returns the maximum numeric value among the arguments passed to it `https://developer.mozilla.org/es/docs/Web/JavaScript/Reference/Global_Objects/Math/max`

- `Math.min()`: Returns the minimum numeric value among the arguments passed to it `https://developer.mozilla.org/es/docs/Web/JavaScript/Reference/Global_Objects/Math/min`

- `Math.floor()`: Returns the resulting number from rounding a number down to the nearest integer that is less than or equal to the given number `https://developer.mozilla.org/es/docs/Web/JavaScript/Reference/Global_Objects/Math/floor`

Other numbers

In JavaScript, there are some special values that are numbers, but they are not real numbers. These values are NaN and `Infinity`.

Not a Number (NaN)

NaN is a special value that represents Not a Number. It is the result of an invalid or undefined mathematical operation, for example, dividing 0 by 0, or multiplying Infinity by 0. You can use isNaN() to check whether a value is NaN (https://developer.mozilla.org/es/docs/Web/JavaScript/Reference/Global_Objects/isNaN).

Infinity

Infinity is a special value that represents infinity. It is the result of a mathematical operation that exceeds the largest possible number. You can use isFinite() to check whether a value is finite (https://developer.mozilla.org/es/docs/Web/JavaScript/Reference/Global_Objects/isFinite).

In the next section, we will explore dates in depth.

Exploring Dates object

Dates are a complex topic for any programming language or system as you need to take into account many things, such as time zones. If you need to work with dates intensively, consider using a library such as Lunox (https://github.com/moment/luxon/) or date-fns (https://date-fns.org/).

For more simple scenarios, you can use the built-in Date object and the Intl API (https://developer.mozilla.org/en-US/docs/Web/JavaScript/Reference/Global_Objects/Intl) to format dates.

The API offers several ways to generate the Date object by using numbers, strings, or several arguments. Also, you have getters and setters to read and modify specific parts, such as the year or milliseconds. It is also possible to perform operations such as comparing or adding time.

For many years, the only way to format dates in JavaScript was using the toLocaleString() method. This method is still valid, but it has a lot of limitations, specifically, when you want to compare dates in a human-readable way (e.g., *3 days ago* or *2 weeks ago*).

In the past, we needed to use external libraries to achieve this, but now we can use the Intl API (https://developer.mozilla.org/en-US/docs/Web/JavaScript/Reference/Global_Objects/Intl) to format dates.

In the following code, you can see how to generate, manipulate, and format dates:

```
const jsDateAnnouncement = new Date(818031600000);
const currentDate = new Date();
const diff = jsDateAnnouncement - currentDate;

const formatter = new Intl.RelativeTimeFormat('en', {
```

```
    numeric: 'auto'
});
const diffInDays = Math.round(diff / 86400000);
const diffInYears = Math.round(diffInDays / 365);
const diffInText = formatter.format(diffInDays, 'day');
console.log(`JavaScript was presented to the world ${formatter.
format(diffInDays, 'day')}`);

// JavaScript was presented to the world 10,094 days ago

console.log(`JavaScript was presented to the world ${formatter.
format(diffInYears, 'year')}`);
// JavaScript was presented to the world 28 years ago.
```

The result may vary on your machine as it will have been some time since I wrote this code. Therefore, keep in mind that the output you observe may differ from mine.

> **Important note**
> The TC39 is doing a great job at consolidating this API, which includes a lot of features to format dates, numbers, currencies, and more. I recommend you follow the proposal's progress and implementation in the JavaScript engines.

In the next section, we will learn how to use conditionals in JavaScript by using several tools that JavaScript provides.

Conditional statements

There are many ways to write conditional statements in JavaScript, but the most common are `if`, `switch`, and the ternary operator (`? :`).

Math comparison operators

For mathematical operations, we have the following operators: `>`, `<`, `>=`, and `<=`. They are used to compare two values and return a Boolean value. Their use is the same as in most modern programming languages.

Equality operators

Equality operators are used to compare two values and return a Boolean value. There are two types of equality operators: strict (`===` and `!==`) and non-strict (`==` and `!=`).

The strict equality operator cannot be used to compare non-primitive types (such as `object`, `array`, and `function`) and certain values such as NaN, as it will always return `false`:

```
console.log([1,2] === [1,2]) // false
console.log({ name: 'John' } === { name: 'John' }); // false
console.log(NaN === NaN); // false
```

It is not recommended to use non-strict equality operators, as they can lead to unexpected results, because this operator does not check the type of the values:

```
console.log(1 == '1'); // true
console.log(1 != '1'); // false
```

Logical operators

It is possible to combine multiple conditions using logical operators. There are three logical operators, `&&`, `||`, and `!`, and some variations of them, `&&=` and `||=`, that are used to reduce the amount of code for certain operations. We won't cover them all in this book.

You can combine operators to build more complex validations:

```
const num = 2
console.log((num == 2) && (3 >= 6)); // false
console.log((num > 3) || (17 <= 40)); // true
```

The NOT operator (!)

The NOT operator is used to invert the value of a Boolean. It will return `true` if the value is false, and `false` if the value is true:

```
console.log(!true); // false
console.log(!false); // true
```

This example is not clear about all the possibilities that are offered, so let's try to build an analogy with a more verbose structure, `Boolean(value) === false`. Basically, the `!` operator converts the value to a Boolean and then compares it with a `false` value.

Equality in JavaScript

Due to the nature of JavaScript, it is possible to use any value as a condition. The condition will be evaluated as a Boolean, and if the value is truthy, the condition will be `true`. If the value is falsy, the condition will be `false`. This can be a bit confusing, so let's explore the `Boolean` method to understand how different data values are transformed:

```
// The truthy values:
console.log("String:", Boolean("Ulises")  );
console.log("1235:", Boolean(1235));
console.log("-1235:", Boolean(-1235));
console.log("Object:", Boolean({text: "hi"}));
console.log("Array:", Boolean(["apple", -1, false]));
console.log("Function:", Boolean(function(){}));
console.log("Arrow function:", Boolean(() => {}));
// The falsy values:
console.log("Empty string:", Boolean("")  );
console.log("0:", Boolean(0));
console.log("-0:", Boolean(-0));
console.log("null:", Boolean(null));
console.log("undefined:", Boolean(undefined));
console.log("NaN:", Boolean(NaN));
```

We can conclude easily that empty values (such as `null`, `undefined`, an empty string, or `NaN`) and 0 are falsy, and values with complex data types (such as objects and functions) or non empty strings and non-zero numbers are truthy.

This is quite convenient when we want to check whether a value is empty or not, as in the following example:

```
function checkValue (value) {
    if(!value) {
        throw new Error ("The value is invalid! Try again.")
    }
}
```

This Boolean transformation and comparison can turn into a very complex situation if you want to compare different data types and values, for example, `Boolean([]) === Boolean({})`. You can explore this topic in detail in the MDN documentation (`https://developer.mozilla.org/en-US/docs/Web/JavaScript/Equality_comparisons_and_sameness`). But in general, you don't need to be an expert in this area to follow along with this book.

> **Note**
> You can get a better understanding of this topic by exploring JavaScript Equality Table by Dorey at `https://github.com/dorey/Javascript-Equality-Table/`.

The nullish coalescing operator (??)

The nullish coalescing operator is a new operator that was introduced in ES2020. It is used to check whether a value is null or undefined; if it is, it will return a default value:

```
const name = null ?? "John Joe";
console.log(name); // John Joe
```

The if statement

The if statement is the most common way to write a conditional statement. It will execute the code inside the block if the condition is true. The else statement allows us to follow up when the condition is not met by executing the code that is in the else statement. The else if statement is a variation of the if statement. It will execute the code inside the block if the condition is true. If the condition is false, it will execute the code inside the else block. You can add as many else if statements as you need:

```
const condition = true
const condition2 = true
if(condition) {
    console.log("The condition is true")
} else if (condition2) {
    console.log("The condition2 is true")
} else {
    console.log("The condition and condition2 are false")
}
```

You can change the values in condition and condition2 in order to get more familiar with the behavior of the conditional structures.

return usage

The return statement is widely used to avoid using else statements and allows for cleaner code. Here is an example:

```
const condition = true;
if(condition) {
    return console.log("The condition is true");
}
console.log("The condition is false");
```

The switch statement

The switch statement is a good option when you want to compare a variable against multiple values. It is good when you want to assign a value to a variable depending on a condition.

The `switch` structure is composed of the `switch` keyword, followed by the variable that you want to compare, and then a block of `case` statements. Each `case` statement is composed of the `case` keyword, followed by the value that you want to compare, "and then a double colon (:). After the double colon," you can write the code that you want to execute if the condition is true. The `default` statement is optional, and it will be executed if none of the `case` statements are true, like `else` when using `if` statements.

The `break` statement is used to stop the execution of the `switch` statement. If you don't add the `break` statement, the code will continue executing the next `case` statement. Here we have a combined example:

```
const extension = ".md";
switch (extension) {
  case ".doc":
    console.log("This extension .doc will be deprecated soon")
  case ".pdf":
  case ".md":
  case ".svg":
    console.log("Congratulations! You can open this file");
    break;
  default:
    console.log(`${extension} is not supported`);
}
```

Ternary operator

The ternary operator is shorthand for the `if` and `else` statements. It is a good option when you want to assign a value to a variable depending on a condition.

The structure is composed of the condition, followed by a question mark, ?, then the value that you want to assign if the condition is true, followed by a double colon (:), and then the value that you want to assign if the condition is false: `condition ? valueIfTrue : valueIfFalse`.

Let's see an example with the `if` and `else` statements:

```
const isMember = true;
console.log(`The payment is ${isMember ? "20.00€" : "50.00€"}`);
// The payment is 20.00€
```

The ternary operator can nest multiple ternary operators, but it is not recommended because it can be extremely difficult to read. Also, it is possible to use the ternary operator to do multiple operations, but it is not recommended because it can be extremely difficult to read even if you use parentheses.

Now that we are clear on how conditional structures work in JavaScript, it is time to explore loops in the next section.

Understanding loops

There are many ways to create loops in JavaScript, but the most common are the `for` and `while` statements and variations of them that are specific to arrays and objects. Also, functions in JavaScript can be used to create loops when using recursion. In this section, we will look at only the `for`, `while`, and `do...while` statements.

while

The `while` statement creates a loop that executes a block of code as long as the condition is true. The condition is evaluated before executing the block of code:

```
let i = 1;
while (i <= 10) {
    console.log(i);
    i++;
};
```

do...while

The `do...while` statement creates a loop that executes a block of code at least once even if the condition is not met, and then repeats the loop as long as the condition is true. The condition is evaluated after executing the block of code:

```
let i = 0;
do {
    console.log(`i value: ${i}`);
    i++;
} while (false);
// i value: 0
```

for

The `for` statement creates a loop that consists of three optional expressions, enclosed in parentheses and separated by semicolons, followed by a statement executed in the loop:

```
for (let i = 0; i < 10; i++) {
    console.log(i);
}
```

The first expression is executed before the loop starts. Usually, it is used to initialize the variable that will act as counter.

The second expression is the condition that is evaluated before executing the block of code. If the condition is true, the block of code is executed. If the condition is false, the loop stops.

The third expression is executed after the block of code is executed. Usually, it is used to increment or decrement the counter variable.

This structure is quite flexible, and some developers tend to abuse it. Let's see an example with bad readability:

```
for (let i = 0, x = 1, z = 2, limit = 10; i <= limit; x *= z, i++ ) {
    console.log(`i: ${i}. x: ${x}. z: ${z}`);
}
// i: 0. x: 1. z: 2
// ...
// i: 10. x: 1024. z: 2
```

The readability issues are due to the large number of variables defined and updated in the `for` loop. It is important to remember that we write code that other programmers can understand in the future. Let's see the same code with a more readable approach:

```
let x = 1;
const z = 2, limit = 10;
for (let i = 0; i <= limit; i++ ) {
    console.log(`i: ${i}. x: ${x}. z: ${z}`);
    x *= z
}
```

You can already notice the difference; it takes less time and effort to understand it. In the next section, we will learn how to use strings.

Using strings in JavaScript

Strings are primitive values. They are a sequence of characters. There are three ways to create strings in JavaScript: using single quotes, ' , double quotes, " , or backticks, ` .

```
console.log('Hello World');
console.log("Hello World");
console.log(`Hello World`);
```

Strings are immutable, which means that once they are created, they cannot be modified, but you can overwrite the variables or references depending on the data structure. So, all the methods that you use to modify a string will return a new string (or array):

Template strings allow you to use placeholders, $ { }, to insert variables or expressions inside a string. There is also added support for multiple lines:

```
const name = "John";
console.log(`Hello ${name}!`) //Hello John!
```

Important methods

There are many ways to perform operations with strings, but in this section, we will see only the most important methods that you will use in your day-to-day work:

- `String.prototype.indexOf()`: Finds the index of the first occurrence of a specified substring within a string `https://developer.mozilla.org/es/docs/Web/JavaScript/Reference/Global_Objects/String/indexOf`

- `String.prototype.lastIndexOf()`: Finds the index of the last occurrence of a specified substring within a string `https://developer.mozilla.org/es/docs/Web/JavaScript/Reference/Global_Objects/String/lastIndexOf`

- `String.prototype.search()`: Searches for a specified substring within a string `https://developer.mozilla.org/es/docs/Web/JavaScript/Reference/Global_Objects/String/search`

- `String.prototype.includes()`: Determines whether one string contains another string `https://developer.mozilla.org/es/docs/Web/JavaScript/Reference/Global_Objects/String/includes`

- `String.prototype.match()`: Extracts matches of a regular expression pattern from a string `https://developer.mozilla.org/es/docs/Web/JavaScript/Reference/Global_Objects/String/match`

- `String.prototype.matchAll()`: Returns an iterator that yields all matches of a regular expression against a string `https://developer.mozilla.org/es/docs/Web/JavaScript/Reference/Global_Objects/String/matchAll`

- `String.prototype.split()`: Splits a string into an array of substrings based on a specified separator `https://developer.mozilla.org/es/docs/Web/JavaScript/Reference/Global_Objects/String/split`

- `String.prototype.slice()`: Extracts a section of a string and returns it as a new string `https://developer.mozilla.org/es/docs/Web/JavaScript/Reference/Global_Objects/String/slice`

- `String.prototype.trim()`: Removes whitespace characters from both ends of a string `https://developer.mozilla.org/es/docs/Web/JavaScript/Reference/Global_Objects/String/trim`

- `String.prototype.replace()`: Finds and replaces substrings within a string `https://developer.mozilla.org/es/docs/Web/JavaScript/Reference/Global_Objects/String/replace`

In the next section, we will learn how to use arrays, one of the most versatile data structures in JavaScript.

Exploring arrays

Arrays are non-primitive values; they are a collection of values. The values can be any type of value, including other arrays. Arrays are mutable, which means that you can modify them and the changes will be reflected in the original array.

Arrays are zero-indexed, which means that the first element is at index 0, the second element is at index 1, and so on.

The `Array.isArray()` method determines whether the passed value is an array:

```
const array = [1, 2, 3];
console.log(Array.isArray(array)); // true
const object = { name: "Ulises" };
console.log(Array.isArray(object)); // false
console.log(typeof array); // object
console.log(typeof object); // object
console.log("are object and array the same type?", typeof(array) ===
typeof(object)); // true
```

As arrays are objects, you need to be careful because they can't be compared with the === or == operator, because it will compare the references, not the values:

```
const array1 = [1, 2, 3];
const array2 = [1, 2, 3];
console.log(array1 === array2); // false
```

Arrays have a `length` property that returns the number of elements in the array and provides an easy way to iterate over the array.

Basic operations

In this section, we will look at the most common operations that you will perform with arrays.

Creating an array

There are many ways to create an array in JavaScript. The most common is using the array literal notation, `[]`, but you can also create an array from other data types, such as when you split a string, or using the `string.prototype.split()` method. The following is an example of creating an array using the array literal notation:

```
const emptyArray = [];
const numbers = [1, 2, 3];
const strings = ["Hello", "World"];
const mixed = [1, "Hello", true];
```

The `Array.of()` method creates a new array instance from a variable number of arguments, regardless of the number or type of the arguments:

```
const array = Array.of( 1, 2, 3 );
```

The `Array.from()` method creates a new array instance from an array-like or iterable object:

```
console.log(Array.from('packt'));    // ['p', 'a', 'c', 'k', 't']
```

The spread operator, `. . .`, can be used to create a new array from an existing array or from a string:

```
console.log([...[1, 2, 3]]);    // [1, 2, 3]
console.log([...'packt']);      // ['p', 'a', 'c', 'k', 't']
```

Also, you can pass a map function as a second parameter so you can perform transformations when the array is created:

```
console.log(Array.from([1, 2, 3], x => x + x)); // [2, 4, 6]
```

Accessing items

You can access an item in an array using the index of the item:

```
const fruits = ['banana', 'apple', 'orange'];
console.log(fruits[0]); // banana
console.log(fruits[1]); // apple
console.log(fruits[2]); // orange
```

Replacing items

You can replace an item in an array using the index of the item:

```
const fruits = ['banana', 'apple', 'orange'];
fruits[0] = 'pear';
console.log(fruits); // ['pear', 'apple', 'orange']
```

Adding items

You can add items to an array using two main methods:

- `Array.prototype.push()`: https://developer.mozilla.org/es/docs/Web/JavaScript/Reference/Global_Objects/Array/push

- `Array.prototype.unshift()`: https://developer.mozilla.org/es/docs/Web/JavaScript/Reference/Global_Objects/Array/unshift

> **Important note**
> It is always preferable to add new items to the end of the array, because adding items to the beginning of the array is an expensive operation. This is because it requires re-indexing all the items in the array.

Removing items

There are several methods that allow you to remove items from the array:

- `Array.prototype.pop()`: https://developer.mozilla.org/es/docs/Web/JavaScript/Reference/Global_Objects/Array/pop

- `Array.prototype.shift()`: https://developer.mozilla.org/es/docs/Web/JavaScript/Reference/Global_Objects/Array/shift

- `Array.prototype.splice()`: https://developer.mozilla.org/es/docs/Web/JavaScript/Reference/Global_Objects/Array/splice

Iterating over an array

As we saw at the beginning of this chapter, it is possible to iterate over an array using a `for` loop, but there are also other ways to iterate over an array.

JavaScript provides great support for declarative programming, which is especially useful when you need to iterate over arrays. So, let's summarize the most common ways to iterate over an array.

Most of these methods receive a function as a parameter, and it is executed for each item in the array. Depending on the method used and the data returned from the function will get one result or another.

Another important thing to remember is that these methods can be chained together, so you can use one method after another and compose more complex operations.

Iteration

As arrays can store a lot of elements, it is important to get familiar with the methods that are provided by the array in order to properly iterate over them. The most common are `Array.prototype.map()` and `Array.prototype.forEach()`. In both cases, we will iterate over the array, but `Array.prototype.map()` will directly return a new array with the applied transformation. Let's see an example comparing both methods:

```
const numbers = [1, 2, 3, 4, 5]
const mapTransformation = numbers.map(el => el * 10)

const forEachTransformation = []
numbers.forEach(el => {
```

```
      forEachTransformation.push(el * 10)
})
console.log(mapTransformation) // 10,20,30,40,50
console.log(forEachTransformation) // 10,20,30,40,50
```

Validation

As arrays can contain any type of data, it is common to need to validate whether an array contains a specific item or whether all the items in the array match a condition. There are several methods, but the most common are as follows:

- `Array.prototype.every()`: https://developer.mozilla.org/es/docs/Web/JavaScript/Reference/Global_Objects/Array/every

- `Array.prototype.some()`: https://developer.mozilla.org/es/docs/Web/JavaScript/Reference/Global_Objects/Array/some

- `Array.prototype.includes()`: https://developer.mozilla.org/es/docs/Web/JavaScript/Reference/Global_Objects/Array/includes

Filtering

Arrays can store a lot of information, and it is quite common to store nested structures such as big objects. There are many ways to do filtering in JavaScript. The most important difference between them is what your expected output is as sometimes we will be interested in a new array with the filtered values, but other times we might want the position (index) of certain elements in the array. The most used method is `Array.prototype.filter()`, which is used to generate a new array with the elements that pass certain criteria. Let's see an example:

```
const numbers = [1, 2, 3, 4, 5]
const filteredNums = numbers.filter(el => el <= 3)
console.log(filteredNums) // [1, 2, 3]
```

There are several methods that you will find relevant in this category:

- `Array.prototype.slice()`: Returns the copy of a portion of the array https://developer.mozilla.org/es/docs/Web/JavaScript/Reference/Global_Objects/Array/slice

- `Array.prototype.find()`: Returns the value of the first item in the array that satisfies the provided criteria https://developer.mozilla.org/es/docs/Web/JavaScript/Reference/Global_Objects/Array/find

- `Array.prototype.findIndex()`: Returns the index of the first item in the array that satisfies the criteria https://developer.mozilla.org/es/docs/Web/JavaScript/Reference/Global_Objects/Array/findIndex

Utilities

Sometimes you need to flatten an array of arrays. You can use the `array.flat()` method to do that:

```
const data = [1, [2, 3], [4, 5]];
const flatData = data.flat();
console.log(flatData); // [1, 2, 3, 4, 5]
```

Another common method is the `array.join()` method, which is used to join all the items in an array into a string:

```
const people = ['Joe', 'Jane', 'John', 'Jack'];
console.log(people.join()); // Joe,Jane,John,Jack
console.log(people.join(' + ')); // Joe + Jane + John + Jack
```

This is very useful when you need to create a string with a list of items, for example, when you need to create a list of items in HTML, XML, Markdown, and so on:

```
const people = ['Joe', 'Jane', 'John', 'Jack'];
const structuredPeople = people.map(person => `<li>${person}</li>\n`);
console.log(`
    <ul>
        ${structuredPeople.join('')}
    </ul>
`)
// <ul>
//     <li>Joe</li>
//       ...
// </ul>
```

While working with data, it is very common that we need to sort the items in the array. This can be done with `array.sort()`. In general, it is better if we provide a function that specifies how to properly sort the items just to avoid unexpected results. Let's see an example:

```
const numbers = [7, 1,10, 3,15,20]
console.log(numbers.sort())
// [1, 10, 15, 20, 3, 7]
console.log(numbers.sort((a, b) => a - b))
// [1, 3, 7, 10, 15, 20]
```

There are several methods that are quite useful and you will find yourself using very frequently:

- `Array.prototype.reverse()`: https://developer.mozilla.org/en-US/docs/Web/JavaScript/Reference/Global_Objects/Array/reverse

- `Array.prototype.concat()`: https://developer.mozilla.org/en-US/docs/Web/JavaScript/Reference/Global_Objects/Array/concat

- `Array.prototype.fill()`: https://developer.mozilla.org/en-US/docs/Web/JavaScript/Reference/Global_Objects/Array/fill

- `Array.prototype.reduce()`: https://developer.mozilla.org/es/docs/Web/JavaScript/Reference/Global_Objects/Array/reduce

Destructuring

ES6 introduced a new syntax for destructuring arrays and objects. The left-hand side of an assignment is now a pattern for extracting values from arrays and objects. This pattern can be used in variable declarations, assignments, function parameters, and function return values. Also, you can use default values (fail-soft) in case the value is not present in the array.

In the following code sample, we can see the classic way to do a fail-soft:

```
const list = [1, 2];
const a = list[0] || 0; // 1
const b = list[1] // 2
const c = list[2] || 4; // 4
```

The following snippet contains the same code but using ECMAScript 6 destructuring:

```
const list = [1, 2];
const [ a = 0, b, c = 4 ] = list;
```

As you can see, this version is more compact. Currently, this is the more popular way to assign default values when it is possible to combine it with destructuring.

Sets

ES6 introduces a new data structure called `Set`. A Set is a collection of values, where each value may occur only once. It can be used to store a collection of values, but it is not an array as it doesn't have indexes. It is quite a common solution to remove duplicate values from an array, as we can see in the following code:

```
let arr = [1,2,2,3,1,4,5,4,5]
let set = new Set(arr)
let uniques = Array.from(set)
console.log(uniques) // [1,2,3,4,5]
```

You can find more information about set-specific methods at https://developer.mozilla.org/en-US/docs/Web/JavaScript/Reference/Global_Objects/Set.

In the next section, we will learn how to use objects, one of the most powerful data structures in JavaScript.

Using objects in JavaScript

Objects are non-primitive values; they are a collection of properties. A property is a key-value pair. The key is always a string, and the value can be any type of value, including other objects.

Basic operations

Objects are the most versatile structure in JavaScript. In this section, we will learn how to create objects, how to access and modify their properties, and how to iterate over the properties of an object.

Creating an object

You can create an object using the object literal syntax, that is, using curly braces:

```
const person = {}
```

You can also create an object and directly add properties:

```
const person = {
    name: 'Jane',
}
```

You can store any type of value in an object, including other objects or functions (methods):

```
const person = {
    name: 'Jane',
    id: 1,
    favoriteColors: ['blue', 'green'],
    address: {
        street: 'Main St',
        number: 1,
    },
    fullName: function() {
        return `${this.name} Doe`
    },
    sayHi: function() {
        console.log('Hello!')
    }
}
console.log(person.fullName()) // Jane Doe
person.sayHi() // Hello!
console.log(person.address.street) // Main St
console.log(person.id) // 1
console.log(person.favoriteColors[0]) // blue
```

Creating and accessing properties

You can create a new property or overwrite existing ones in an object by assigning a value:

```
const person = {
    id: 12
}
person.name = 'Jane'
console.log(person.name) // Jane
person.id = 1
console.log(person.id) // 1
```

You can also access the properties of an object using the bracket notation, which is useful when using programmatic access or when using keys with special characters or whitespaces:

```
const person = {
    id: 12
}
console.log(person['id']) // 12
const specialKey = 'first name with spaces'
person[specialKey] = 'Jane'
console.log(person[specialKey]) // Jane
```

Deleting properties

You can delete a property from an object using the `delete` operator or overwrite it to `undefined`:

```
const person = {
    id: 12,
    name: 'Jane'
}
delete person.id
person.name = undefined
console.log(person.id) // undefined
console.log(person.name) // undefined
```

Iteration

Let's see how to iterate over the properties of an object, and how to get an array with the keys and values of an object.

This is our base object:

```
const users = {
    admin: 'Jane',
    moderator: 'Joe',
```

```
        user: 'Billy',
}
```

You can iterate over the properties of an object using the `for...in` loop:

```
for (let role in users) {
    console.log(`${users[role]} is the ${role}`)}
// Jane is the admin
// Joe is the moderator
// Billy is the user
```

You can also use the `Object.keys()` method to get an array with the keys of an object, so you can use array-specific methods to manage the iteration, such as `array.prototype.forEach()`:

```
const roles = Object.keys(users)
console.log(roles) // ['admin', 'moderator', 'user']
roles.forEach(role => {
    console.log(role) // admin
    console.log(users[role]) // Jane
})
```

You can also use additional methods introduced recently in the language:

- `Object.values()`: https://developer.mozilla.org/en-US/docs/Web/JavaScript/Reference/Global_Objects/Object/values

- `Object.entries()`: https://developer.mozilla.org/en-US/docs/Web/JavaScript/Reference/Global_Objects/Object/entries

Shallow copy versus deep copy

The way JavaScript works means that sometimes we don't get the expected copy of a variable. Let's see a simple example:

```
const name = "Jane"
const number = 1
const array = [1, 2, 3]
const object = { id: 1, name: 'Jane' }

// Copy
let nameCopy = name
let numberCopy = number
const arrayCopy = array
const objectCopy = object
```

```
// Modify the copy
nameCopy = 'Joe'
numberCopy = 2

arrayCopy.push("additional item")
objectCopy.name = 'Joe'

// Check the original
console.log(name) // Jane
console.log(nameCopy) // Joe
console.log(number) // 1
console.log(numberCopy) // 2
console.log(array) // [1, 2, 3, "additional item"]
console.log(arrayCopy) // [1, 2, 3, "additional item"]
console.log(object) // { id: 1, name: 'Joe' }
console.log(objectCopy) // { id: 1, name: 'Joe' }
```

This is quite a specific behavior of JavaScript that frustrates many developers. How is it possible that the original variable is modified when we modify the copy? The answer is that we are not copying the variable (*deep copy*) in all the scenarios; we are copying the reference to the variable (*shallow copy*).

Only the primitive types (*string, number, Boolean, null, undefined,* and *symbol*) are copied by value; the rest are copied by reference, so you actually get a reference to the original variable, like a shortcut.

This allows you to do some interesting things, such as create shortcut references for very nested objects:

```
const data = {item: {detail: { reference: {id: '123'} }}}
// make a shortcut reference
const ref = data.item.detail.reference
ref.name = 'Jane'

// check the original
console.log(data.item.detail.reference) // {id: '123', name: 'Jane'}
```

But, as you can see, this can lead to changes in the original object. This can be an unexpected behavior if we are not clear how the original structure was copied. It can be trickier to detect if you are using nested structures.

If you want to get a deep copy of a simple object, you can use `Object.assign()` or the spread operator, . . .:

```
const array = [1, 2, 3]
const object = { id: 1, name: 'Jane' }
// Copy
```

```
const arrayCopy = [...array]
const objectCopy = Object.assign({}, object)
// Modify the copy
arrayCopy.push("additional item")
objectCopy.name = 'Joe'
// Check the original
console.log(array) // [1, 2, 3]
console.log(arrayCopy) // [1, 2, 3, "additional item"]
console.log(object) // { id: 1, name: 'Jane' }
console.log(objectCopy) // { id: 1, name: 'Joe' }
```

But the nested objects will be copied by reference, so you will get the same behavior as before:

```
const data = [{ 'a': 1 }, { 'b': 2 }];
const shallowCopy = [...data];
shallowCopy[0].a = 3;
console.log(data[0].a); // 3
console.log(shallowCopy[0].a); // 3
```

An alternative is to use a specialized library such as Lodash (`https://lodash.com/docs/4.17.15#cloneDeep`) or transform it into JSON and digest the structure, but this has some limitations, such as not being able to copy functions or items that are not defined in the JSON specs (`https://datatracker.ietf.org/doc/html/rfc7159`).

Merging objects

Merging two objects can be done with `Object.assign`, but you need to understand two things:

- The order is important, so the first item will be overwritten by the next item when they share common properties

- If the objects are complex data structures such as nested objects or arrays, then the final object will copy the references (shallow copy)

Let's see an example:

```
const dst  = { quux: 0 }
const src1 = { foo: 1, bar: 2 }
const src2 = { foo: 3, baz: 4 }
Object.assign(dst, src1, src2)
console.log(dst) // {quux: 0, foo: 3, bar: 2, baz: 4}
```

Destructuring

Since ES6, JavaScript has provided destructuring assignment for objects, which is very handy for extracting and including values in objects. Let's see an example with a simple object:

```
const name = "Jane";
const age = 25;
const data = { item: "Lorem Ipsum", status: "OK" };
```

If we didn't use destructuring, we would have to do something like this:

```
const user = {
  name: name,
  age: age,
  data: data,
};
const item = data.item;
const status = data.status;
```

But with destructuring, we can do it in a more concise way:

```
const user = { name, age, data };
const { item, status } = data;
```

Optional chaining (?.)

The optional chaining operator is a new operator introduced in ES2020. It allows you to access deeply nested properties of an object without worrying about whether the property exists or not. Before the optional chaining operator, you had to check whether the property exists before accessing it. This was quite tedious for very nested structures. Let's see a practical example:

```
const user = {
  name: "John",
  address: {
    street: "Main Street",
  },
};

const otherUser = {
  name: "Jane",
};

console.log(user.address?.street); // Main Street
console.log(otherUser.address?.street); // undefined
```

```
// without optional chaining:
console.log(user.address.street); // Main Street
console.log(otherUser.address.street); // TypeError: Cannot read
properties of undefined (reading 'street')
```

Now that we are familiar with most of the data structures, it is time to explore functions in the next section.

Exploring functions

Functions are one of the more meaningful structures in JavaScript. There are certain characteristics that make them different from other programming languages; for example, they are first-class citizens, which means that they can be assigned to a variable, passed as an argument to another function, or returned from another function.

The basics

There are many advanced concepts related to functions, but in this section, we will just look at the basics of functions in JavaScript. We will start with the declaration, execution, and arguments using the function keyword. Then, we will focus on arrow functions and closures.

Declaration

In essence, a function is a block of code that can be executed when it is called. In JavaScript, we can declare a function using the function keyword. The syntax is the following:

```
function myFunction() {
  console.log("This is a function body")
  // code to be executed
}
```

Execution

The function is not executed when it is declared; it is executed when it is called. To call a function, we just need to write the name of the function followed by parentheses. Take the following example:

```
const myFunction = function() {
  console.log("This is a function body")
  // code to be executed
}
myFunction() // This is a function body
```

Anonymous functions

Functions can also be declared as a function expression. This is known as anonymous functions. A simple example is when we pass the function as an argument to another function, like when we use timers – `setTimeout`, in this case:

```
setTimeout(function() {
    console.log('1 second later')
}, 1000);
```

Return values

A function can return a value using the `return` keyword. This value can be assigned to a variable or used in another function. Take the following example:

```
function isEven(number) {
   return number % 2 === 0
}
const result = isEven(2)
const otherResult = isEven(3)
console.log(result) // true
console.log(otherResult) // false
```

Arguments

Functions can receive arguments; these arguments are passed to the function when it is called. Take the following example:

```
function sayHi (name) {

   console.log(`Hi ${name}!`);
};
sayHi('John'); // Hi John!
```

You don't need to specify the arguments; you can use the rest operator (. . .) to access the arguments. In this example, we will sum all the numbers passed to the function:

```
function sum (...numbers) {
  console.log("First Number:", numbers[0])
  console.log("Last Number:", numbers[numbers.length - 1])
  let total = 0
  for (let number of numbers) {
    total += number
  }
  console.log("Total (SUM):", total)
```

```
}
const result = sum(1, 2, 3, 4, 5)
// First Number: 1
// Last Number: 5
// Total (SUM): 15
```

Arrow functions

One of the most important features introduced in ES6 is arrow functions. They are a new syntax for writing JavaScript functions, but they also introduce certain changes that are important to be aware of:

- Arrow functions introduce a new syntax for writing functions

- Arrow functions are always anonymous

Syntax

Since the beginning of JavaScript, we declared functions using the `function` keyword, as in the following example:

```
const sampleFunction = function () { }
const sayHelloNow = function (name) {
  const now = new Date()
  console.log(`Hello ${name}, at ${now}!`)
}
```

The new syntax for writing arrow functions uses `=>` and does not use the `function` keyword. The following example is the same as the previous one but with the new syntax:

```
const sampleFunction = () => {}
const sayHelloNow = name => {
  const now = new Date()
  console.log(`Hello ${name}, at ${now}!`)
}
```

The new syntax has an implicit return, so if you want to return a value, you can do it without using the `return` keyword:

```
const alwaysTrue = () => true

const getData = (name, age) => ({ name: "John", age: 25 })
```

The previous example can be translated to the previous syntax as follows:

```
const alwaysTrue = function () { return true }
const getData = function (name, age) {
```

```
    return { name: "John", age: 25 }
}
```

Arrow functions can receive arguments, but if you want to receive more than one argument, you need to use parentheses:

```
const sum = function (a, b) { return a + b }
// Arrow function translation
const sum = (a, b) => a + b
```

Behavior changes

Due to the fact that JavaScript has retro compatibility with older versions, arrow functions introduce certain changes in the behavior of the functions. The most important one is related to the `this` keyword.

Also, arrow functions do not have a `prototype` property, which means that they cannot be used as constructors or method handlers.

> **Important note**
>
> The management of `this` in JavaScript can be a bit confusing and is quite advanced for the objectives of this book. If you want to learn more about it, you can read the MDN documentation: `https://developer.mozilla.org/en-US/docs/Web/JavaScript/Reference/Operators/this`.

Closures

This is one of the most popular and important concepts in JavaScript, but it is a bit advanced, and it is not easy to understand.

So, what is a closure?

Basically, a closure is a function returned by another function. Here, we have an example:

```
const outerFunction = function () {
  console.log("This is the outer function")
  const innerFunction = function () {
    console.log("This is the inner function")
  }
  return innerFunction
}
```

In this example, `outerFunction` returns `innerFunction`, so we can call `innerFunction` after calling `outerFunction`:

```
const innerFunction = outerFunction() // This is the outer function
innerFunction() // This is the inner function
```

Now, let's achieve the same result using less code by doing both executions in the same statement:

```
// Execution in single line
outerFunction()()
```

But how is this useful?

The most important thing about closures is that they can access and even modify the scope of the parent function (code block and arguments), even after the parent function has returned. Let's see a practical example:

```
const createCounter = (initialValue = 0) => {
  let counter = initialValue
  return (incrementalValue) => {
    counter += incrementalValue
    console.log(counter)
  }
}
```

In this example, we added the `initialValue` and `incrementalValue` arguments to the functions, and also, we defined the `counter` variable to store the counter's current value. In practice, we can use this function to create a counter that starts from a specific value, and then we can increment it by a specific value. We can't access the `counter` variable directly because it lives only in the scope within the function and not outside, but we can use the closure to access it and even manipulate the value:

```
const addToCounter = createCounter(10)

addToCounter(12) // 22
addToCounter(1)  // 23
```

In this example, we saw the basic usage of closures, but they can be used for many other things. One of the most common usages is to create abstractions to manage third-party services such as databases and APIs.

We will use this structure in the following chapters when using MongoDB and Express.

In the next section, we will learn how to create and manage classes, as well as how prototypical inherence works in JavaScript.

Creating and managing classes

Classes were introduced in ES6. They are syntactic sugar over the prototype-based inheritance. Historically, JavaScript did not have formal classes as we can expect from the typical Object Oriented Programing (OOP) languages.

In this section, we will learn how to create classes and how to use them with ES6. Also, we will explore how the prototypical inheritance is a key feature in maintaining retro compatibility and extends JavaScript's core features.

Creating a class

To create a class, we need to use the `class` keyword, and then we can define the default properties of the class using the `constructor` method:

```
class Human{
  constructor(name, age) {
    this.name = name;
    this.age = age;
  }
}
const jane = new Human ("Jane", 30);
console.log(jane.name); // Jane
console.log(jane.age); // 30
```

In this example, we created a class called Human and then we created an instance of the class called jane. We can access the properties of the class using dot notation.

Class methods

To define a method in a class, we need to use a similar syntax as we use for defining methods in objects:

```
class Human {
  constructor(name, age) {
    this.name = name;
    this.age = age;
  }
  sayHello() {
    console.log(`Hello, my name is ${this.name}!`);
  }
}
const jane = new Human ("Jane", 30);
jane.sayHello(); // Hello, my name is Jane!
```

In this example, we defined a method called `sayHello` in the Human class, then we created an instance of the class, and we called the method.

Extending classes

We can extend classes using the `extends` keyword. This will allow us to inherit the properties and methods of the parent class:

```
class Colleague extends Human {
  constructor(name, age, stack) {
    super(name, age);
    this.stack = stack;
    this.canCode = true;
  }
  code() {
    console.log(`I can code in ${this.stack}!`);
  }
}
const jane = new Colleague ("Jane", 30, ['JavaScript', 'React',
'MongoDB']);
console.log(jane.name); // Jane
console.log(jane.canCode); // true
jane.sayHello(); // Hello, my name is Jane!
jane.code(); // I can code in JavaScript, React and MongoDB!
```

In this example, we created a class called `Colleague` that extends the Human class, then we created an instance of the class, and we called the methods and properties inherited from both classes.

Static methods

Static methods are methods that can be called without instantiating the class. They are defined using the `static` keyword:

```
class Car {
  constructor(brand) {
    this.brand = brand;
  }
  move() {
    console.log(`The ${this.brand} is moving!`);
  }
  static speedLimits() {
    console.log("The speed limit is 120 km/h for new cars");
  }
}
```

Now, we can call the `speedLimits` method without instantiating the class:

```
Car.speedLimits(); // The speed limit is 120 km/h for new cars
```

Getters and setters

As in other languages that support object-oriented programming, you can define getters and setters using the `get` and `set` keywords, respectively. This will allow you to access and modify the properties of the instance in a more classic way:

```
class Rectangle {
    constructor (width, height) {
        this._width  = width
        this._height = height
    }
    set width  (width)  { this._width = width            }
    get width  ()       { return this._width             }
    set height (height) { this._height = height          }
    get height ()       { return this._height            }
    get area   ()       { return this._width * this._height }
}
const shape = new Rectangle(5, 2)
console.log(shape.area) // 10
console.log(shape.height) // 2
console.log(shape.width) // 5
shape.height = 10
shape.width = 10
console.log(shape.area) // 100
console.log(shape.height) // 10
console.log(shape.width) // 10
```

Summary

In this chapter, we explored JavaScript's history and current state. We learned about the different versions of the language and how the language has evolved over time. We also learned about how the new features are added to the language.

Also, we learned how to find the best documentation about the language and how to use it to learn about the language in more depth.

Additionally, we explored how to use numbers, dates, conditional statements, loops, strings, arrays, objects, and functions, among others, in detail.

Furthermore, we learned about classes and prototype-based inheritance and how it is a key feature to maintain retro compatibility and extends JavaScript's core features.

In the next chapter, we will learn about asynchronous programming with JavaScript. You will apply all the knowledge learned in this chapter to manage asynchronous code using different approaches, such as callbacks, promises, and async/await.

Further reading

- The Weird History of JavaScript: `https://www.youtube.com/watch?v=Sh6lK57Cuk4`

- A Brief History of JavaScript, talk by Brendan Eich (creator of JavaScript): `https://www.youtube.com/watch?v=qKJP93dWn40`

- TC39 Demystified, by Ujjwal Sharma: `https://www.youtube.com/watch?v=YLHhRpaPly8`

- Documenting the Web Platform, by Florian Scholz: `https://www.youtube.com/watch?v=f_M0vQcKiW4`

- TC39: From the Proposal to ECMAScript, Step by Step, by Romulo Cintra: `https://www.youtube.com/watch?v=h5pUuz2qqVQ`

4

Asynchronous Programming

This chapter will explain in detail how to use all the asynchronous mechanisms that JavaScript offers today, including how to convert callbacks to promises and perform bulk asynchronous operations.

You will gain an in-depth understanding of all the tools at your disposal for managing both simple and complex asynchronous activities. We'll begin with callbacks following Node.js Core conventions, then progress to effectively handling asynchronous operations using promises, and `async/await`. Toward the end of the chapter, we'll employ the **Immediately Invoked Function Expression (IIFE)** pattern to execute asynchronous code. Additionally, we will provide a comprehensive overview of how to convert asynchronous operations between different handlers, including callbacks and promises.

To sum up, here are the main topics that we will explore in this chapter:

- Asynchronous programming in JavaScript
- Understanding callbacks and how to avoid callback hell
- Mastering promises
- Using `async` and `await` for handling asynchronous code

Technical requirements

The code files for the chapter can be found at `https://github.com/PacktPublishing/NodeJS-for-Beginners`.

Check out the code in action video for this chapter on `https://youtu.be/FHzqWr4dK7s`

Asynchronous programming in JavaScript

In JavaScript, asynchronous programming is a fundamental part of the language. It is the mechanism that allows us to perform operations in the background, without blocking the execution of the main thread. This is especially important in the browser, where the main thread is responsible for updating the user interface and responding to user actions.

Overall, asynchronous programming is a complex topic that requires a lot of practice to master, but in my opinion, it requires a change in your mindset. You will need to start thinking about how to break down your code into small chunks that can be executed in the background, and how to combine them to achieve the desired result. You'll encounter asynchronous programming regularly while coding with JavaScript. Most operations involving interactions with external resources, such as sending and receiving data from a server or a database and reading the content from a file, will necessitate its use.

> **Previous knowledge**
>
> In *Chapter 1* we introduced the concept of the event loop, which is the mechanism that allows JavaScript to be asynchronous. In this chapter, we will see how to use this mechanism to our advantage.
>
> In *Chapter 3*, we learned how to use JavaScript in detail; this chapter requires a solid knowledge of functions and arrays.

Let's begin by exploring how asynchronous programming differs from conventional programming and how we need to adopt a different mindset.

This chapter uses isomorphic JavaScript snippets, so the code can be executed in Node.js or in the browser.

The asynchronous mindset

The first step in mastering asynchronous programming is to change your mindset. You need to start thinking about your code in a non-linear way; you will think more about "what should happen next" rather than "what should happen first."

When we learned about functions in *Chapter 3*, we saw that a function is *just* a piece of code that can be executed at any time. In this section, we will connect that piece of code to previous events, and to future events.

There are many ways to perform asynchronous operations in JavaScript. In this chapter, we will focus on the most common ones, which are as follows:

- **Callbacks**: A callback is a function that is passed as an argument to another function, and it is executed when a certain event happens. This is the most basic way to perform asynchronous operations in JavaScript, and it is the foundation of all the other mechanisms.

- **Promises**: ES6 introduced the concept of promises, which you can use to handle asynchronous operations in an advanced way because they use a state machine with several states (pending, fulfilled, and rejected) to keep track of operations. Promises have many advantages over callbacks in terms of readability, reusability, and overall simplicity. This is the most common way to perform asynchronous operations in modern JavaScript today. For more details, check out the *Mastering promises* section in this chapter.

- **Async/await**: Async/await acts as a wrapper over promises to make code more readable (syntax sugar). Currently is the most popular way of handling asynchronous operations.

In the next section, we will explore how we can use callbacks effectively in our applications, the error first pattern, and other good practices to follow. Later on, we will explore how to wrap callbacks inside promises.

Understanding callbacks

Callbacks exploit JavaScript's capability to pass functions. There are two essential parts to this technique:

- A function that is passed as an argument to another function
- The passed function is executed when a certain event happens

Let's create a basic example to illustrate this concept. In the following code snippets, we will show how the callback is defined as an argument and how a function is passed as an argument when the execution occurs:

1. In this example, we will define a function (doSomething) that expects a function as an argument:

    ```
    const doSomething = (cb) => {
      console.log('Doing something...');
      cb();
    };
    ```

2. At this point, we have a function called doSomething that receives a function as an argument and executes it as the last step, this illustrates the idea that the callbacks are just a pattern where we expect that the next function to the executed is actually called as the final step (call me back when you are done - callback) . Let's see how we can use this function:

    ```
    const nextStep = () => {
      console.log('Callback called');
    };
    doSomething(nextStep);
    ```

3. Once the function is executed, the expected output will be the following:

    ```
    Doing something...
    Callback called
    ```

Now, we have a function called nextStep that is passed as an argument to doSomething. When doSomething is executed, it will print Doing something..., and then it will execute the function that was passed as an argument, which will print Callback called as the last step.

It is important to note that the function that is passed as an argument is not executed immediately , as we only want to execute them when the operation is complete. On the other hand, the immediate execution will require the use of parentheses (doSomething(nextStep())) and will produce a different result and an error:

```
doSomething(nextStep())
// Callback called
// Doing something...
// Error: cb is not a function
```

We can also pass an anonymous function as an argument. This is the most common way to use callbacks, as we don't need to define the functions previously. In most cases, we don't reuse that function later:

```
doSomething(() => {
    console.log('Callback called');
});
```

It is also possible to pass a function that receives arguments:

```
const calculateNameLength = (name, cb) => {
  const length = name.length;
  cb(length);
};


calculateNameLength('John', (length) => {
  console.log(`The name length is ${length}`); // The name length is 4
});
```

As you can see, the callback technique is very simple, but we haven't seen any asynchronous operations yet. At the end of the day, we assume that a callback is literally a "call me back when you are done" approach. Now, let's see how this can be used to manage asynchronous operations with timers and intervals.

Timers and intervals

There are two functions that are commonly used to delay the execution of a function, setTimeout and setInterval. Both functions receive a callback as an argument and execute it after a certain amount of time. Now, let's define and use these functions in examples.

The setTimeout function is employed to defer the execution of a function by a specified amount of time.

Let's see how `setTimeout` works with a simple example:

```
console.log('Before setTimeout');
const secondInMilliseconds = 1000;
setTimeout(() => {
   console.log('A second has passed');
}, secondInMilliseconds);
console.log('after setTimeout');
```

If we execute this code, we will see the following output:

```
Before setTimeout
after setTimeout
A second has passed
```

As you can see, the callback is executed after the rest of the code, even though it was defined before. This is because the callback is executed asynchronously, which means that it is executed in the background, and the rest of the code is executed in the main thread.

The `setTimeout` function receives two arguments. The first one is the callback, and the second one is the amount of time that the callback should be delayed. The amount of time is expressed in milliseconds, so in this case, we are delaying the execution of the callback by 1,000 milliseconds, which is 1 second.

The `setInterval` function is used to execute a function repeatedly, with a fixed time delay between each execution.

Let's see how `setInterval` works with a simple example:

```
const secondInMilliseconds = 1000;
let totalExecutions = 0
console.log('Before setInterval');
setInterval(() => {
    totalExecutions++;
    console.log(`A second has passed, this is the ${totalExecutions}
execution`);
}, secondInMilliseconds);
console.log('After setInterval');
```

If we execute this code, we will see the following output:

```
Before setInterval
After setInterval
A second has passed, this is the 1 execution
...
A second has passed, this is the 50 execution
```

As you can see, the callback is executed every second, and it is executed in the background, so the rest of the code is executed in the main thread.

The set Interval function receives two arguments. The first one is the callback, and the second one is the amount of time that the callback should be delayed. The amount of time is expressed in milliseconds, so in this case, we are delaying the execution of the callback by 1,000 milliseconds, which is 1 second.

Error first callbacks

In the examples in the preceding sections, we saw how to use callbacks to manage asynchronous operations, but we didn't see how to handle errors. In this section, we will see how to handle errors in callbacks.

The most common way to handle errors in callbacks is to use the error first pattern. This pattern consists of passing an error as the first argument of the callback, and the result as the second argument. Let's see how this works with a simple example:

```
const doSomething = (cb) => {
  const error = new Error('Something went wrong');
  cb(error, null);
};

doSomething((error, result) => {
  if (error) {
    console.log('There was an error');
    return;
  }
  console.log('Everything went well');
});
```

The output of this code will be as follows:

```
There was an error
```

In this example, we have a function called doSomething that receives a callback as an argument. This callback receives two arguments. The first one is an error, and the second one is the result. In this case, we are passing an error as the first argument, and null as the second argument because an error occurred. When the callback is executed, we check if the first argument is an error, and if it is, we print There was an error. Otherwise, we print Everything went well.

Let's see how this works when everything goes well:

```
const doSomething = (cb) => {
  const result = 'It worked!';
  cb(null, result);
};
```

```
doSomething((error, result) => {
  if (error) {
    console.log('There was an error');
    return;
  }
  console.log(result);
  console.log('Everything went well');
});
```

The output of this code will be as follows:

```
It worked!
Everything went well
```

In this case, we are passing `null` as the first argument as there is no error, and the result as the second argument. When the callback is executed, we check if the first argument is an error, and if it is, we print `There was an error`. Otherwise, we print the result, and `Everything went well`.

Callback hell

Previously, we saw how to use callbacks to manage asynchronous operations and how to handle errors with the error first pattern.

The problem with callbacks is that they are not very easy to read, and when we have a lot of nested callbacks, the code becomes very difficult to read. This is called callback hell, and it is a very common problem when using callbacks.

In the following pseudocode example, you can see how the functions are generated in an inclined pyramid with nested callbacks that make the code really hard to follow. In the following code example, observe how the functions are structured in an inclined pyramid with nested callbacks, making the code challenging to comprehend:

```
readFile("docs.md", (err, mdContent) => {

    convertMarkdownToHTML(mdContent, (err, htmlContent) => {
        addCssStyles(htmlContent, (err, docs) => {
            saveFile(docs, "docs.html",(err, result) => {
                ftp.sync((err, result) => {
                    // ...
                })
            })
        })
    })
})
```

As you can see, the code is very difficult to read, and it is very easy to make mistakes. This is why we need a better way to manage asynchronous operations. There are some ways to prevent callback hell, such as using named functions instead of anonymous functions, but one of the most common ways to avoid callback hell is to use promises.

Promises are a great solution when you need to chain asynchronous operations, let's explore it in the next section.

Mastering promises

A promise functions as a state machine, symbolizing the eventual success or failure of an asynchronous operation, along with its resultant value. It can exist in any of three states: pending, fulfilled, or rejected.

When a promise is created, it is in the pending state. When a promise is fulfilled, it is in the fulfilled state. When a promise is rejected, it is in the rejected state.

The following diagram shows the various states of a promise and the connections between them:

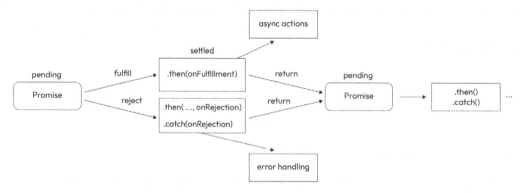

Figure 4.1 – Attributions and copyright licensing by Mozilla Contributors is licensed under CC-BY-SA 2.5. https://developer.mozilla.org/en-US/docs/MDN/Writing_guidelines/Attrib_copyright_license

After a promise is fulfilled or rejected, it becomes unchangeable. To manage fulfillment, the `then` method is employed, while the `catch` method is used to address the rejection of the promise.

Now that it is clear what the promises are and how the states are related, it is time to observe them in action. In the next section, we will explore how to use them and control any asynchronous flow effortlessly in JavaScript.

Using promises

Let's see how this works with a simple example using `fetch` to make a request to an external **application programming interface (API)**. This example will be using my simple-api project (`https://github.com/UlisesGascon/simple-api`), which is available at `https://api.demo.foo/__/docs/` and is a fake online **Representational State Transfer (REST)** API for testing and fast prototyping.

So, in the following code example, we will perform a network request and bring data to our application using the internet, as this operation requires network I/O, it is asynchronous, so we will need to use promises:

```
fetch('https://api.demo.foo/v1/todo')
  .then(response => response.json())
  .then(json => console.log(json))
  .catch(error => console.log(error));
```

The output of this code will be as follows:

```
[{
  "id": "fc3f31b9-8d98-42e9-aab3-1586f2273c3a",
  "title": "We need to input the digital DNS capacitor!",
   "completed": true  }
...
]
```

In this example, we are using the `fetch` function to make a request to the API. The function yields a promise, allowing us to employ the `then` method to manage successful fulfillment and the `catch` method to handle potential rejections. In this case, we are using the `then` method twice: the first time to parse the response as JSON, and the second time to print the result to the console. We are also using the `catch` method to print the error to the console.

Creating promises

You can create a promise using the `Promise` constructor, which receives a callback as an argument. This callback receives two arguments, `resolve` and `reject`. The `resolve` function is used to resolve the promise, and the `reject` function is used to reject the promise. Let's see how this works with a simple example:

```
const setTimeoutPromise = (time) => {
  return new Promise((resolve, reject) => {
    setTimeout(() => {
      resolve();
    }, time);
  });
```

```
};

console.log('Before setTimeoutPromise');
setTimeoutPromise(1000).then(() => console.log('one second later'))
console.log('After setTimeoutPromise');
```

The output of this code will be as follows:

```
Before setTimeoutPromise
After setTimeoutPromise
one second later
```

In this example, we have a function called `setTimeoutPromise` that receives a `time` as an argument. This function returns a promise that will be resolved after the specified time. When the promise is resolved, we print `one second later` to the console.

Callback hell with promises

Promises are a great way to deal with the limitations that callbacks introduce when we need to perform multiple asynchronous operations that should be executed in a consecutive order.

Promises will handle errors more easily, so the readability of the code should be clearer and easier to maintain in long term.

In the previous section, we saw that callback hell is a very real thing in JavaScript. By now, you should be more familiar with the inclined pyramid and nested callbacks. Here is the snippet that we used to explain how Callback hell can be easily achieved in a previous section:

```
readFile("docs.md", (err, mdContent) => {
    convertMarkdownToHTML(mdContent, (err, htmlContent) => {
        addCssStyles(htmlContent, (err, docs) => {
            saveFile(docs, "docs.html",(err, result) => {
                ftp.sync((err, result) => {
                    // ...
                })
            })
        })
    })
})
```

Now let's see how we can solve this problem using promises:

```
readFile("docs.md")
  .then(convertMarkdownToHTML)
// shortcut for .then(mdContent => convertMarkdownToHTML(mdContent))
```

```
.then(addCssStyles)
.then(docs => saveFile(docs, "docs.html"))
.then(ftp.sync)
.then(result => {
  // ... other things
})
.catch(error => console.log(error));
```

As you can see, the code is much easier to read, and it is much easier to make changes to. This is one of the main advantages of using promises. Now the errors are handled in the last `catch` method, so we don't need to handle the errors in each `then` method, which makes the code much cleaner.

Parallel promises

Another advantage of using promises is that we can run multiple promises in parallel. Basically, we provide an array of promises and we choose a strategy to handle the results (`Promise.race()` or `Promise.all()`). This is a great way to reduce the execution time, as we are using Node.js' abilities to manage I/O operations asynchronously.

In the following examples, we will use this function to generate a random timeout promise as an example of an asynchronous operation:

```
const randomTimeOutPromise = () => {
  return new Promise((resolve, reject) => {
    const time = Math.floor(Math.random() * 100);
    setTimeout(() => {
      console.log(`Promise resolved after ${time}ms`);
      resolve(time);
    }, time);
  });
};
```

This function will return a promise that will be resolved after a random time between 0 and 100 milliseconds. Now that we have an asynchronous function, we can employ various strategies to group multiple requests together based on our specific needs. In this instance, our goal is to initiate several requests in parallel and await their resolution.

`Promise.all()`: The `all` method produces a singular promise that resolves once all the promises are resolved or if any of the promises are rejected:

```
Promise.all([
  randomTimeOutPromise(),
  randomTimeOutPromise(),
  randomTimeOutPromise(),
  randomTimeOutPromise(),
```

```
  randomTimeOutPromise(),
]).then((results) => {
  console.log("results:", results);
});
```

The output of this code will be something like this when all the promises are resolved successfully:

```
Promise resolved after 0ms
Promise resolved after 26ms
Promise resolved after 31ms
Promise resolved after 37ms
Promise resolved after 62ms
results: [37, 31, 26, 62, 0]
```

As you can see, the then method will be called when all the promises are resolved, and it will receive an array with the results of each promise in the order they are being added in the promise array, not by the order in which they are resolved.

In the previous example, all the promises were successfully resolved as they are based on timer operation. But when we relay on promises to access external resources like files in our system or fetching data from the Internet, then we need to take into account that these resources might not be always available. For example, if the Internet is down, then one or multiple promises can fail and this will make our application to crash. Obviously, this crashing situation can be avoided if we handle the errors using a catch statement, but even in that case, it is very important to remember that when we use this parallelism approach, we need to take into account that if a single promise generates an error, the resolved ones will be ignored just the same as if we were using a single promise.

An alternative approach to Promise.all() is to aggregate all the requests but resolve the promise as soon as the first one is complete. This way, there's no need to wait for the fulfillment of all requests.

Promise.race(): The race method returns a single promise that is fulfilled or rejected as soon as one of the promises gets fulfilled or rejected. This can lead to unexpected results if not carefully managed, as the promises won't stop running even if one of the promises was rejected or fulfilled already:

```
Promise.race([
  randomTimeOutPromise(),
  randomTimeOutPromise(),
  randomTimeOutPromise(),
  randomTimeOutPromise(),
  randomTimeOutPromise(),
]).then((result) => {
  console.log("result:", result);
});
```

The output of this code will be something like this:

```
Promise resolved after 30ms
results: 30
Promise resolved after 33ms
Promise resolved after 60ms
Promise resolved after 79ms
Promise resolved after 83ms
```

As you can see, the then method will be called when the first promise is resolved, and it will receive the result of the first promise that is resolved. The other promises will continue running, but the then method will not be called again.

Error handling

In the previous examples, we saw how to handle errors using the catch method, but there is another way to handle errors: using the reject function. Let's see how this works with this example:

```
const generatePromise = shouldFail => {
  return new Promise((resolve, reject) => {
    if (shouldFail) {
      return reject(new Error("Rejected!"));
    }
    resolve("Success!");
  });
};

generatePromise(true).catch(error => console.log("Error message:",
error));
// Error message: Error: Rejected!
// ...
```

It's important to notice that the reject function will not stop the execution of the code, so we need to return the function after calling the reject function.

The final approach is when we need to perform an action once a promise has been concluded, regardless of whether it was successful or rejected. It is important to remember that unhandled promise rejections can lead to runtime errors that will crash your application. We will learn more about this in *Chapter 15*.

Promise.finally(): Sometimes, we don't care if the promise is resolved or rejected; we just want to know when the promise has been resolved or rejected. For this case, we can use the finally method:

```
generatePromise(true)
  .then(result => console.log("Result:", result))
  .catch(error => console.log("Error message:", error))
  .finally(() => console.log("Promise settled"));
```

Chaining promises

We can also chain promises; we can return a promise in the then method, and this promise will be resolved before calling the next then method. The catch method will be called if any of the promises in the chain are rejected. Let's see an example:

```
generatePromise()
  .then(generatePromise)
  .then(result => {
    return generatePromise(true);
  })
  .then(() => console.log("This will not be called"))
  .catch(error => console.log("Error message:", error));
```

When the third generatePromise is called, it will return a promise that will be rejected, so the catch method will be called and then the last then won't be executed.

We have been utilizing promises for some time, and the syntax can be quite verbose, requiring keywords such as then and catch consistently. A more advanced and aesthetically pleasing syntax involves using async and await. We will delve into this approach in the next section.

Using async and await to handle asynchronous code

ES2017 introduced a new way to handle asynchronous code, the async and await keywords. These keywords are syntactic sugar for promises; they are not a new way to handle asynchronous code, but they make the code much easier to read and write.

Essentially, the async keyword is employed to define an asynchronous function, while the await keyword is used to pause and await the resolution of a promise within that function. Even if you use the word async it doesn't make you code asynchronously, that will only occur when you actually have asynchronous code on it (a promise). To make it more simple, we can say that in order to use await, we need to define the code block using async. Let's explore more in detail how we can use async.

async

When a function is defined with the async keyword, it will always return a promise that can be handled as any regular promise. Let's see an example:

```
const asyncFun = async (generateError) => {
    if (generateError) {
        throw new Error("Error generated");
    }
    return 1;
```

```
};

asyncFun().then((result) => console.log(result));
asyncFun(true).catch((error) => console.log(error));
```

As this is syntactic sugar for promises, we can build a similar function using promises:

```
const asyncFun =  (generateError) => new Promise((resolve, reject) =>
{
    if (generateError) {
        reject(new Error("Error generated"));
    }
    resolve(1);
});

asyncFun().then((result) => console.log(result));
asyncFun(true).catch((error) => console.log(error));
```

Now, let's acquaint ourselves with `await`; we'll be able to seamlessly combine both keywords and eliminate the need to use `then` or `catch`.

await

Let's see how we can use the `await` keyword in order to wait for promises:

```
// Promises
fetch(' https://api.demo.foo/v1/todo')
  .then(response => response.json())
  .then(json => console.log(json))
  .catch(error => console.log(error));

// Async/Await
const fetchData = async () => {
  try {
    const response = await fetch('https://api.demo.foo/v1/todo');
    const json = await response.json();
    console.log(json);
  } catch (error) {
      console.log(error);
  }
}
fetchData(); // [{userId: 1, id: 1, title: 'delectus aut autem',
completed: false}]
```

As you can see, the code is much easier to read and write using `async` and `await`. The `await` keyword can only be used inside an `async` function. We need to use the `try/catch` block to handle the errors.

`try/catch` is a mechanism provided by JavaScript that allows us to encapsulate certain code inside the `try` block, and handle any possible errors with the `catch` block. So, in the previous example, as we are doing an HTTP request we depend on external factors such as connectivity to the internet or the ability of the external server to return the information that we are asking for in our request. In our specific case, we are "silently failing" this error because in the `catch` block we only print the information about the error, but in other scenarios we might show an alert message in the UI or trigger a retry strategy to try to perform this HTTP request again. It is important to remember that If we don't handle errors properly, our application might crash. We will explore this topic in detail in *Chapter 15*.

Now, let's explore how we can blend **Immediately Invoked Function Expressions (IIFEs)** with `async` to employ this syntactic sugar even in older Node.js versions.

IIFEs

In some cases, we want to use the `await` keyword outside an `async` function, for example, when we are using the `await` keyword in the top level of a module. In this case, we can use an IIFE to wrap the `await` keyword inside an `async` function. An IIFE is a function that is executed immediately after it is created. It is a design pattern that is used to avoid polluting the global scope with variables and functions. In the subsequent example, we can observe the fundamental syntax:

```
(function () {
  // ... some code here
})();
```

The idea is to create an anonymous function and execute it immediately after it is created. In order to achieve this, we need to wrap the function between parentheses, and then add another pair of parentheses to execute the function: `(...)()`.

We can use `async` and `await` inside an IIFE easily:

```
(async () => {
    const response = await fetch(' https://api.demo.foo/v1/todo ');
    const json = await response.json();
    console.log(json);
})()
```

This guarantees that the code will be executed immediately after it is created, and we can use the `await` keyword inside the IIFE.

Summary

In this chapter, we learned about asynchronous programming in JavaScript. We explored asynchronous APIs such as setTimeout and fetch, and we learned how to handle asynchronous code using callbacks, promises, and async/await. Additionally, we learned about the error first callback convention and how to prevent callback hell using named functions and promises. Finally, we learned how to manage promises, how to bulk operations using the Promise.all and Promise.race methods, and how to use the async and await keywords to handle asynchronous code in a cleaner way.

In the next chapter, we will learn about HTTP and how the modern web works using REST APIs.

Further reading

Asynchronous programming in JavaScript is a broad topic that necessitates a considerable amount of time to master and comprehend fully. With the following links, you will discover valuable resources that will aid you in delving deeper into the subjects covered in this chapter:

- *JavaScript Promise in 100 Seconds*: https://www.youtube.com/watch?v=RvYYCGs45L4

- *Asynchrony: Under the Hood – Shelley Vohr – JSConf EU*: https://www.youtube.com/watch?v=SrNQS8J67zc

- *async/await in JavaScript – What, Why and How – Fun Fun Function*: https://www.youtube.com/watch?v=568g8hxJJp4

Part 2:
Node.js Ecosystem
and Architecture

In *Part 2*, you will learn how to use the Node.js core libraries and third-party libraries by using the vast npm ecosystem ecosystem. Also, you will learn how to use and implement event-driven architectures in detail, and you will understand how to use testing and implement unit testing in your projects.

This part includes the following chapters:

- *Chapter 5, Node.js Core Libraries*

- *Chapter 6, External Modules and npm*

- *Chapter 7, Event-Driven Architecture*

- *Chapter 8, Testing in Node.js*

5
Node.js Core Libraries

In this chapter, we delve into the core libraries of Node.js and explore the techniques for modularizing your code. JavaScript has come a long way from being limited to browsers, and Node.js has offered us new ways to structure our code. We'll begin by understanding the historical limitations of organizing code in the browser and how they led to the development of various module systems. We'll primarily focus on two module systems, **CommonJS (CJS)** and **ECMAScript Modules (ESM)**, and discuss their usage, importation, and exportation. Achieving interoperability between these two systems is crucial, and we'll explore strategies to make it work seamlessly.

Understanding how core libraries in Node.js are structured is key. We'll take a closer look at core libraries including `fs` and `http`, which deal with file operations, and explore the use of callbacks, synchronous functions, and promises for asynchronous I/O operations.

Also, more advanced topics related to extending Node.js functionality with C++ addons and executing external commands using the `child_process` library will be discussed. We'll also review various command-line options (including to enable experimental features and control memory allocation) and environmental variables that allow you to customize the Node.js behavior. We'll provide examples of how to use these options to enable experimental features, control memory allocation, and fine-tune your Node.js applications.

To sum up, here are the main topics that we will explore in this chapter:

- How to create and consume modules using the ESM and CJS approaches
- How to interoperate between ESM and CJS modules
- How the Node.js core libraries interfaces are structured
- What the most relevant Node.js core libraries are when starting with Node.js

How to extend the Node.js functionality by using command-line options and the `NODE_OPTIONS` environment variable

Technical requirements

The code files for the chapter can be found at `https://github.com/PacktPublishing/NodeJS-for-Beginners`.

Check out the code in action video for this chapter on `https://youtu.be/WQzdXAFxdsc`

Modularizing your code (ESM versus CJS)

For many years JavaScript was limited to the browser, and the only way to organize our code was using script files that were loaded in the correct order in a HTML page. This was done by including specific references in the HTML files, such as the following:

```html
<!-- External Sources -->
<script src="https://code.jquery.com/jquery-3.7.0.min.js"></script>
<!-- Other files -->
<script src="script1.js"></script>
<!-- Direct Scripts -->
<script>
console.log("Hello world");
</script>
```

This approach was not scalable, and it was very easy to pollute the global scope. To solve this problem, historically we used the IIFE pattern and the module pattern. As the adoption of JavaScript started to grow and the amount of JavaScript required for a modern website was dramatically rising, the community began to create libraries and frameworks to solve these aforementioned problems. The outcome included results such as RequireJS (`https://requirejs.org/`).

For many years, we had four different ways to organize our code:

- **CommonJS (CJS)**
- **ECMAScript Modules (ESM)**
- **Asynchronous Module Definition (AMD)**
- **Universal Module Definition (UMD)**

In this book, we will focus on the first two approaches, CJS and ESM. Currently CJS is the default module system in Node.js, but since the release of Node.js 12, ESM is now available. In this section, we will explore how to create and consume modules using both approaches.

> **Important note**
>
> Today, in the browser environment is very common to consolidate our code using a module bundler such as webpack or Rollup. However, in Node.js we keep using CJS or ESM directly. In this section, we will explore how to create and consume modules using both approaches.

CommonJS (CJS)

CommonJS is the module system that Node.js uses by default. This module system is synchronous, and is based on the `require` and `module.exports` functions. It is important to note that this module system is not part of the ECMAScript specification, but it is the most used module system in the Node.js ecosystem, especially if you are looking for documentation or tutorials.

There are two aspects here of CJS use that we need to understand: the importation and the exportation. Let's start with the importation.

Importation

So, we have two files in our project, `utils.js` and `index.js`. In this example, we are importing the `sayHello` function from the `utils.js` file in the `index.js` file, as follows:

```
const sayHello = require('./utils.js');
sayHello();
```

The `require` function is a global function that is available in Node.js and is used to import modules. The `require` function receives a string as a parameter, and this string is the path to the module that we want to import. In this case, we are using a relative path, but we can also use absolute paths or even the name of a module that is installed in the `node_modules` folder.

Exportation

In this example, we are exporting the `sayHello` function in the `utils.js` file:

```
function sayHello() {
  console.log('Hello world');
}
module.exports = sayHello;
```

`module.exports` is a global object that is available in Node.js, and it is used to export modules. In this case, we are exporting the `sayHello` function, but we can export any type of value.

If you execute the `index.js` file, you will see the following output:

```
$ node index.js
Hello world
```

But if we execute the `utils.js` file, we will see nothing. Even if the file is executed, the `sayHello` function itself is not executed, just defined:

```
$ node utils.js
```

Export object structures

The most popular structure to use while exporting modules is the object structure, as it is very flexible and allows us to export multiple values. If we want to export multiple values, we can use the `exports` object:

```
// You can export directly
exports.sayHello = () => {
  console.log('Hello world');
}

function sayGoodbye() {
  console.log('Goodbye world');
}

// You can also export using references
exports.sayGoodbye = sayGoodbye;
```

But we can also export an object directly using `module.exports = {}`:

```
const sayHello = () => {
  console.log('Hello world');
}

function sayGoodbye() {
  console.log('Goodbye world');
}

module.exports = {
  sayHello,
  sayGoodbye
}
```

I recommend the preceding option as it is more readable when working with larger files. In order to import the exported values, we can use the destructuring syntax:

```
const { sayHello, sayGoodbye } = require('./utils.js');

sayHello();
sayGoodbye();
```

JSON support

Yep, you can add JSON files directly to your project in Node.js and you don't need to use any external library or parse the content:

```json
{
    "name": "John",
    "lastName": "Doe"
}
```

Now we can require the file directly:

```
const user = require('./user.json');

console.log(user);
// { name: 'John', lastName: 'Doe' }
```

The way that modules work in Node.js is very similar to the IIFE pattern. When we import a module, the code is executed and the module is cached. If we import the same module again, the code is not executed again, and the module is retrieved from the cache. Basically, the module is executed only once (singleton pattern).

So, for example, if we make changes to the imported JSON file, the changes will not be reflected in the imported module once it has already been imported, because it is read once and the content is cached in the program memory.

ECMAScript Modules (ESM)

Node.js 12 introduced the support for **ECMAScript Modules** (**ESM**). ESM is the module system that is part of the ECMAScript specification. This module system supports asynchronous (dynamic modules) and is based on the import and export keywords.

In order to use modules with Node.js 20.11.0 you will need to create a package.json file and add the following configuration:

```json
{
    "type": "module"
}
```

> **Important note**
>
> In *Chapter 6*, we will explore how to create a package.json file and how to configure it in depth.

Basic usage

In this example, we are exporting the sayHello function in the utils.js file:

```
export default function sayHello() {
  console.log('Hello world');
}
```

The export keyword is used to export modules. In this case, we are exporting the sayHello function, but we can export any type of value. Note that we are using the default keyword, this is because we are exporting a single value. If we want to export multiple values, we can use the export keyword without the default keyword.

In this example, we are importing the sayHello function from the utils.js file:

```
import sayHello from './utils.js';
sayHello();
```

Export object structures

The most popular structure to use while exporting modules is the object structure, as it is very flexible and allows us to export multiple values. If we want to export multiple values, we can use the export keyword:

```
const sayHello = () => {
  console.log('Hello world');
}

function sayGoodbye() {
  console.log('Goodbye world');
}

export { sayGoodbye, sayHello };
```

In this example, we are importing the sayHello and sayGoodbye functions from the utils.js file in several ways:

```
// Import values directly
import { sayHello, sayGoodbye } from './utils.js';
// Use wildcards to import all the exported values
import * as utils from './utils.js';
sayHello();
utils.sayHello();
```

Support for JSON files

While using ESM, it is not possible to import JSON files directly as we did for CJS. If we try to import a JSON file, we will get the following error:

```
TypeError [ERR_IMPORT_ASSERTION_TYPE_MISSING]: Module "file:///
{REDACTED}/user.json" needs an import assertion of type "json"
```

In the future, it will be possible to import JSON files directly, there is a proposal (`https://github.com/tc39/proposal-import-attributes`) that will allow us to use import attributes, such as `import json from "./foo.json" with { type: "json" };`. But for now, we need to use a workaround to import JSON files. We can fix this error by understanding how interoperability works between ESM and CJS.

Understanding how interoperability works

While ESM is the future, there are many libraries and frameworks that still use CJS. The good news is that Node.js supports both module systems, and it is possible to use both in the same project without any problem, but there are some considerations that we need to take into account in order to make it work.

> **Important note**
> Interoperability has been a very controversial topic in the Node.js community, and there are many discussions about it. If you want to know more about it, I recommend you to read this article by Gil Tayar: `https://medium.com/@giltayar/native-es-modules-in-nodejs-status-and-future-directions-part-i-ee5ea3001f71`.

JSON files in ESM

In the previous section, we saw that it is not possible to import JSON files directly in ESM today. But we can use the `module` library built into Node.js to import JSON files. The `module` library is a global object that is available in all the modules and contains the `createRequire` method that allows us to create a `require` function that can be used to import CJS modules:

```
import { createRequire } from "module";
const require = createRequire(import.meta.url);
const user = require("./user.json");
console.log(user);
// { name: 'John', lastName: 'Doe' }
```

File extensions (.cjs and .mjs)

In order to use both module systems in the same project, we need to use different file extensions in our files. The `.mjs` extension is used for ESM modules, and the `.cjs` extension is used for CJS modules.

> **Important note**
>
> If you are using .js extension for your files, Node.js will try to use the CJS module system by default, like if you were using .cjs extension.

Here is the file structure of a project that uses both module systems:

```
├── index.cjs
├── index.mjs
├── utils.cjs
└── utils.mjs
```

The utils.cjs file is a CJS module:

```
const sayGoodbye = () => {
  console.log('Goodbye world');
}
module.exports = { sayGoodbye }
```

The utils.mjs file is an ESM module:

```
const sayHello = () => {
  console.log('Hello world');
}
export { sayHello }
```

The index.mjs file is an ESM module. We can combine both module systems in the same file as long as we use different file extensions:

```
import { sayHello } from './utils.mjs';
import { sayGoodbye } from './utils.cjs';
sayHello();
sayGoodbye();
```

The index.cjs file is a CJS module. In this case, ESM modules can not be imported directly because require was designed as a synchronous function, and ESM modules are asynchronous. But we can use the import function to import ESM modules asynchronously:

```
const { sayGoodbye } = require('./utils.cjs');
import("./utils.mjs").then(({ sayHello }) => {
    sayHello();
    sayGoodbye();
});
```

> **Important info**
>
> This way of importing modules is part of the standard, and it is called dynamic import (`https://developer.mozilla.org/en-US/docs/Web/JavaScript/Reference/Statements/import#dynamic_imports`).

In this book, we use ESM modules by default, but we will use CJS modules when we need to use interoperability with other libraries and frameworks.

Now that we have a clearer idea of how to create modules in the different formats, let's explore in the next section how the Node.js core APIs use a similar approach to expose tons of functionalities that we will use very often in our projects.

Structuring core libraries

Over the years, Node.js has grown a lot, and the core libraries too. There are many libraries available for us to use, and it is important to know how they are structured to be able to use them properly.

Most of the core libraries are quite simple and are structured in a similar way so you know what to expect in practical terms. Once you know how to use one of them, you will be able to use the rest of them without any problem.

Furthermore, you will be able to create your own libraries and publish them in npm, and other developers will be able to use them easily, but we will talk about this in the next chapter.

The library structure

Let's look at the `fs` library as an example. The `fs` library is used to work with the file system, and it is one of the most used libraries in Node.js.

Any library that performs I/O operations is asynchronous. Historically, Node.js has offered two ways to handle I/O operations: callbacks or synchronous functions. While callbacks are still supported, Node.js currently offers the same functionality providing a promise interface.

In this example, we will use the `readFile` function to read a file asynchronously. This function receives the path of the file to read, and a callback function that will be called when the file is read. The callback function receives two arguments: an error object and the content of the file:

```
import { readFile } from 'node:fs';

readFile('hello.txt', (err, content) => {

  if (err) {
    console.error("OMG, there is an error:", err);
    return;
  }
```

```
        console.log(`File content: ${content}`);
        // File content: Hello world
    });
```

When you run the previous example, it will throw an error, as the file does not exist. However, we manage the error using the error first pattern in the callback. You can see the `OMG, there...` `error message`. Now, if you create the `hello.txt` file with the content `Hello world` and you run again the script, you will see the content printed as expected.

In the next example, we will use the `readFileSync` function to read a file synchronously. This function receives the path of the file to read, and it returns the content of the file:

```
import { readFileSync } from 'node:fs';

try {
    const content = readFileSync('hello.txt');
    console.log(`File content: ${content}`);
    // File content: Hello world
} catch (err) {
    console.error("OMG, there is an error:", err);
};
```

And finally, in this example, we will use the `readFile` function to read a file asynchronously. This function receives the path of the file to read and returns a promise that will be resolved when the file is read. The promise will be resolved with the content of the file:

```
import { readFile } from 'node:fs/promises';

readFile('hello.txt')
    .then(content => console.log(`File content: ${content}`))
    .catch(err => console.error("OMG, there is an error:", err))
```

Core libraries without prefix

Historically, Node.js has provided the core libraries without the `node:*` prefix, such as `const { readFile } from 'fs'`. This is mainly for backward compatibility. But it is recommended to use the new syntax with the prefix `node:*`. You will find many examples on the internet that use the old syntax. More information can be found at `https://nodejs.org/api/modules.html`.

CJS support

All the core libraries are available as CJS modules, so you can use them in your projects without any problem. You can use the require function to import them:

CJS	ESM
const { readFile } = require('node:fs')	import { readFile } from 'node:fs'
const { readFileSync } = require('node:fs')	import { readFileSync } from 'node:fs'
const { readFile } = require('node:fs/promises')	import { readFile } from 'node:fs/promises'
const { readFile } = require('node:fs')	import { readFile } from 'node:fs'
const { readFileSync } = require('node:fs')	import { readFileSync } from 'node:fs'

Additional interfaces

Other core libraries that you will use frequently, such as http or https, are structured similarly and provide an interface to work with events. We will cover this topic in depth in *Chapter 7*.

Stability index

The stability index is a number that indicates the stability of the core libraries. The stability index is a number between 0 and 3, where 0 means deprecated, 1 means experimental, 2 means stable, and 3 means legacy.

You can find the stability index of each core library in the official documentation, along with more details about the stability index at https://nodejs.org/dist/latest-v20.x/docs/api/documentation.html#stability-index.

> **Important note**
> If you are just starting with Node.js, you should use the core libraries with stability index 2 or 3. The core libraries with a stability index of 0 or 1 are not recommended for production environments.

Let's see some examples from Node.js 20:

- Permission Model (`https://nodejs.org/docs/latest-v20.x/api/permissions.html#permission-model`): This is an API that allows us to restrict access to system resources such as network or files. Currently, it is in active development (stability=1), so you can experiment with it, but it is not yet mature enough to use for building production systems as the API might change or have unexpected behavior.

- http (`https://nodejs.org/docs/latest-v20.x/api/http.html#http`): This is the API used since the beginning of Node.js to build web server applications and make HTTP requests to external resources. Currently, it is stable (stability=2), but some methods are legacy (stability=3). This library is perfect for use in production systems.

Other core libraries

The `fs` library is just an example; in this book, we will cover the most important core libraries, but you can find the documentation of all the core libraries in the Node.js documentation at `https://nodejs.org/docs/latest-v20.x/api/index.html`.

In my humble opinion, the most important core libraries when you are starting with Node.js are the following, in alphabetical order:

- `Buffer` handles binary data efficiently in memory, commonly used for tasks such as file operations and network communication.

- `Crypto` provides cryptographic functionality, such as encryption, decryption, hashing, and digital signatures.

- `Events` allows us to create, emit, and listen for events inside our applications.

- `File System` provides a solid interface to deal with the file system (files, folders, creation, deletions, etc.).

- `HTTP` allows us to create HTTP servers and perform HTTP requests.

- `OS` offers various utilities to retrieve information about the system's architecture, platform, CPU, memory, network interfaces, and much more.

- `Path` provides utilities for working with file paths and directory paths.

- `Process` provides information and control over aspects of the current Node.js process, including environmental variables, lifecycle events, and more.

- `Stream` provides readable and writable streams, as well as transform streams for modifying data as it passes through. This module is essential for building scalable and memory-efficient applications that work with large volumes of data in Node.js.

- `Timers` includes functions such as `setTimeout()`, `setInterval()`, and `setImmediate()`.

There are other core libraries that are very important to extend the functionality of Node.js, but they are not so important when you are just starting out with Node.js.

For example, the `child_process` library is essential to execute external commands such as `ls` and `cat` from Node.js, complex applications such as `ffmpeg` and `imagemagick`, and even directly execute Python scripts.

The C++ Addons (`https://nodejs.org/dist/latest-v20.x/docs/api/addons.html`) are very important to extend the functionality of Node.js with C++ code. This is very useful when you need to use a C++ library in your Node.js application.

Command-line options

Node.js provides a lot of command-line options and environmental variables that you can use to customize the behavior of Node.js. You can find the complete list of command-line options in the Node.js documentation at `https://nodejs.org/dist/latest-v20.x/docs/api/cli.html#cli_command_line_options`.

For example, you can use the `--experimental-json-modules` command-line option to enable the JSON modules in ESM, such as `node --experimental-json-modules index.js`.

The code of the `index.js` file is as follows:

```
import data from './data.json' assert { type: 'json' };
console.log(data);
```

This does work, and the terminal output will remark that the JSON modules are experimental:

```
(node:21490) ExperimentalWarning: Import assertions are not a stable
feature of the JavaScript language. Avoid relying on their current
behavior and syntax as those might change in a future version of Node.
js.
(Use `node --trace-warnings ...` to show where the warning was
created)
(node:21490) ExperimentalWarning: Importing JSON modules is an
experimental feature and might change at any time
```

Aside from enabling experimental features, you can use the `--max-old-space-size` command-line option to increase the RAM usage limit of Node.js. This is very useful when you are working with large files, have a lot of data in memory, or are debugging a complicated memory leak.

For example, you can use the `--max-old-space-size=4096` command-line option to increase the RAM limit to 4GB: `node --max-old-space-size=4096 index.js`.

> **Important note**
> You can't use all the RAM in your computer, because the operating system and other applications also need some RAM to work properly.

Environmental variables

You can use environmental variables to customize the behavior of Node.js. You can find the complete list of environmental variables in the Node.js documentation at `https://nodejs.org/dist/latest-v20.x/docs/api/cli.html#cli_environmental_variables`.

Sometimes it is more convenient to use environmental variables instead of command-line options directly, such as when using UNIX-based systems:

```
# Define the environmental variable
export NODE_OPTIONS='--experimental-json-modules,--max-old-space-size=4096'
# Run the Node.js application as usual
node index.js
```

The preceding code lets you use the `NODE_OPTIONS` environmental variable to set the command-line options that you want to use. This is very useful when you are using a tool such as `nodemon` or `pm2` to run your Node.js application. We will use a lot of environmental variables from *Chapter 12*.

Summary

In this chapter, we have covered how modules work in Node.js, the differences between CJS and ESM, and how to interoperate between them.

Additionally, we have covered the core libraries of Node.js, how to use them, their structure, and the stability index. We listed the most important core libraries when starting out with Node.js and other libraries that become essential in more advanced projects.

Finally, we learned how to use the command-line options and environmental variables to modify the Node.js behavior.

In the next chapter, we will learn how to use the **node.js package manager** (**npm**) in depth. We will publish our first package and we will see how we can integrate the huge module ecosystem available for us in our Node.js projects.

Further reading

- Node.js documentation: `https://nodejs.org/dist/latest-v20.x/docs/api/documentation.html#documentation_stability_index`

- Keeping the Node.js core small: `https://medium.com/the-node-js-collection/keeping-the-node-js-core-small-137f83d18152`

- Moz://a Hacks | ES6 In Depth: Modules: `https://hacks.mozilla.org/2015/08/es6-in-depth-modules`

- Promises API in Node.js Core: Part "Do", the Update! - Joe Sepi, IBM: `https://www.youtube.com/watch?v=f7YSsYQmNSI`

6

External Modules and npm

Node Package Manager (**npm**) is one of the most popular software registries around the world. There are more than two million packages available for us to use. In this chapter, we will explore how to use npm commands and NPX, as well as what the isomorphic libraries are and how to choose the correct dependencies for our project, so we can minimize the risks. As a final practice, you will publish a package to npm.

In this chapter, we will explore how to use external modules in our projects. This will allow us to reuse code from other developers and save time and effort. We will explore together the vast ecosystem of Node.js modules, and we will learn how to choose the correct modules for our projects.

To sum up, here are the main topics that we will explore in this chapter:

- Managing the application with `package.json`
- Choosing the correct dependencies for your project
- Installing dependencies
- Removing dependencies
- Understanding `package-lock.json`
- Managing dependencies versions
- Building Isomorphic JavaScript
- Using npm scripts
- Executing packages directly with NPX
- npm alternatives
- Publishing your first package

Technical requirements

The code files for the chapter can be found at `https://github.com/PacktPublishing/NodeJS-for-Beginners`

Check out the code in action video for this chapter on `https://youtu.be/B-7vZyAfi2U`

Managing the application with package.json

When you install Node.js, npm is installed as well. npm is the package manager for Node.js. It is used to install, update, and remove packages from our projects. It also allows us to publish our own packages.

A package is a JavaScript library that we can use in our applications to speed up the process of developing our own projects. There are many different types of packages, from very simple ones such as a function that can tell us whether a number is odd or not (`https://www.npmjs.com/package/is-odd`), to very complex libraries that can help us to use Firebase (`https://firebase.google.com/?hl=es`) to store information from our users (`https://www.npmjs.com/package/firebase`). It is quite common to use many libraries in a single project, and some companies create their own private libraries to distribute utilities, configurations, and many more things across their many code bases.

The `package.json` file is the manifest file for our project. It contains the metadata of our project, such as the name, version, description, author, and license. It also contains the dependencies of our project, both the runtime dependencies and the development dependencies, and it contains the scripts that we can run with npm.

In order to create a `package.json` file, we can run the following command:

```
npm init
```

This command will ask us a few questions, and then it will create the `package.json` file. For an even faster creation, you can use `npm init -y` to automatically create the file with the default values suggested.

We can also create the `package.json` file manually, but it is recommended to use the `npm init` command.

The `package.json` file can be very simple, like this one:

```
{
  "name": "my-project",
  "version": "1.0.0",
  "description": "My project",
  "main": "index.js",
  "scripts": {
    "test": "echo \"Error: no test specified\" && exit 1"
```

```
    },
    "author": "John Doe",
    "license": "MIT"
}
```

But it can also be a large file, with one or many dependencies, scripts, and additional metadata. Currently, there is no official standard for the `package.json` file, but there are efforts to create it in the Standards Working Group from the OpenJS Foundation (`https://github.com/openjs-foundation/standards/issues/233`).

Currently, we can use the npm documentation to know what fields we can use in the `package.json` file. The documentation is available at `https://docs.npmjs.com/cli/v7/configuring-npm/package-json`.

In the next sections, we will see some of the most important fields in the `package.json` file and how to use them in our projects.

Choosing the correct dependencies for your project

It is true that the npm ecosystem is very solid and growing every day. But it is also true that many packages are not maintained anymore, or that include security vulnerabilities and performance issues.

The community is aware of this and there are plenty of jokes and memes about this topic. For example, the following image:

Figure 6.1 – npm Delivery by MonkeyUser – a classic meme that shows how many dependencies
we tend to include in our projects (https://www.monkeyuser.com/2017/npm-delivery/)

While this is a joke based on the huge number of dependencies and sub-dependencies that we install on an average project, it is true that we need to be careful when choosing the dependencies for our projects. In this section, we will see how to choose the correct dependencies for our projects.

> **Note**
>
> Most modules depend on other modules, and those modules depend on other modules, and so on. This is called the **dependency tree**. When we install a module, we are installing all the dependencies of that module, and all the dependencies of the dependencies, and so on. This is why it is important to choose the correct dependencies for our projects.

Before choosing a dependency, we need to ask ourselves the following questions:

- What are the risks associated with choosing a bad dependency?

- What are the criteria that I should use to choose a dependency?

Let's see the answers to these questions!

Risks

In our modern world, we are used to using dependencies. It will be very hard or directly impossible to build modern web applications without using dependencies.

When we choose a dependency, we are taking a risk. Let's see what the main risks associated with choosing a bad dependency are:

- **Security vulnerabilities**: A dependency can have security vulnerabilities or even be a malicious piece of code.

- **Performance issues**: A dependency can have performance issues and generate memory leaks that can affect the performance of our application and even crash it.

- **Maintenance issues**: A dependency cannot be maintained anymore, and it can be deprecated in the future. This can cause our application to stop working in the future or prevent us from upgrading other dependencies or Node.js itself.

In 2020, I published a controversial blog post called *What is a backdoor? Let's build one with Node.js* (`https://snyk.io/blog/what-is-a-backdoor/`). In that blog post, I explained that a backdoor is a piece of code that allows us to access a system without going through the authentication process. I also explained how to build a backdoor with Node.js using a few lines of code and I demonstrated how easy was to publish and distribute a malicious package.

I know that security is a very sensitive topic, especially if you are starting your journey in web development. *Chapter 15* of this book is dedicated to security, and we will explore security in depth there.

In order to minimize the risks, we need to choose the correct dependencies for our projects. Let's see how to do that.

Good criteria

There are many criteria that we can use to choose the correct dependencies for our projects. In this section, we will see some of the most important ones.

What are we trying to avoid?

We try to avoid the following things:

- Packages that are not maintained anymore
- Packages that have known security vulnerabilities and are not patched
- Packages that depend on a lot of packages or have low-quality dependencies
- Packages that are not popular or are low quality
- Packages with license issues

What evidence do we have?

We are going to do some basic OSINT before we install any package, and we are going to check two data sources in detail: the npm website and the GitHub or code repository.

> *OSINT is intelligence produced by collecting and analyzing public information with the purpose of answering a specific intelligence question. (Ritu Gill,* `https://www.sans.org/blog/what-is-open-source-intelligence/`*.)*

Real example

In this book, we are going to use the Express library. Express is a very popular library for Node.js, and it is used to build web applications and APIs. In this image, we can see in detail how the Express library is showcased on the npm website:

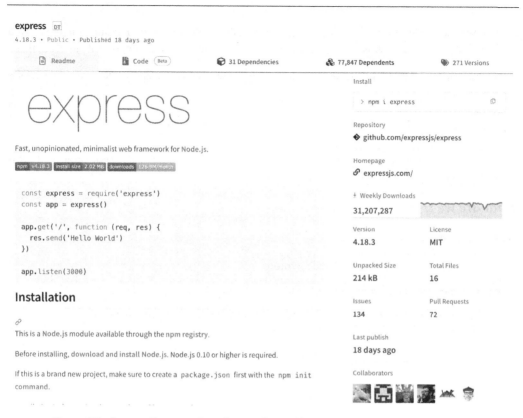

Figure 6.2 – Express library package in npm (https://www.npmjs.com/package/express)

From the npm website, we can see the following information:

- There are 31 dependencies, most of which are very popular and well-maintained by the same Express maintainers

- There are +77k dependents, which means that many other package authors are using Express in their projects

- There are 271 versions published

- There are almost 31M weekly downloads, which means that Express is a very popular package for the Node.js community

- An MIT license, which is a permissive license and valid as open source

- Clear and solid documentation

- It was last published few days ago, which means that the package is maintained and updated regularly

From npm, we can access the GitHub repository of the package. In the following image, we can see in detail how the Express library is showcased on the GitHub website:

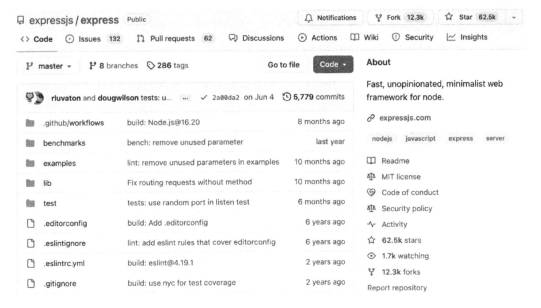

Figure 6.3 – Express library repository in GitHub (https://github.com/expressjs/express)

From the GitHub website, we can see the following information:

- It has +10k forks, which means that many other developers are contributing to the project

- It has +60k stars, which means that the project is popular in the community

- It has +5k commits, which means that the project has a long history

- It has +3k issues closed, +120 issues open, +1k pull requests closed, and +60 pull requests open, which means that the project is active

- It has almost 300 contributors, which means that many other developers are contributing to the project and evolving it

As we can see, we have a lot of information from the npm website and the GitHub repository at least to make a first decision, especially if we want to compare several packages. The offer is huge and sometimes it is difficult to choose the correct package.

Exceptions to the rules

We need to be quite flexible with the rules that we have seen before because very often we can find exceptions to the rules.

For example, johnny-five (https://www.npmjs.com/package/johnny-five) is a great library to use when working with Arduino and Raspberry Pi in Node.js. But the total download per week is very low. In this case, we need to consider that there are much less developers working with Arduino and Raspberry Pi than developers working with Express, for example.

Another example is Lodash (https://www.npmjs.com/package/lodash), which is a very popular library and is used by many other packages. But the last version was published three years ago. In this case, we need to consider that the project is mostly completed, and it is not evolving anymore and only making new releases when needed.

Deprecation notices

Sometimes, we can find a package that is deprecated. In this case, we should avoid using it. We can find a deprecation notice in the npm website, in the GitHub repository, or when we install the package.

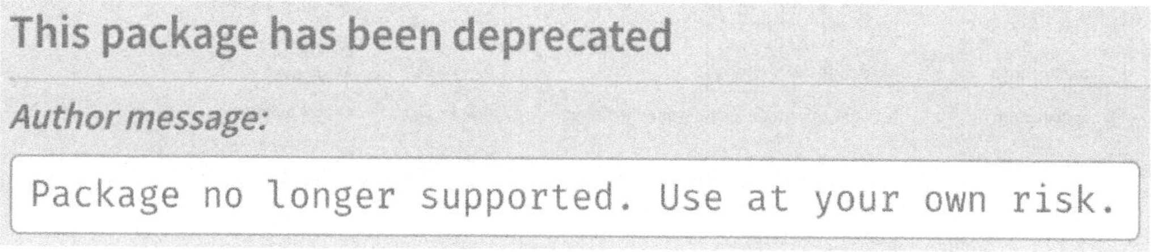

This package has been deprecated

Author message:

Package no longer supported. Use at your own risk.

Figure 6.4 – Image from the npm documentation that shows how the deprecation warnings are shown in npm (https://docs.npmjs.com/packages-and-modules/updating-and-managing-your-published-packages/deprecate-package.png)

Very often, in the deprecation notice, we can find a recommendation to use another package. In this case, we should follow the recommendation.

Tooling

In the previous OSINT analysis, we answered most of our questions, but we didn't answer questions regarding known vulnerabilities. These days, I use two tools to check known vulnerabilities: *Snyk* (https://snyk.io/) and *socket.dev* (https://socket.dev/).

In *Chapter 15*, we will see how they are used in detail. In order to use these tools properly, you will need to understand how the dependency tree works and how the vulnerabilities are classified. Otherwise, these tools can be very confusing for beginners.

I will suggest to say "In the next section, we will learn how to install the dependencies in our projects.

Installing dependencies

Now that we know how to choose the correct dependencies for our projects, and we have a `package.json` we can start installing our dependencies.

Locally or globally

We can install dependencies in two ways: locally or globally:

- **Locally**: These are dependencies that are installed in the `node_modules` folder of our project. For example, `express` is a local dependency of our application.

- **Globally**: These are dependencies that are installed in the global folder of our system, so they become available from anywhere in our system, such as Node.js binary, which is available as soon as we open the terminal.

We would prefer to install dependencies locally because it is easier to manage the dependencies of our project and to avoid conflicts between different projects. We will install dependencies globally only when it is strictly necessary.

One example of a dependency that we will install globally is `yeoman`, a scaffolding tool, which we will use to generate a new project.

Dependency or development dependency

We can install the local dependencies in two ways: as a dependency or as a development dependency:

- **Dependency**: Dependencies that are required to run the application. For example, `express` is a dependency of our application.

- **Development dependency**: Dependencies that are required to develop the application. For example, `standard`, which is a linter library, will be used only while developing the code but not when running.

> **Note**
>
> There is an additional mode to install dependencies: **peer dependencies**. We will not cover this mode in this book, but you can find more information and use cases in this blog post: `https://nodejs.org/en/blog/npm/peer-dependencies`.

The segmentation of dependencies is very important because it allows us to install only the dependencies that we need in each environment and to reduce the size of our application and attack surface.

Adding new dependency

For example, if we want to install the `express` package, we can use the following command:

```
# npm install <package-name>
npm install express
```

We can install the `standard` package as a development dependency. Development dependencies are those dependencies that we need when we are actually coding the project, but they are not used when the project is being deployed or distributed as a library. As `standard` is a linting tool, we will use it only when adding or changing code, but we won't use it while the application is running. This segmentation of the dependencies has a lot of benefits as our final applications will be smaller (ignoring the development dependencies) and more secure as we have less external code. We can use the `-D` or `--save-dev` for installing development dependencies arguments:

```
# npm install --save-dev <package-name>
# npm install  -D <package-name>
npm install --save-dev standard
```

We can see that the `package.json` file has been updated with the new dependencies in two different sections: `dependencies` and `devDependencies`:

```
{
  "dependencies": {
    "express": "^4.18.3"
  },
  "devDependencies": {
    "standard": "^17.1.0"
  }
}
```

One new file, `package-lock.json`, has also been added and the `node_modules` folder has been created with the dependencies structured in folders and files.

We will explore in the next section how the `package-lock.json` file works.

> **Note**
>
> The `node_modules` should not be included with the project source code if you are using Git or any other system to distribute your source code. It is good practice to include the `node_modules` folder in the `.gitignore` file to avoid including it in the repository. If you need a solid `.gitignore` file for Node.js, you can generate one (`https://www.toptal.com/developers/gitignore/api/node`). We should ignore `node_modules` because the folder can be huge, and have many files and a heavy weight, but also because we can install the dependencies at any time, as soon as we keep our changes in `package.log`, we will be able to install the correct dependencies

Global dependencies are installed with the -g or –global argument:

```
# npm install --global <package-name>
# npm install -g <package-name>
# Install yeoman globally
npm install --global yo
```

You can see the list of global dependencies with the list or ls command:

```
# npm list --global
# npm ls --global
npm list --global
```

The output of this command will be something like this:

```
/Users/ulises/.nvm/versions/node/v20.11.0/lib
├── corepack@0.23.0
├── npm@10.2.4
└── yo@5.0.0
```

Installing all the dependencies

If we want to install all the dependencies that are listed in the package.json file, we can use the install or i command without any argument:

```
npm install
```

We can also use the --only argument to install only the dependencies or the development dependencies:

```
# Prod Only
npm install --only=prod
npm install --only=production
# Dev Only
npm install --only=dev
npm install --only=development
```

In the production environments, we want to avoid using development tools because, although this will make our applications smaller and more secure, in our development environments we will require all the dependencies to properly do our job.

In the next section, we will explore how to properly remove dependencies from our projects.

Removing dependencies

You can remove a dependency using the `uninstall` command:

```
# npm uninstall <package-name>
npm uninstall express
```

This command will remove the dependency from the `package.json` and `package-lock.json` files and the `node_modules` folder.

Global dependencies are removed with the `-g` or `--global` argument:

```
# npm uninstall --global <package-name>
# npm uninstall -g <package-name>
# Remove yeoman globally
npm uninstall --global yo
```

In the next section we will explore how the `package-lock.json` file can help us to manage our dependencies.

Understanding the package-lock.json

Historically, the `package.json` file was the only file that we needed to manage the dependencies of our project. But this file has a problem: it doesn't contain the exact version of each sub-dependency that we have installed in our project and was also quite slow to install the dependencies.

Not having the exact version of each sub-dependency can be a problem because if we install the same dependency in two different environments, we can end up with different versions of the same dependency. The lack of immutability in our dependencies can lead to unexpected errors and bugs that are quite complicated to debug.

Also, by default, when we install a dependency the version that is recorded in `package.json` includes a caret `^` symbol, such as `"express": "^4.18.3"`. This symbol means that we can install any version of the dependency that is compatible with the version that is recorded in `package.json`.

The `package-lock.json` file is a file that is automatically generated when we install a new dependency and also speeds up the installation of the dependencies because it contains the exact version of each dependency and the source where it comes from.

The file can be huge, but the structure per dependency is quite simple:

```
{
    "node_modules/express/node_modules/debug": {
        "version": "2.6.9",
        "resolved": "https://registry.npmjs.org/debug/-/debug-
2.6.9.tgz",
        "integrity": "sha512-bC7ElrdJaJnPbAP+1EotYvqZsb3ec15wi6Bfi6BJT
```

```
UcNowp6cvspg0jXznRTKDjm/E7AdgFBVeAPVMNcKGsHMA==",
        "dependencies": {
            "ms": "2.0.0"
        }
    }
}
```

As you can see, the exact `version` is included, as well as the `resolved` and `integrity` fields that are used to validate the origin of the dependency and to avoid manipulations with the data in transit as `integrity` provides a checksum. Also, the `dependencies` field is included to list the sub-dependencies with the exact version.

> **Note**
>
> `package-lock.json` should be distributed with the source code of the project and should be committed to the repository; basically, it should be treated as `package.json` in terms of distribution.

Now that we know how to classify and organize the dependencies in our projects, it is time to explore how to install specific versions and notice outdated dependencies.

Managing dependencies versions

If we want to install a specific version of a package, we can use the @ symbol. You can be as specific as you want:

```
# npm install <package-name>@<version>
npm install express@4
npm install express@4.17
npm install express@4.17.1
```

Outdated dependencies

Eventually, the dependencies that we have installed in our project will be outdated, and we will need to update them. To check if we have any outdated dependencies, we can use the `outdated` command:

```
npm outdated
```

This command will list all the outdated dependencies, as well as the current version, the wanted version, and the latest version:

```
Package  Current  Wanted  Latest  Location                Depended by
express  3.21.2   3.21.2  4.18.3  node_modules/express    my-project
```

Now that we are clear on how to handle outdated dependencies it is time to explore in the next section how to create isomorphic JavaScript code that can be executed in all environments (browsers and Node.js)

Building Isomorphic JavaScript

Isomorphic JavaScript is a term that is used to describe JavaScript code that can run both in the browser and in Node.js. In other words, it is a library that can be used in both environments. In order to do that, you will limit yourself to the features that are available in both environments.

For example, you can't use the `fs` module in the browser, and you can't use the `window` object in Node.js.

Sometimes, we install dependencies in our projects that are designed to be used in the browser and we try to use them in Node.js, and vice versa. This is a common mistake that we need to avoid.

Most of the projects will specify which environment they are designed for. Here is an example from Lodash (`https://lodash.com/`):

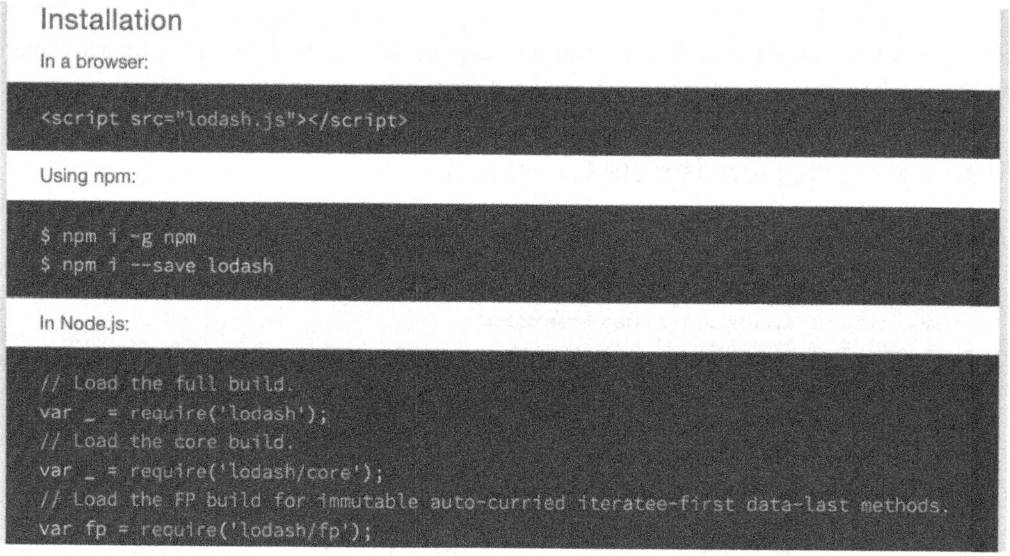

Figure 6.5 – Image from the Lodash documentation that explains in detail how to install the library in both environments (https://lodash.com/)

It is quite clear that lodash is designed to be used in Node.js and in the browser, and from the figure you can see how to install it in each environment.

In the next section, we will learn how we can use npm scripts to improve our developer experience while building Node.js projects.

Using npm scripts

npm scripts are commands that we can define in the package.json file. These commands can be executed using the run command:

```
# npm run <script-name>
npm run lint
```

This is great because we can define our own commands and we can use them to automate tasks. For example, we can define a command to run the linter in our project:

```
{
    "scripts": {
        "lint": "standard",
        "lint:fix": "standard --fix"
    },
    "devDependencies": {
        "standard": "^12.0.1"
    }
}
```

Then we can run the following command:

```
npm run lint
npm run lint:fix
```

npm scripts are basically shortcuts to run commands that we can run manually in the terminal. So, you can build quite complex things such as starting/stopping a server, running tests, preparing infrastructure, and deploying your application.

This is a very powerful feature that we can use to automate tasks in our projects, especially when we are working in a team, and we want to make sure that everyone is running the same commands or with continuous integration tools.

We will use npm scripts in the next chapters to automate tasks in our projects.

Executing packages directly with NPX

Since version 5.2.0, npm comes with a new tool called npx, which allows us to execute packages without installing them globally. This is great for one-time commands.

Let's say that we have a project with outdated dependencies, and we want to update them:

```
{
  "dependencies": {
    "express": "^3.21.2",
```

```
    "lodash": "^1.3.1"
  },
  "devDependencies": {
    "standard": "^17.1.0"
  }
}
```

As we saw in the previous section, we can use the `npm outdated` command to check which dependencies are outdated, but the upgrade process is a bit more complex as we need to upgrade each dependency manually or modify the `package.json` directly.

Fortunately, there is a package called npm-check-updates (`https://www.npmjs.com/package/npm-check-updates`), which allows us to upgrade all the dependencies in our project. Let's learn how to use it:

```
npx npm-check-updates
```

This command will list all the outdated dependencies, and will show the new version that is available:

```
express   ^3.21.2  →   ^4.18.3
lodash    ^1.3.1   →   ^4.17.21
```

Then we can use the `-u` flag to upgrade all the dependencies:

```
npx npm-check-updates -u
```

> **Note**
>
> The `npm-check-updates` package offers a lot of options to customize the upgrade process, you can check the documentation at `https://www.npmjs.com/package/npm-check-updates` for more information.

The dependencies were upgraded in `package.json`, we just need to run `npm install` to make the changes take effect:

```
{
  "dependencies": {
    "express": "^4.18.3",
    "lodash": "^4.17.21"
  },
  "devDependencies": {
    "standard": "^17.1.0"
  }
}
```

Now, we can take an extra step and automate this process using npm scripts, so in the future, we can speed up this process, and we do this just by adding the following scripts to your `package.json` file:

```
{
    "scripts": {
        "deps:check": "npx npm-check-updates",
        "deps:upgrade": "npx npm-check-updates -u && npm install"
    }
}
```

This was a great example of how you can combine npm scripts and npx to automate tasks in your projects and increase the developer experience for other contributors as they can run the same command to upgrade the dependencies when needed.

Also, this combination is great for continuous integration tools, as you can run the same commands in your CI pipeline.

But the most important thing is that you don't need to install any global or local packages, so you keep your dependencies to a minimum.

In the next section we are going to learn more about the current alternatives to npm.

npm alternatives

Over the years, npm has become the standard package manager for JavaScript, but there are other alternatives that you can use in your projects.

Most of the alternatives are compatible with the npm registry, so you can use the same packages that you use with npm and you can switch between them without any problem.

Each alternative has its own advantages and disadvantages, so you need to evaluate which one is the best for your project. Most of the time, npm will be the best option, but it is good to know that there are other alternatives designed to solve very specific scenarios.

Let's introduce some of them:

Yarn

Yarn (`https://yarnpkg.com/`) is a package manager created by Facebook and released in 2016. It was created to solve some specific problems that npm had at that time, but over the years, npm has improved a lot and it has solved most of the problems that Yarn solved originally.

PNPM

PNPM (`https://pnpm.js.org/`) is a package manager that uses a different approach to install dependencies. Instead of installing the dependencies in the `node_modules` folder, it creates a single folder for all the dependencies in the project. This approach has some advantages such as disk space usage and network usage.

Verdaccio

Verdaccio (`https://verdaccio.org/`) is a private npm registry that you can use to host your own packages. This is great if you want to have a private registry for your company or if you want to have a mirror of the npm registry.

> **Note**
>
> Verdaccio is a great tool if you have connectivity issues or if you want to experiment with the npm registry before publishing the packages.

In the next section we will learn how to publish and distribute our own packages so we can re-use our code across projects. Also, other developers can use the libraries that we built.

Publishing your first package

We have seen how to install packages from the npm registry, but we can also publish our own packages. This is great if we want to share our code with other developers or if we want to reuse our code in other projects.

So, let's see how to publish our first package in the npm registry.

Registries

Before we start, we need to understand how the npm registry works. The npm registry is a public repository where all the packages are stored. This is the default registry that npm uses, but you can also use other registries such as Verdaccio (`https://verdaccio.org/`) or GitHub Packages (`https://github.com/features/packages`).

We will use the npm registry in this chapter, but the process is very similar for other registries. Some developers publish their packages in multiple registries, so you can choose the one that you prefer.

> **Note**
>
> If you want to publish a private package, it is more common to use a private registry such as Verdaccio or GitHub Packages, but if you want to publish a public package, the npm registry is the best option.

npm account

Before we can publish our packages, we need to create an account in the npm registry. You can create an account on the npm website (`https://www.npmjs.com/signup`) by following the steps in the next section (`https://docs.npmjs.com/creating-a-new-npm-user-account`).

Prepare the package

So, let's start by creating a new folder for our package with the name `my-first-package`.

We will create a `package.json` file with the following content:

```
{
  "name": "@USERNAME/demo-package",
  "version": "1.0.0",
  "description": "Sample package: Node.js for beginners",
  "main": "index.mjs",
  "scripts": {
    "test": "echo \"Error: no test specified\" && exit 1"
  },
  "author": "YOUR NAME",
  "license": "MIT"
}
```

You will need to replace @USERNAME with your npm username, which is `@ulisesgascon` in my case, and also change the `author` field with your name.

Then, we will create an `index.mjs` file with the following content:

```
function sum(a, b) {
  return a + b
}

export { sum }
```

The last step is to include a `README.md` file with some information about the package:

```
# Sample package: Node.js for beginners

This is a sample package to learn how to publish packages in npm.

## Installation

```bash
npm install @USERNAME/demo-package
```
```

```
```

Usage

```js
import { sum } from '@USERNAME/demo-package'
console.log(sum(1, 2))
```
```

Replace @USERNAME with your npm username as we did previously with the `package.json`.

This is a very simple package, but it is enough to show how to publish a package in the npm registry.

## Reviewing the package

Now that we have our package ready, we can publish it in the npm registry. To do that, we need to run the following command in the terminal:

```
npm publish --dry-run
```

The `--dry-run` flag is optional, but it is a good idea to use it the first time to see what is going to happen. This command will show you the files that are going to be published and some information about the package.

```
npm notice
npm notice 📄   @ulisesgascon/demo-package@1.0.0
npm notice === Tarball Contents ===
npm notice 188B .vscode/settings.json
npm notice 267B README.md
npm notice 55B  index.mjs
npm notice 272B package.json
npm notice === Tarball Details ===
npm notice name:          @ulisesgascon/demo-package
npm notice version:       1.0.0
npm notice filename:      ulisesgascon-demo-package-1.0.0.tgz
npm notice package size:  617 B
npm notice unpacked size: 782 B
npm notice shasum:        cb55a05cdfb52f9dbd4b074d4940bfb5ad698d8f
npm notice integrity:     sha512-MDdDzLyysuWJS[...]H92x5C6Vvi0iA==
npm notice total files:   4
npm notice
npm notice Publishing to https://registry.npmjs.org/ with tag latest
and default access (dry-run)
+ @ulisesgascon/demo-package@1.0.0
```
```

As you can see, there is a file that is not needed, the `.vscode/settings.json` file. This file is used by Visual Studio Code to configure the editor, but it is not needed in the package. We can remove it by adding a `.npmignore` file with the following content:

```
.vscode
```

This file will tell npm to ignore the `.vscode` folder when publishing the package. If you run the command again, you will see that the file is not included in the package:

```
npm notice === Tarball Contents ===
npm notice 267B README.md
npm notice 55B  index.mjs
npm notice 272B package.json
npm notice === Tarball Details ===
```

Publish the package

Now that we have our package ready, we can publish it in the npm registry. To do that, we need to run the following command in the terminal:

```
npm publish --access public
```

The `--access public` flag makes this package available to the world, so anyone with internet access can download your package.

You can see in the output that the package is published in the npm registry:

```
npm notice
npm notice Publishing to https://registry.npmjs.org/ with tag latest
and public access
+ @ulisesgascon/demo-package@1.0.0
```

Now, if you go to the npm website (`https://www.npmjs.com/`) and search for your package, you will see it in the search results. You can also access the package page directly using the following URL: `https://www.npmjs.com/package/@USERNAME/demo-package` (replace @USERNAME with your npm username, which is @ulisesgascon in my case).

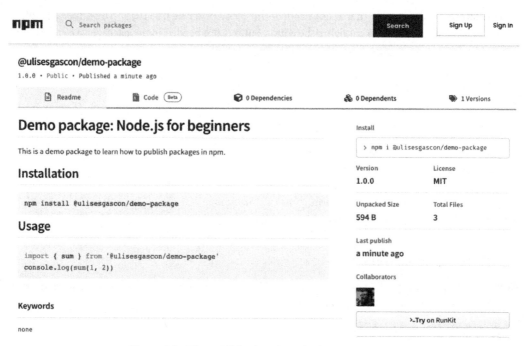

Figure 6.6 – The published package in the npm registry

Avoid the scoped packages

It is possible to publish packages without a scope in the npm registry, but it is difficult to find a name that is not already taken. For that reason, it is a good idea to use the scoped packages, such as @ulisesgascon/demo-package in our case.

But nothing stops you from publishing a package without a scope such as my-great-demo-package if the name is not already taken. But if you do that, you will need to be careful with the name, because once you publish a package, you can't change the name. So, if you want to change the name, you will need to publish a new package with the new name and deprecate the old one.

Release new versions

Let's make some changes to improve our package. We will add a new multiply function to the index.mjs file:

```
function sum(a, b) {
    return a + b
}
```

```
function multiply(a, b) {
    return a * b
}

export { sum, multiply }
```

We will also include it in the README.md file:

```
## Usage

```js
import { sum, multiply } from '@ulisesgascon/demo-package'
console.log(sum(1, 2))
console.log(multiply(5, 2))
```
```

Now, we are ready to publish again the package using npm publish --access public again, but there is an error:

```
npm notice Publishing to https://registry.npmjs.org/
npm ERR! code E403
npm ERR! 403 403 Forbidden - PUT https://registry.npmjs.org/@
ulisesgascon%2fdemo-package - You cannot publish over the previously
published versions: 1.0.0.
```

We forgot to change the version number in the package.json file, so we need to do that before publishing the package again. We should always follow semantic versioning (https://semver.org/), so in this case we will change the version number to 1.1.0 as it is a minor change, we can make this change using the npm version minor command and as a result, we can see that package.json has been updated as expected:

```
{
  "version": "1.1.0",
}
```

Now, we can publish the package again and we will see the new version on the npm website and in the terminal:

```
npm notice
npm notice Publishing to https://registry.npmjs.org/
+ @ulisesgascon/demo-package@1.1.0
```

If we check the npm URL again, we can see the new version available and the changes we made:

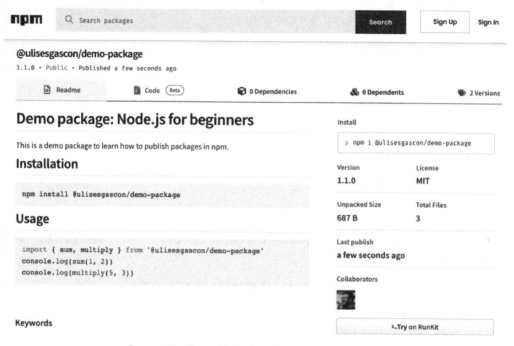

Figure 6.7 – The published package updated in npm

Prevent accidental publishing

While not very common, it is possible to publish a package by mistake, so it is a good idea to prevent that by adding the `private` flag to the `package.json` file if you don't plan to publish the package:

```
{
  "private": true
}
```

Best practices

Now that we know how to create and publish a package, it is time to talk about quality. The best packages have a high-level standard and follow the best practices.

Some of the best practices are quite advanced, so we will not cover them in this book, but here are two great resources to learn more about them:

- Best practices for creating a modern npm package with security in mind (https://snyk.io/blog/best-practices-create-modern-npm-package/)

- 10 npm Security Best Practices (`https://snyk.io/blog/ten-npm-security-best-practices/`)

Summary

In this chapter, we explored how to create a package from scratch, and how to install and maintain our dependencies over time. We learned how to use the `package.json` file to manage our dependencies, and how to use the `package-lock.json` file to lock the dependencies versions.

Additionally, we learned how to use npm scripts to automate tasks, and how to use global dependencies and `npx` to run commands without installing them globally.

Finally, we learned how to create our own packages and publish them in the npm registry, and how to update them over time.

In the next chapter, we will learn how to take advantage of the event-driven architecture in Node.js to create our own events and listen to them, and how core libraries such as HTTP use events to notify us about incoming requests and much more. We will build our first web server using the HTTP library.

Further reading

- *Happy Developers, Healthy Modules - Together We Can Do This - Michael Dawson, IBM* (`https://www.youtube.com/watch?v=e7tj_IbHEF4`)

- *What is npm, and why do we need it? | Tutorial for beginners* (`https://www.youtube.com/watch?v=P3aKRdUyr0s`)

- *Package.json vs Package-lock.json* (`https://www.atatus.com/blog/package-json-vs-package-lock-json/`)

- *Best practices for creating a modern npm package with security in mind* (`https://snyk.io/blog/best-practices-create-modern-npm-package/`)

- *What is a backdoor? Let's build one with Node.js* (`https://snyk.io/blog/what-is-a-backdoor/`)

- *Juan Picado @ NodeTLV 22 - Deep dive into Verdaccio, a lightweight Node.js registry* (`https://www.youtube.com/watch?v=qRMucS3i3kQ&`)

- *Isaac Schlueter: How npm Works* (`https://www.youtube.com/watch?v=ShRDgdvlZQ8`)

- *Leveling up Monorepos with npm Workspaces - Ruy Adorno, DevOps.js Conference 2022* (`https://www.youtube.com/watch?v=A-pWrajferM`)

- *Ashley Williams | You don't know npm* (`https://www.youtube.com/watch?v=g3_e5Sp9vd4`)

7
Event-Driven Architecture

Events are one of the most powerful ways to use Node.js. Node.js was designed from the ground up to build event-driven modules. Many core libraries offer an events interface that can be used and extended easily. Also, Node.js provides a powerful events library that can be used to build event-driven modules.

In this chapter, we delve into events in Node.js. We will learn how to use events from the core libraries, from event listener registration to event emission, and handling multiple listeners for the same event.

We will build our first HTTP server using events, and we will discuss the organization of event listeners and the cleanup.

To sum up, here are the main topics that we will explore in this chapter:

- Introducing events
- Watching for file changes
- The Node.js event emitter library
- Your first HTTP server
- Adding an event layer to your modules

By the end of this chapter, you will know how to use events and even how to include an event interface in your modules.

Technical requirements

The code files for the chapter can be found at `https://github.com/PacktPublishing/NodeJS-for-Beginners`

Check out the code in action video for this chapter on `https://youtu.be/opZER2MY1Yc`

Introducing events

In the real world, events are occurrences. For example, when you click a button, a click event is triggered. When you receive a message, a message received event is triggered. When you save a file, a file saved event is triggered. Events are present everywhere. In Node.js, events are also present everywhere.

So, when we talk about events in Node.js, we are talking about the same concept as in the real world. Events are occurrences, and we produce them or consume them. In some cases, one entity produces an event, and another entity consumes it. In other cases, the same entity produces and consumes the event. This can be very flexible; it is even possible that many entities consume the same event, or many entities produce the same event.

If you are familiar with the frontend world, you may have implemented handlers when a button is clicked, something like this:

```
document.getElementById('my-button').addEventListener('click', () => {
    console.log('Button clicked');
});
```

In this case, the `addEventListener` method receives two arguments, the event name and the callback function. The callback function will be called when the event is triggered. In this case, the event name is `click`, but you can subscribe to many other events, such as `mouseover`, `mouseout`, `keydown`, `keyup`, `change`, and `submit`.

If you have worked with other programming languages, you may have heard about the Observer, Publish/Subscribe, and mediator patterns. In this chapter, we will explore how to use the Node.js events library to build event-driven modules and explore how the core libraries are using this architecture.

One of the best ways to get familiar with events is by using the Node.js core API to handle files. We can subscribe to events and react when a file is modified. So, in the next section, we will explore this topic in detail.

Watching for file changes

As we are already familiar with the Node.js filesystem library, let's build a simple script that watches for file changes. We will use the `fs.watch` method to watch for file changes. This method receives two arguments, the path to the file to watch and a callback function that will be called when the file changes. The callback function receives two arguments, the event type and the filename. The event type can be `rename` or `change`. The `rename` event is triggered when the file is renamed or deleted. The `change` event is triggered when the file is modified.

Now, we will create a simple program to detect file changes:

1. Let's create a file called `watch.mjs` and add the following code:

    ```
    import { watch } from 'node:fs';

    console.log('Watching for file changes...');
    watch('./watch.txt', (eventType, filename) => {
        console.log('--------------------------');
        console.log(`Event type is: ${eventType}`);
        if (filename) {
            console.log(`Filename provided: ${filename}`);
        }
    });
    ```

2. Create a file called `watch.txt` and run the script with the following command:

    ```
    node watch.js
    ```

3. Open the watch.txt file, add some text, and save the changes. You will see that the script prints the following output:

    ```
    Watching for file changes...
    ----------------------------
    Event type is: change
    Filename provided: watch.txt
    ```

As you can see, the `change` event is triggered, and the filename is provided. Now, rename the file and save the changes. You will see that the script prints the following output:

```
----------------------------
Event type is: rename
Filename provided: watch2.txt
```

In the next section, we will learn how we can implement custom events inside of our application and how we can emit and consume them.

The Node.js event emitter library

Now that we know how to watch for file changes, let's explore the Node.js events library. This library provides an `EventEmitter` class that can be used to build simple interface to register and unregister event listeners and emit events.

Let's create a file called `event-emitter.mjs` and add the following code:

```
import { EventEmitter } from 'node:events';
const emitter = new EventEmitter();
```

```
emitter.on('message', (message) => {
    console.log(`Message received: ${message}`);
});
emitter.emit('message', 'Hello world!');
```

In this example, we created an instance of the EventEmitter class and registered an event listener for the message event. Then, we emit the message event with the message Hello world!. If you run the script, you will see that the message is printed in the console.

You can also register multiple event listeners and emitters for the same event; this is a common practice when you want to modularize code and/or you want from the same event to trigger multiple actions. Let's say that you receive an incoming request, and you want to store a copy of that message and also notify that to the final user; by using events, you can handle both actions in parallel. Let's modify the previous example by adding the following code:

```
setInterval(() => {
    emitter.emit('message', `Interval (${Date.now()})`);
}, 1000);

emitter.on('message', (message) => {
    console.log(`Additional listener received: ${message}`);
});

emitter.once('message', (message) => {
    console.log(`Once listener received: ${message}`);
});

setTimeout(() => {
    emitter.emit('message', 'Timeout says hello!');
}, 2500);
```

Let's analyze the code. First, we use the setInterval method to emit the message event every second. Then, we register an additional event listener for the message event. This event listener will be called every time the message event is emitted. Then, we register an event listener using the once method. This event listener will be called only once, but if you want to keep listening for more than one message, you can use on – for example, when you listen for incoming request in an HTTP server application. Finally, we use the setTimeout method to emit the message event after 2.5 seconds. If you run the script, you will see that the following output is printed:

```
Message received: Hello world!
Message received: Interval (1691771547260)
Additional listener received: Interval (1691771547260)
Once listener received: Interval (1691771547260)
```

```
Message received: Interval (1691771548258)
Additional listener received: Interval (1691771548258)
Message received: Timeout says hello!
Additional listener received: Timeout says hello!
```

Preventing chaos by organizing the listeners

One important thing to note is that the event listeners are called synchronously. This means that the event listeners are called in the same order that they are registered. Also, remember that you can use more channels to communicate between processes. In our example, we used message, but you can use any name you want or have multiple channels to better segment communication.

Removing listeners when they are not needed

The EventEmitter class provides removeListener and off methods that can be used to remove an event listener, as well as a removeAllListeners method that can be used to remove all event listeners for a given event. You can find more information about it in the official documentation: https://nodejs.org/docs/latest-v20.x/api/events.html.

In the next section, we will create our first HTTP server with Node.js, which is one of the most commons ways to use events while doing web applications in Node.js.

Your first HTTP server

Now that we know how to use the EventEmitter class, let's build a simple HTTP server. We will use the http core library to create the server and the EventEmitter class to handle the requests. In *Chapter 9*, we will explore in more detail how to build HTTP servers and clients, but for now, let's focus on building our first HTTP server.

Let's create a file called server.mjs and add the following code:

```
import { createServer } from 'node:http';

const port = 3000;
const server = createServer();

server.on('request', (request, res) => {
  res.writeHead(200, { 'Content-Type': 'text/html' });
  res.end('<h1>This is my first HTTP server in Node.js. Yay</h1>!');
});

server.listen(port, () => {
  console.log(`Server running at http://localhost:${port}/`);
});
```

In this example, we created an instance of the `http.Server` class and registered an event listener for the `request` event. This event listener will be called every time a request is received. Then, we use the `writeHead` method to set the status code and the content type of the response. Finally, we use the `end` method to send the response. If you run the script, you will see that the following output is printed:

```
Server running at http://localhost:3000/
```

And if you open the URL in any browser, you will see your first HTTP server in action:

This is my first HTTP server in Node.js. Yay!

Figure 7.1 – A screenshot from the application running

In the next section, we will learn how to encapsulate the events in our modules and a lot other components to emit and consume those events easily. This technique is quite popular and extendable to many libraries.

Adding an event layer to your modules

Now that we know how to use the `EventEmitter` class, let's add an event layer to our modules. In this example, we will create a module that will be used to save files and emit an event every time a file change is saved.

Let's create a file called `utils.mjs` and add the following code:

```
import { writeFile } from 'node:fs/promises';
import { EventEmitter } from 'node:events';

const emitter = new EventEmitter();

const on = emitter.on.bind(emitter);
const save = async (location, data) => {
  await writeFile(location, data);
  emitter.emit('file:saved', { location, data });
};
export { save, on };
```

In this example, we created an instance of the `EventEmitter` class and exported the `save` function. This function will be used to save the file and emit the `file:saved` event. Then, we export the `on` method of the `EventEmitter` class. This method will be used to register event listeners for the `file:saved` event.

> **Important info**
>
> In the example, we used `bind` to check that the `this` value is correct. You can find more information about it in the official documentation at `https://developer.mozilla.org/en-US/docs/Web/JavaScript/Reference/Global_Objects/Function/bind`. The use of `bind` is quite advanced, so you can skip it for now.

Now, let's create a file called `index.mjs` and add the following code:

```
import { save, on } from './utils.mjs';

on('file:saved', ({ location, data }) => {
  console.log(`File saved at ${location}`);
});

console.log('Saving file...');
save('test.txt', 'Hello world!').catch('Error saving file');
console.log('The file is being saved but is not blocking the
execution...');
```

If you run the script, you will see that the following output is printed:

```
Saving file...
The file is being saved but is not blocking the execution...
File saved at test.txt
```

As you can see, the `file:saved` event is emitted after the `save` function is completed. This means that the `save` function does not block the execution of the script. In previous examples in the book, we used `then` to handle the result of a promise; in this case, we offered an alternative, using events that will allow you to decouple the logic of your application more easily.

Summary

In this chapter, we learned about how to use events in Node.js. We learned about the `EventEmitter` class and how to use it to emit and listen to events. We also learned how to use events to decouple the logic of our applications.

Additionally, we built a script to watch for changes in files in our system, and we also built our first HTTP server and learned how to handle requests using events.

Finally, we built a simple library that exports an event layer to decouple the logic of our applications. This will allow us to build more robust applications in future chapters.

In the next chapter, we will learn how to add tests to our applications. This will help us to build more robust applications, avoid bugs, and overall, consolidate our knowledge about Node.js while learning it.

Further reading

- *Refactoring Guru – the Mediator pattern*: `https://refactoring.guru/design-patterns/mediator`

- *Refactoring Guru – the Observer pattern*: `https://refactoring.guru/design-patterns/observer`

- *NodeConf Remote 2020 - Anna Henningsen - Node.js and the struggles of being an EventTarget*: `https://www.youtube.com/watch?v=SOPC3aLoD4U`

- *The Node.js event emitter*: `https://nodejs.org/en/learn/asynchronous-work/the-nodejs-event-emitter`

8

Testing in Node.js

Testing is one of the most relevant practices these days; it has become much more popular in the last couple of decades than in the past. Today, we build complex software with many dependencies and requirements that evolve over time. I strongly believe that testing is key when you are learning a new language or tool because it will provide you with a security net that will allow you to take more risks and move faster without breaking the previous code.

In this chapter, we will dive into the importance of testing and how to choose the right type of testing for your application. You will write your first test, and then we will learn about creating test suites by grouping related tests, demonstrating both Node.js core testing and the Jest library.

Writing good tests is not easy, but by the end of this chapter, you will have a clear idea of what principles to follow every time and how you can use a testing coverage tool to extend and refactor your tests over time.

Finally, we will introduce **Test-Driven Development** (**TDD**) by solving some edge cases.

To sum up, here are the main topics that we will explore in this chapter:

- Why is testing important?
- Test approach and philosophy
- How should I test my code?
- Writing our first test suite
- Mastering code coverage tooling
- TDD in action

Technical requirements

The code files for the chapter can be found at `https://github.com/PacktPublishing/NodeJS-for-Beginners`

Check out the code in action video for this chapter on `https://youtu.be/aK572sFboEM`

Why is testing important?

As we saw in the previous chapters, modern applications are complex, have many moving parts, and will have dependencies.

Overall, we can say that testing is important because it helps us to ensure that our code is working as expected and that we are not introducing bugs when we are adding new features or fixing bugs.

Testing is a complex culture

Testing is much more than just writing some code to validate your application. It's a culture that has many ideas, principles, practices, and tools... Have you heard of TDD? BDD? Unit tests? Integration tests? End-to-end tests? Mocks? Stubs? Spies? There are many concepts to learn and understand, and we will explore some of them in this chapter.

Testing has to be a team activity

Testing will help you to onboard new developers to your team easily. You can join other teams to help them build new features or fix bugs even if you don't know the code base in depth.

I love to see tests as documentation for the application, or even better, as the agreement to the world of how your application should behave in certain scenarios.

But testing is a team effort. It's not just the developer's responsibility to write tests, the same way that it's not just the developer's responsibility to write secure code. The whole team should be involved in the process, and the team should have a culture of testing and stick to it over time.

Automating your tests is essential. Without automation, we would need to test our applications manually. It means that we will do a lot of repetitive tasks that are prone to errors, and we will need to spend a lot of time ensuring that our application is working as expected.

With tests, we can automate the process and ensure that our application is working as expected. We can run the tests on our local machine, or on a remote machine before a pull request is merged or we deploy the software. We can run the tests in different environments, and we can run them in parallel to speed up the process.

Take advantage now

I am used to doing tests in my day-to-day work, and I can say that they're a great tool that has helped me to build better software. But overall, they have helped me to learn new things and improve my skills.

When you must use a new language or tool, you can use tests to learn how it works and explore the features. You can use tests to learn how this new thing works and do your own experiments while learning.

But if you are not used to doing tests, it can be a little bit hard to learn Node.js and testing at the same time. So, I recommend you learn Node.js first and then take a more in-depth look at testing.

In the next chapters, we will build a web application and use tests to ensure that our application is working as expected.

You will face many challenges while adopting the testing culture. As with any cultural change, it's not easy to start doing tests. It's a challenge that you will need to overcome, and you will need to invest time to learn how to do it. But I can say that it's worth it.

If you work with a team, you will need to convince your team to start doing tests and consolidate the culture over time. It's not easy, but it's possible.

You can always start doing tests in your own code and show the benefits to your team. You can start with a pet project or a proof-of-concept test and convince the whole team.

Note that you will need to invest time to learn how to do it, and even when you know how to do it, you will need to invest time to write the tests. That time will always be bigger in comparison with the time that you will need to just write the code. But you will save time in the long term when you need to fix bugs or add new features and in preventing bugs in the first place.

Now that we are clear on the motivations behind the adoption of testing, it is time to learn, in the next section, about the different types of tests that are available for our applications and how other industries have built solid products using different testing frameworks.

Testing approach and philosophy

One of the things that we don't realize when we are starting to learn about testing is that there are many different kinds of tests, and each one has a different purpose.

Testing is wildly used in the world

In the real world, testing is used in many industries. For example, if we want to test the quality of a car being manufactured in a factory, we can do the following:

- Test the engine in isolation
- Test the car in a controlled environment to ensure that it's working as expected
- Test the car in a real environment to ensure that it's working as expected
- Test the individual components of the car to ensure certain quality standards
- Test the car against a wall or other objects to ensure that it's safe

- The automobile industry has one of the most interesting testing frameworks in terms of engineering in the world. Most cars that are manufactured today, for the vast majority of end users, were previously tested in many ways, including crash simulations to evaluate the potential damages. In the following figure, you can see how one of these tests

Figure 8.1 – Image by Wikimedia https://en.wikipedia.org/wiki/
Crash_test#/media/File:Honda_Fit-Impact_Still.jpg

Software products are no different. Just to give you an idea, we can test the web application components in isolation, or we can test the whole application from the perspective of the end user. There's also the option to just test the performance of our application by making a lot of requests with different structures to our application and detecting any bottlenecks and inefficiencies. We can even test the security of our application by doing penetration tests and trying to hack our application.

The test pyramid

So, we can say that there are many different types of tests and each one has a different purpose. Let's have a look at the test pyramid:

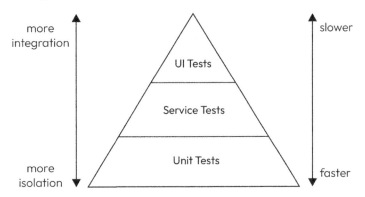

Figure 8.2 – Image by Martin Fowler in "The practical test pyramid" https://martinfowler.com/articles/practical-test-pyramid.html

As we can see, the base of the pyramid is unit tests, which are more isolated and faster to run. At the top of the pyramid, we have UI tests, which are more expensive (as they require more integration) and are slower to run.

Using the car example, we can say that unit tests are like testing the engine in isolation, and UI tests are like testing the car in a real environment.

We can easily understand that testing the engine in isolation is faster and cheaper than testing the car in a real environment because we don't need to build the whole car to test the engine, prepare paperwork, coordinate with the insurance companies, or bring on more staff such as drivers and mechanics. Also, testing the car in a real environment can lead to impacts by external factors such as the weather, traffic, and road conditions.

In comparison, we can just build the engine and test it in isolation inside the factory with the tools and necessary people. We can do it faster and cheaper, but this test won't be able to detect some issues that we can have when we are testing the car in a real environment.

So, in the same way, we can say that unit tests are faster and cheaper to run than UI tests, but UI tests will be able to detect some issues that we can't detect with unit tests.

In this chapter, we will focus on unit tests, but we will have a look at other types of tests as well in the following chapters when we will build the web application.

Now that we are clear on the different types of tests, it is time to be pragmatic and explore how to build our first test case using different libraries together in the next section.

How should I test my code?

Due to the history of JavaScript, most developers didn't have the culture of testing their code while JavaScript was limited to the browser and used almost exclusively to build relatively simple scripts.

However, with the evolution of the language and the community, we now have a lot of tools and frameworks to help us build tests.

Frameworks and libraries

When you have a clear idea of how to test your code, you can easily migrate from one tool to another until you find the one that fits your needs best.

In this chapter, we will explore the promising Node.js test core library and the most popular test framework for web development, Jest.

> **Important note**
>
> We are living in a transitional period where the Node.js core library is evolving to provide a better experience to developers. So, probably in the future, it will be the default tool to use. But for now, if you are new to testing, I recommend you use Jest because there are more tutorials and blog posts and the API is more stable.

Our first test

Let's have a look at a simple test, and then we'll explore the different parts of it:

```
import { describe, it } from 'node:test';
import assert from 'node:assert';

const sum = (a, b) => a + b;
describe('Utils Test Suite', () => {
  it('Should sum two numbers', () => {
    assert.strictEqual(sum(1, 2), 3);
  });
});
```

In this example, we are testing the sum function. First, we import the `describe` and `it` functions from the `node:test` module. Then, we import the `assert` function from the `node:assert` module.

The `describe` function is used to group tests. In this case, we are grouping all the tests related to the `utils` module.

The `it` function is used to define a test. In this case, we are defining a test that should sum two numbers.

Finally, we are using the `assert` function to check that the result of the `sum` function is the expected one.

So, we can say that a test is composed of three parts:

- **Arrange**: Where we define the data that we need to run the test
- **Act**: Where we run the code that we want to test
- **Assert**: Where we check that the result of the code is the expected one

Testing principles and goals

There are some principles that we should follow when we are building tests. For me, these principles can be summarized into three goals, which are fast, trustable, and maintainable.

Fast

The tests should be fast to run and write. We will run this test many times, so if the test is slow to run, we will lose a lot of time waiting for it to finish. But the worst part is that we will be tempted to run the test less frequently or write fewer tests.

Then, testing will be a frustrating experience for you and your team. In small projects, you will have a few dozen tests, but in big projects, you can have thousands of tests.

> **Important note**
>
> If you have a test that on average takes one second to run, you will lose one second every time you run the test. If you have 1,000 tests, you will lose 1,000 seconds, which is more than 16 minutes! In most cases, you will have the option to use concurrency and run the tests in parallel, so the total time will be much lower. But it requires an extra step to set up (`https://nodejs.org/api/test.html#runoptions`).

You will need to dedicate time and resources to refactor and improve your tests in big projects to keep them fast.

Trustable

The tests should be trustable. If you have flaky tests (that is, tests that fail randomly), your team will be very frustrated and will lose confidence in the tests.

In order to avoid this situation, we should follow these principles:

- **Isolated**: We need to isolate the tests from external factors such as the network, filesystem, database, and time
- **Repeatable and deterministic**: We need to be able to run the tests many times and get the same results
- **Self-contained and independent**: We need to be able to run any tests in isolation and get the same results

Maintainable

Tests are code as well, so we need to maintain them in the same way as we maintain our production code. We should follow these principles:

- **Readable and explicit**: Tests should be easy to read and understand. They have to be flexible in order to evolve with the code that we are testing.

- **Focused**: A single test should test a single thing. If we have a test that is testing more than one thing, we won't be able to know exactly what is failing.

- **Small and simple**: It is better to have many small and simple tests than a few big and complex tests.

Congratulations! You wrote your first test and now the mechanics should be clearer. In the next section, we will learn how we can build a full test suite to cover multiple cases and how to automate some steps.

Writing our first test suite

In this section, we will build our first test suite. We will build a test suite for the `utils` module that we created and published in the previous chapter.

We will use the `node:test` and `node:assert` modules to build our test suite, and then we will build the same tests using the `Jest` framework, so we can compare both approaches and see the differences.

Utils module

Let's start by creating a new folder and then initialize a new Node.js project with `npm init`. Then we will create a `utils.js` file with the following code:

```
export const sum = (a, b) => a + b
export const multiply = (a, b) => a * b
```

The code is very simple. The `sum` function will sum two numbers and the `multiply` function will multiply two numbers. Then the tests should be very simple as well.

Basically, we need to test that the `sum` function is summing two numbers and the `multiply` function is multiplying two numbers.

Test core library

Recently, Node.js has introduced a new core library to help us to build tests. This library is called `assert` and it's a core library, so we don't need to install it. We can just import it and use it.

Adding the npm scripts

Let's add the following NPM scripts to our package.json file and add type: "module" as well:

```json
{
  "type": "module",
  "scripts": {
    "node-test": "node --test node_test/"
  }
}
```

In this case, we have chosen type: "module" to enable the ESM syntax by default, so we can use the import keyword in the files directly. You can find more information about how to import modules in *Chapter 6*.

Adding the test suite

Let's create a new folder, node_test, and include a new file, utils.test.js, inside it with the following code:

```js
import { describe, it } from "node:test";
import assert from "node:assert";
import { sum, multiply } from "../utils.js";

describe("Utils Test Suite: sum", () => {
  it("Should sum two numbers", () => {
    assert.strictEqual(sum(1, 2), 3);
  });
});

describe("Utils Test Suite: multiply", () => {
  it("Should multiply two numbers", () => {
    assert.strictEqual(multiply(5, 3), 15);
  });
});
```

It is important to notice that we are using ../ to refer to parent directories from the current file. That way, we can import files from anywhere on the computer. It is also possible to use the absolute path to a specific resource. You can find more details about the differences at https://www.redhat.com/sysadmin/linux-path-absolute-relative.

Running the tests

Now, we can run the tests with the following command:

```
npm run node-test
```

We should see the following output:

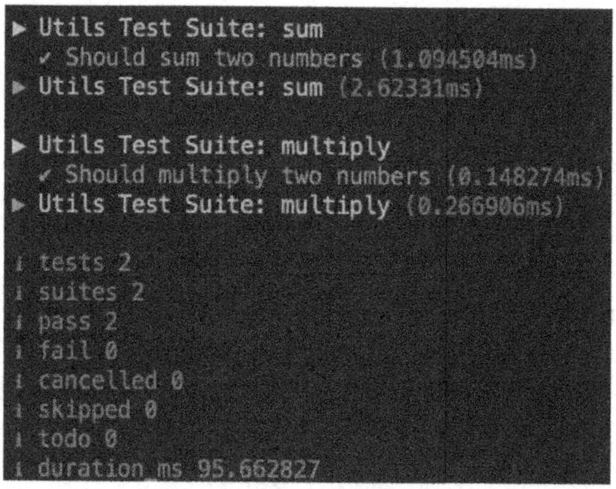

Figure 8.3 – Terminal output

Notice that the terminal uses distinct colors to show us the results of the tests. In this case, we have two tests and both are passing. As you can see, the output is very simple and is using the texts that we defined in the `describe` and `it` functions.

Using the Jest library

Jest is a JavaScript testing framework that is very popular in the JavaScript community. It's very easy to use and has a lot of features that will help us to build and maintain our test suite, especially if you are doing frontend development using modern frameworks as libraries, such as Angular, React, or Vue.

Installing Jest

The first step is to install `Jest` in our project as a development dependency. We can do it with the following command:

```
npm install --save-dev jest@29
```

Configuring Jest

As we had the test previously set up for the Node.js core library, we will need to use a custom configuration for Jest. In a real project, we will use only one testing framework, and in that case, we can configure Jest using `npx jest@29 --init`.

The `npx` command will execute the `Jest` command that we have installed in our project. The `--init` flag will create a configuration file for us.

We will create a new file, `jest.config.js`, with the following content:

```
export default {
    modulePathIgnorePatterns: ['<rootDir>/node_test/' ]
}
```

`modulePathIgnorePatterns` will ignore the `node_test` folder, so we can ignore the tests that we have created with the Node.js core library. `<rootDir>` is a reference to the folder where `jest.confg.js` is in this case, so it is easier to reference other resources.

As Jest does not support ESM modules yet, we will use Babel (`https://babeljs.io/`) to transpile the code. We will create a new file, `.babelrc`, with the following content:

```
{
  "presets": ["@babel/preset-env"]
}
```

We will install the following dependencies:

```
npm i -D @babel/preset-env@7
```

Adding the npm scripts

Let's add the following npm scripts to our `package.json` file:

```
{
  "scripts": {
    "node-test": "node --test node_test/",
    "jest-test": "jest"
  }
}
```

Adding the test suite

Let's create a new folder, `jest_test`, and include a new file, `utils.test.js`, inside it with the following code:

```js
import { sum, multiply } from "../utils.js";

describe("Utils Test Suite: sum", () => {
  it("Should sum two numbers", () => {
    expect(sum(1, 2)).toBe(3);
  });
});

describe("Utils Test Suite: multiply", () => {
  it("Should multiply two numbers", () => {
    expect(multiply(5, 3)).toBe(15);
  });
});
```

As you can see, the code is very similar to the code that we created for the Node.js core library. The only difference is in how we manage the assertions.

> **Important note**
>
> Note also that we are not importing the `describe` and `it` functions. This is because Jest provides these functions for us and we don't need to import them.

Running the tests

Now, we can run the tests with the following command: `npm run jest-test`.

We should see the following output:

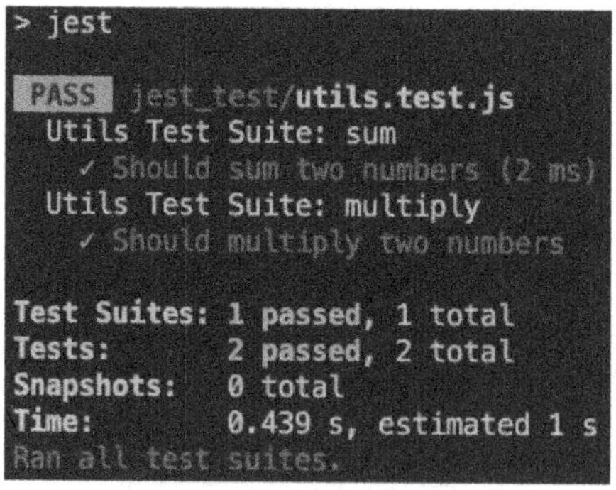

Figure 8.4 – Terminal output

As you can see, the output is very similar to the output that we saw with the Node.js core library. The only difference is that the output is using different colors, and the text is slightly different. But the most important thing is that we have the same information.

Now we are quite confident about our tests, but when the source code is growing every day, you need an additional tool that helps you know what code has been covered by tests or not. So, in the next section, we will learn in detail how we can use the test coverage to generate reports that will help us to improve the tests in our projects.

Mastering code coverage tooling

When we are building a test suite, we need to make sure that we are covering all the code that is critical in scenarios that make sense for our purpose. This is called **code coverage** and it's a very important metric to measure the quality of our test suite.

Some people say that we need to have 100% code coverage, but this is not always true or practical. In my opinion, code coverage is a metric that helps us to detect the code that is not covered by our tests or code that has been over-tested.

Overall, it is a metric that can help us to skim the code and detect potential tests that we need to add or remove.

Configuration

Historically, code coverage was a feature that was provided by third-party libraries such as Istanbul (`https://istanbul.js.org/`). But now, Node.js and Jest provide this feature out of the box, so we don't need to install any third-party library.

Jest library

Let's add the following npm script to our `package.json` file:

```
{
  "scripts": {
    "node-test": "node --test node_test/",
    "jest-test": "jest",
    "jest-test:coverage": "jest --coverage"
  }
}
```

Node.js

Node.js has an experimental feature that we can use to generate code coverage. We need to use the
`--experimental-test-coverage` flag to enable this feature:

```
{
  "scripts": {
    "node-test": "node --test node_test/",
    "jest-test": "jest",
    "jest-test:coverage": "jest --coverage",
    "node-test:coverage": "node --test --experimental-test-coverage
node_test/"
  }
}
```

Running the tests

Let's add a new function, `substract`, to our `utils.js` file:

```
export const sum = (a, b) => a + b
export const multiply = (a, b) => a * b
export const subtract  = (a, b) => a - b
```

Now, let's run the code coverage for both Node.js and Jest to see the results.

Node.js report

By default, Node.js will generate a `coverage` folder with the results. We can open the `index.html`
file in our browser to see the results:

```
npm run node-test:coverage
```

The output should be similar to the following figure:

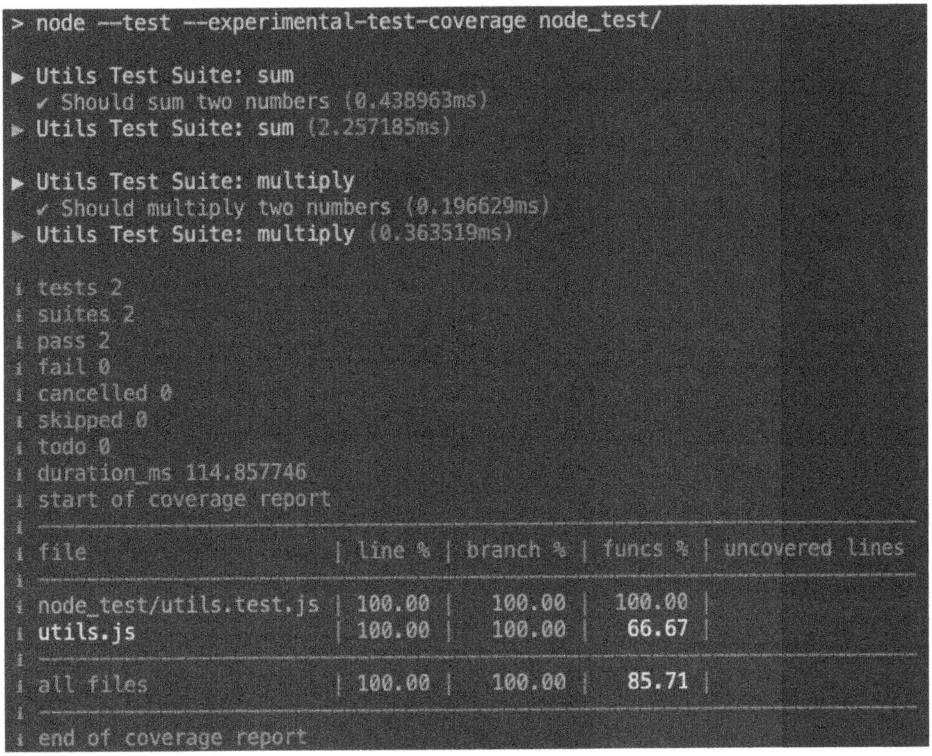

```
> node --test --experimental-test-coverage node_test/

▶ Utils Test Suite: sum
  ✓ Should sum two numbers (0.438963ms)
▶ Utils Test Suite: sum (2.257185ms)

▶ Utils Test Suite: multiply
  ✓ Should multiply two numbers (0.196629ms)
▶ Utils Test Suite: multiply (0.363519ms)

ℹ tests 2
ℹ suites 2
ℹ pass 2
ℹ fail 0
ℹ cancelled 0
ℹ skipped 0
ℹ todo 0
ℹ duration_ms 114.857746
ℹ start of coverage report
ℹ
ℹ file                     | line % | branch % | funcs % | uncovered lines
ℹ
ℹ node_test/utils.test.js  | 100.00 |   100.00 |  100.00 |
ℹ utils.js                 | 100.00 |   100.00 |   66.67 |
ℹ
ℹ all files                | 100.00 |   100.00 |   85.71 |
ℹ
ℹ end of coverage report
```

Figure 8.5 – Terminal output

As you can see, we have 66.67% code coverage for the functions, as we don't have any coverage for the `subtract` function.

Jest report

Running the code coverage with Jest is very similar to running the tests:

```
npm run jest-test:coverage
```

The output should be similar to the following figure:

```
> jest --coverage

PASS  jest_test/utils.test.js
  Utils Test Suite: sum
    ✓ Should sum two numbers (2 ms)
  Utils Test Suite: multiply
    ✓ Should multiply two numbers (1 ms)

----------|---------|----------|---------|---------|-------------------
File      | % Stmts | % Branch | % Funcs | % Lines | Uncovered Line #s
----------|---------|----------|---------|---------|-------------------
All files |   83.33 |      100 |   66.66 |     100 |
 utils.js |   83.33 |      100 |   66.66 |     100 |
----------|---------|----------|---------|---------|-------------------
Test Suites: 1 passed, 1 total
Tests:       2 passed, 2 total
Snapshots:   0 total
Time:        0.896 s, estimated 1 s
Ran all test suites.
```

Figure 8.6 – Terminal output

As you can see, we have the same code coverage as with Node.js. This is because both tools are used in the same way to calculate the code coverage.

Coverage UI report

In both cases, we have generated a coverage folder with the results. We can open the index.html file located in coverage/lcov-report in our browser to see the results.

All files

83.33% Statements 5/6   **100%** Branches 0/0   **66.66%** Functions 2/3   **100%** Lines 3/3

Press *n* or *j* to go to the next uncovered block, *b, p* or *k* for the previous block.

Filter: [   ]

File ▲		Statements			Branches			Functions			Lines	
utils.js		83.33%	5/6		100%	0/0		66.66%	2/3		100%	3/3

Figure 8.7 Web browser report

We can explore in detail what is and is not covered in utils.js.

All files utils.js

83.33% Statements 5/6   **100%** Branches 0/0   **66.66%** Functions 2/3   **100%** Lines 3/3

Press *n* or *j* to go to the next uncovered block, *b, p* or *k* for the previous block.

```
1  1x  export const sum = (a, b) => a + b
2  1x  export const multiply = (a, b) => a * b
3  1x  export const subtract  = (a, b) => a - b
```

Figure 8.8 – Web browser report

As you can see, the subtract function is not covered by our tests. So, here we have the opportunity to improve our tests.

The code coverage report is a great way to understand your tests, especially when you are working with a large code base. So, I encourage you to use it as much as possible.

In the next section, we will change the approach. We are going to learn about the additional value that we receive when we define the tests before we write the code. While that might sound complicated, it will help you a lot to clarify what you need to build next and how to do it in a way where you can test it. You will be amazed at how much time you can save when you follow this approach. It is called test-driven development.

TDD in action

There are some edge cases that we are not covering in our utils module. For example, what happens if we pass a string to the sum function?

```
import { sum } from "../utils.js";
const result = sum("1", 2); // 12
```

This is not the expected behavior when we use the sum function, so we need to fix it.

Let's add some tests to cover these edge cases in our jest-tests/utils.test.js file:

```
describe("Utils Test Suite: sum", () => {
  it("Should sum two numbers", () => {
    expect(sum(1, 2)).toBe(3);
  });

  it("Should throw an error if we don't provide a valid number", () =>
{
    expect(() => sum("1", 2)).toThrow("Please provide a valid
number");
  });
});
```

As you can see, we are using the toThrow matcher to test that the function is throwing an error. Now, let's run the test coverage with npm run jest-test.

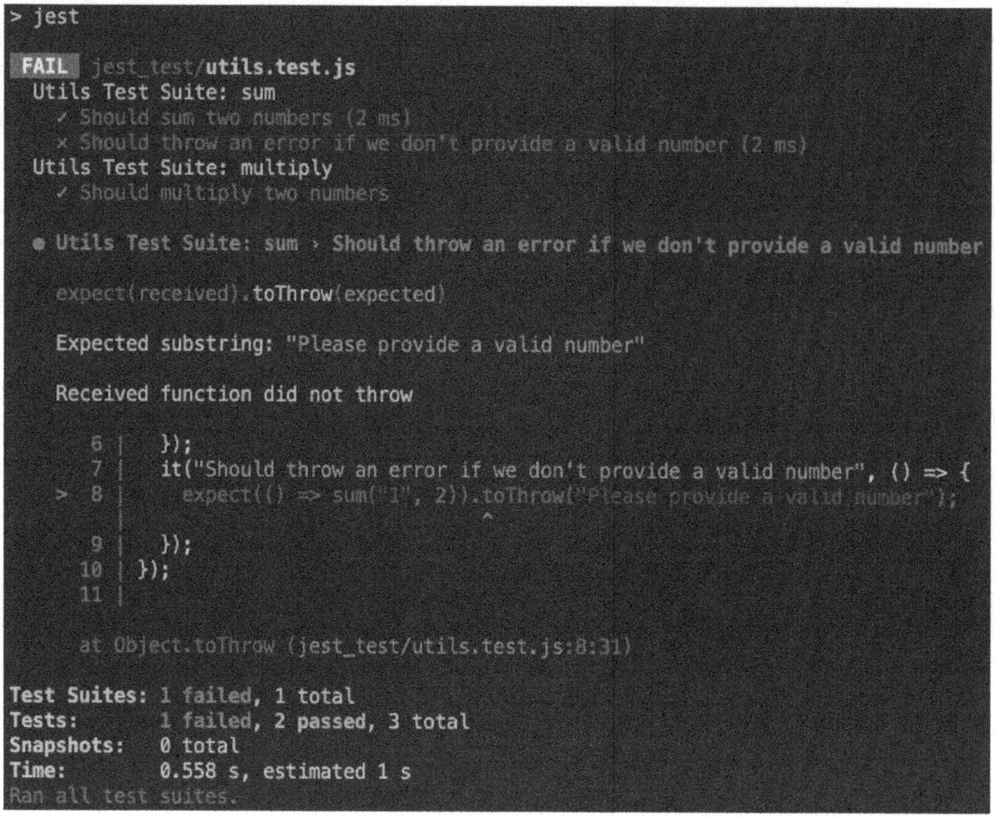

```
> jest

FAIL  jest_test/utils.test.js
  Utils Test Suite: sum
    ✓ Should sum two numbers (2 ms)
    × Should throw an error if we don't provide a valid number (2 ms)
  Utils Test Suite: multiply
    ✓ Should multiply two numbers

  ● Utils Test Suite: sum › Should throw an error if we don't provide a valid number

    expect(received).toThrow(expected)

    Expected substring: "Please provide a valid number"

    Received function did not throw

       6 |   });
       7 |   it("Should throw an error if we don't provide a valid number", () => {
    >  8 |     expect(() => sum("1", 2)).toThrow("Please provide a valid number");
         |                               ^
       9 |   });
      10 | });
      11 |

      at Object.toThrow (jest_test/utils.test.js:8:31)

Test Suites: 1 failed, 1 total
Tests:       1 failed, 2 passed, 3 total
Snapshots:   0 total
Time:        0.558 s, estimated 1 s
Ran all test suites.
```

Figure 8.9 – Terminal output

Our new test is failing because our code didn't meet our requirements, so let's make some changes in utils.js:

```
export const sum = (a, b) => {
    if(typeof(a) !== 'number' || typeof(b) !== 'number') {
        throw new Error('Please provide a valid number')
    }
    return a + b
}
export const multiply = (a, b) => a * b
export const subtract  = (a, b) => a - b
```

Now, let's run the tests again.

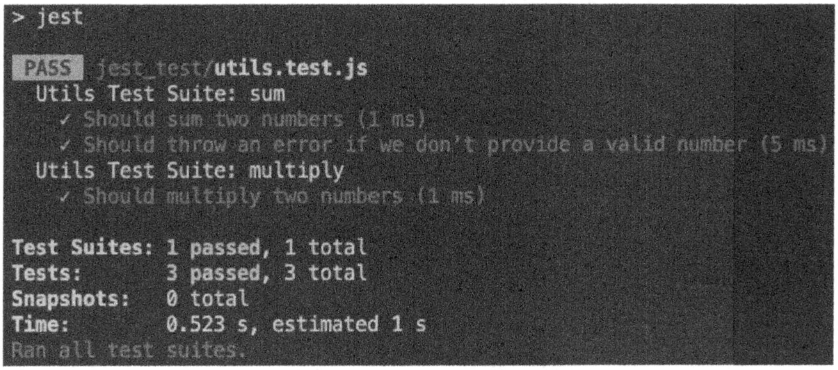

Figure 8.10 – Terminal output

Our tests are passing again, so we can say that our code is working as expected. This interactive process of writing the tests first and then writing the code to make the tests pass is called test-driven development, or TDD.

While TDD is a vast topic, we can take this simple example as an exploratory introduction to the benefits of TDD without following it strictly. For example, we can test edge cases and then use them to improve our code.

I personally find TDD a great approach in Node.js, as it helps me a lot with dividing complex tasks into smaller pieces that have their own well-defined and tested functionality. While this may seem obvious to more senior developers, due to the nature of JavaScript, it is very easy to build overengineering solutions. Testing will help us a lot in this matter.

Also, testing can be a great ally when you are working in isolation, for example, when you need to build an HTTP API for a web application, but the frontend team is not planning to start until the API is ready. So, testing is a great way to validate the implementation with the frontend team. Also, tests are a great way to onboard new members to a team, as they can easily follow what is expected to happen in the application just by running and reading the tests.

For more advanced cases, it is also a great way to debug applications and recreate bugs reported by clients or team members. Overall, I think that the return on investment is very high, especially in dynamic languages such as JavaScript.

Summary

In this chapter, we learned about the testing principles and how we can combine different types of tests to build a robust test suite. We also explored how the test pyramid can help us to build a test suite that is easy to maintain and understand.

Additionally, we discussed the differences between unit tests and integration tests and how we can use them to test our code. We also explored strategies to evangelize testing in our teams.

After that, we explored how to add unit tests to our code using Node.js core modules and Jest.

Finally, we learned how to use code coverage as an interactive tool to help us refine our tests and keep our code base robust. Then, we did a little exercise using TDD to fix a bug in our library.

In the next chapter, we will explore how the HTTP protocol works in detail and how we can build RESTful APIs with Node.js.

Further reading

- *The Practical Test Pyramid by Martin Fowler*: `https://martinfowler.com/articles/practical-test-pyramid.html`

- *Test-Driven Development // Fun TDD Introduction with JavaScript*: `https://www.youtube.com/watch?v=Jv2uxzhPFl4`

- *Delightful JavaScript Testing with Jest*: `https://www.youtube.com/watch?v=-cAKYQpTC7MA`

- *Migrating from Jest to Node.js Native Test Runner by Erick Wendel*: `https://www.youtube.com/watch?v=2YfIB4gia60`

- *TDD, Where Did It All Go Wrong (Ian Cooper)*: `https://www.youtube.com/watch?v=EZ05e7EMOLM`

- *Unit testing in JavaScript Part 1 - Why unit testing?*: `https://www.youtube.com/watch?v=Eu35xM76kKY&list=PL0zVEGEvSaeF_zoW9o66wa_UCNE3a7BEr`

Part 3:
Web Application
Fundamentals

In *Part 3*, you will learn how web applications are built by using modern patterns and techniques that are adopted by most companies. You will also learn how to build solid RESTful APIs.

This part includes the following chapters:

- *Chapter 9, Handling HTTP and REST API*
- *Chapter 10, Building Web Applications with Express*

9

Handling HTTP and REST APIs

In this chapter, we will learn about the internet from both a historical point of view and a practical understanding of the infrastructure behind the internet that we know and use every day.

We will deep dive into the protocols and architectures that make it possible to create web projects and will explore the RFCs that are the backbone of the current web browsing experience.

We will master all the components and theoretical concepts around HTTP, URLs, and REST APIs.

To sum up, here are the main topics that we will explore in this chapter:

- The history of the internet and how the internet infrastructure works

- What **Requests for Comments** (**RFCs**) are and how to use them

- HTTP communications between the server and clients (**Single-Page Applications** (**SPAs**) versus server-side rendering)

- Mastering HTTP (headers, status codes, payloads, verbs, and more)

- Using tools to debug HTTP requests

- How REST APIs are structured

- How the JSON spec works

- How the modern web works under the hood

By the end of this chapter, you will have a clear idea of all the pieces in place that constitute the current internet and how you should build your web projects by applying this knowledge learned in this chapter.

Technical requirements

The code files for the chapter can be found at https://github.com/PacktPublishing/NodeJS-for-Beginners.

Check out the code in action video for this chapter on https://youtu.be/GleRpaaR2PQ

How the internet works under the hood

We use the internet every day, but do we know how it works? Wikipedia defines the internet as follows:

> *"The Internet (or internet) is the global system of interconnected computer networks that uses the Internet protocol suite (TCP/IP) to communicate between networks and devices. It is a network of networks that consists of private, public, academic, business, and government networks of local to global scope, linked by a broad array of electronic, wireless, and optical networking technologies. The Internet carries a vast range of information resources and services, such as the interlinked hypertext documents and applications of the World Wide Web (WWW), electronic mail, telephony, and file sharing."*

Basically, the internet is a global system that connects computers together through networks and employs certain protocols and techniques to enable that communication in a resilient way. The internet is used by all kinds of entities and people to share information resources and services using tools such as electronic mail, file sharing, and so on.

But to be honest, this definition is just scratching the surface. To understand how the internet works, we need to go back in time and understand how it started.

History of the internet

The internet as we know it today was not created by a single person or specific group of people. The internet is the product of the work of many people who contributed to the creation of different technologies and ideas that, over time, became what we know today as the modern internet.

There are two main concepts that we need to keep in mind when we try to understand how the internet works from the engineering perspective. These concepts are the following:

- **Access to information**: While the computer world was stuck in the mainframe era, user terminals had to be connected to a mainframe. The idea of remote access started to grow. Over time, humanity discovered that if we connect computers together, we can share information and resources between them. Basically, we can segment and distribute information and computer resources. We can connect with other people and share information with them faster than ever before in the history of humanity.

- **Resilience**: In the 1960s, the US government was concerned about the possibility of a nuclear attack that could destroy the communication infrastructure. This concern was the seed of the idea of a distributed network without a single point of failure that could survive a nuclear attack, and that is the reason why the internet is very often referred to as a network of networks.

Many more things needed to happen since the 20th century to make the internet a reality, but these two concepts remain strong in the architecture of the internet today.

Important info

There is a great video that explains the history of the internet in a very simple way. You can watch it here: `https://www.youtube.com/watch?v=9hIQjrMHTv4`.

Internet Infrastructure

Just to give you an idea of the dependency that we all have on the internet, there are hundreds of optic fiber cables connecting the world across the oceans and seas to make internet connectivity possible. Here is a map of the submarine cables that connect the world:

Figure 9.1 – Our world is connected by dozens of fiber optic cables across the oceans.
Screenshot from (https://www.submarinecablemap.com/) CC BY-SA 4.0.

Optic fiber cables are not the only way to connect to the internet. Other ways include satellites and radio waves. Over the years, the speed of the internet has increased and the cost of a connection has decreased thanks to endless research and innovation in the field of telecommunications.

Request for Comments (RFC)

In this chapter, we will focus a lot on the specifications, protocols, and standards that we need to get familiar with in order to make our applications work.

If this is the first time that you're exploring such exotic topics, you may feel overwhelmed by the amount of information that you need to digest. But don't worry, we will explore all these topics in a very simple and functional way.

The Internet Engineering Task Force (IETF) defines an Request for Comments (RFC) as follows (`https://www.ietf.org/standards/rfcs/`):

> *" RFC documents contain technical specifications and organizational notes for the Internet."*

Basically, RFC is a document that describes some kind of specification/protocol/standard to be designed as part of the internet architecture. Any person can submit an RFC to the IETF and if the RFC is approved, it becomes a standard while this sounds simple, this process can take a long time as the refinement and review process is exhaustive.

Here is a simple extract from RFC 2616 (`https://www.rfc-editor.org/rfc/rfc2616.txt`) that describes the **Hypertext Transfer Protocol – HTTP/1.1** in 175 pages:

```
Network Working Group                          R. Fielding
Request for Comments: 2616
  UC Irvine
Obsoletes: 2068


  J. Gettys
Category: Standards Track                       Compaq/
W3C                                                   J. Mogul
                                                  Compaq
                                              H. Frystyk
                                                 W3C/MIT
                                              L. Masinter
                                                   Xerox
                                                P. Leach
                                                Microsoft
                                          T. Berners-Lee
                                                 W3C/MIT
                                                June 1999


          Hypertext Transfer Protocol -- HTTP/1.1


Status of this Memo

   This document specifies an Internet standards track protocol for
the
   Internet community, and requests discussion and suggestions for
   improvements.  Please refer to the current edition of the "Internet
```

```
    Official Protocol Standards" (STD 1) for the standardization state
    and status of this protocol.  Distribution of this memo is
unlimited.

Copyright Notice

    Copyright (C) The Internet Society (1999).  All Rights Reserved.

Abstract

    The Hypertext Transfer Protocol (HTTP) is an application-level
    protocol for distributed, collaborative, hypermedia information
    systems. It is a generic, stateless, protocol which can be used for
    many tasks beyond its use for hypertext, such as name servers and
    distributed object management systems, through extension of its
    request methods, error codes and headers [47]. A feature of HTTP is
    the typing and negotiation of data representation, allowing systems
    to be built independently of the data being transferred.

    HTTP has been in use by the World-Wide Web global information
    initiative since 1990. This specification defines the protocol
    referred to as "HTTP/1.1", and is an update to RFC 2068 [33].
```

Yeah, I know… this is not an easy read. I don't expect you to read the whole RFC but we will explore some parts of it in this chapter in a practical way.

The best aspect of RFCs is that they are free and you can read them online. You can find lots of quality information that can help you understand specific parts of the internet architecture when you need it.

Other RFCs

Just to get rid of that overwhelming feeling, I would like to share with you other RFCs that are more fun to read:

- **RFC 2324** (`https://tools.ietf.org/html/rfc2324`): Hyper Text Coffee Pot Control Protocol (HTCPCP/1.0)

- **RFC 1149** (`https://tools.ietf.org/html/rfc1149`): A Standard for the Transmission of IP Datagrams on Avian Carriers

And my favorite one:

- **RFC 2549** (`https://datatracker.ietf.org/doc/html/rfc2549`): IP over Avian Carriers with Quality of Service; an iteration of RFC 1149

These funny RFCs can give you familiarity and an idea of the power of the RFC discussion format. Basically, if you want to create a new protocol, you can submit an RFC to the IETF and if the RFC is approved, it becomes a standard. You can read more about the RFC process here: `https://www.rfc-editor.org/about/independent/`.

One of the most important protocols that you will need to know as a web developer is HTTP. In the next section, we will explore this protocol in detail and will learn the different architectures and components it involves and that are in use today as the backbone of the internet as we know it.

HTTP – server and client relationship

While web development can be a very complex topic, we can simplify it by understanding the relationship between the server and the client in the typical web applications.

We have two main actors, the server and the client:

- **Server**: The server is the computer that is running the application, dealing with the database queries, and many other things. This server is often called the backend.

- **Client**: The client is the piece of software that the end user executes on the local machine in the case of web applications. The user employs a web browser to execute the software (HTML, CSS, JS, etc.). The client is often called the frontend.

The communication between the server and the client is done through HTTP. The client sends a request to the server and the server replies with a response. This is the typical request/response cycle

Request and response

The request and response are the two main parts of HTTP. The request is sent by the client to the server and the server returns a response. The request and response are composed of different parts that we will explore in the following sections.

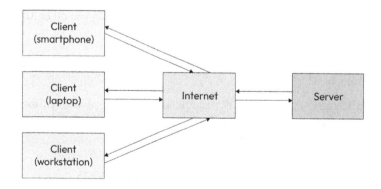

Figure 9.2 – The relationship between the server, internet, and multiple clients

As we can see in the preceding diagram, one server can handle multiple clients at the same time. This is the typical architecture of a web application. The server handles the requests from clients and responds with the corresponding response.

But very often, one client will send multiple requests to a single server or multiple servers. Let's take a look at the following HTML snippet:

```
<head>
<link rel="stylesheet" type="text/css" href="https://server1.com/
style.css">
</head>
<body>
<img src="https://server3.com/image.png">
<script type="text/javascript" src="https://server2.com/script.js"></
script>
</body>
```

As we can see, the client sends three requests to three different servers (`server1.com`, `server2.com`, and `server3.com`) asking for specific resources. Each server will eventually respond with the requested resource.

As a simple example, let's go to `https://packtpub.com` and open the developer tools in our browser. In the **Network** tab, we can see all the requests that the browser is sending to the server and the responses from the server:

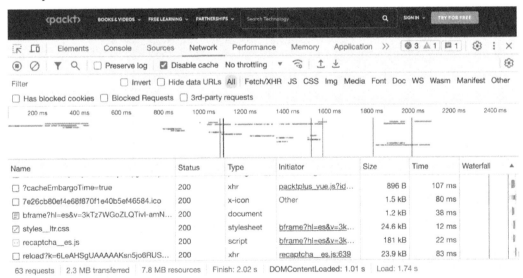

Figure 9.3 – Web browser screenshot

If you pay attention to the bottom part of *Figure 9.3*, you can easily see that this page is sending more than 60 requests targeting different servers to render the page. This is a very common scenario in web applications: the client sends multiple requests to the server(s) to get key resources including favicons, CSS files, JS files, images, videos, and raw data. If we look at the table, we can see each item that is loaded, and can debug and explore each request that was made. This can be intimidating at the beginning, but once you know how the filter works and you spend some hours working with it you will feel more comfortable.

Server-side rendering

In the beginning, web applications were very simple, and JavaScript was very limited in its usage. Web applications were rendered on the server and the client just received the HTML, CSS, and JS files. This is called server-side rendering, and it is still used in many applications.

While this model is still used today, there are some clear disadvantages. Any time the user wants to interact with the application, the server needs to render the page again and send it to the client. This generates a lot of traffic and the user experience is not the best, as there are moments where the website appears blank between refreshes.

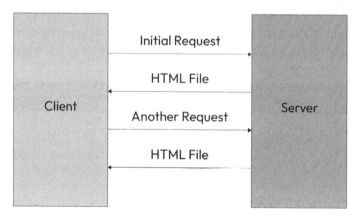

Figure 9.4 – The relationship between the server and client in the server-side rendering approach

This pattern was especially bad in the early days of smartphones, when mobile devices were not powerful enough to render the pages and the connection was not very good. The user experience was very bad. The solution was to move the rendering to the client side, this is called client-side rendering.

Single-Page Applications (SPAs)

In client-side rendering, the server sends the initial HTML, CSS, and JS files to the client. Then, JavaScript takes control of the application and renders the views on the client side. Thus, the server only sends the data to the client and the client renders the page. This is called a **Single-Page Application** (**SPA**) and it is the most common pattern today.

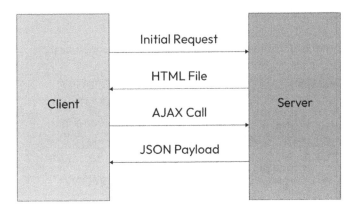

Figure 9.5 – The relationship between the server in the AJAX approach

At first, this pattern was very complicated to implement, but with the evolution of JavaScript frameworks, this pattern has become very popular. Today, we have a lot of frameworks that can help us to build SPAs easily. Some of the most popular frameworks are Angular, React, and Vue.js. The SPA pattern uses the same HTTP but in a different way via **Asynchronous JavaScript and XML (AJAX)** requests.

This new technique introduced a lot of changes and innovations in the way we build the backend applications. Backend applications became more like an **Application Programming Interface (API)** that responds with data to the client, and not only to the typical web clients, but now even servers can also use this API to exchange information with each other.

Now that we have a clear idea of the components and possible web architectures, it is time to deep dive into HTTP so we can build solid projects using standardized communication between the server and the clients.

Mastering HTTP

Now that we have a better understanding of the HTTP concept, let's take a look at the different parts of HTTP that we need to understand in order to build a web application.

We have already seen the request and response, but let's take a deeper look at the different parts that compose the request and the response (headers, payloads, versions, and methods).

HTTP headers

Each request and response has a set of headers. These are key-value pairs and provide additional information about the request or the response.

While both the request and response headers may look similar, they are not the same, although they do share common key-value pairs.

Request headers

We will start by analyzing in *Figure 9.6* what is included in the request header:

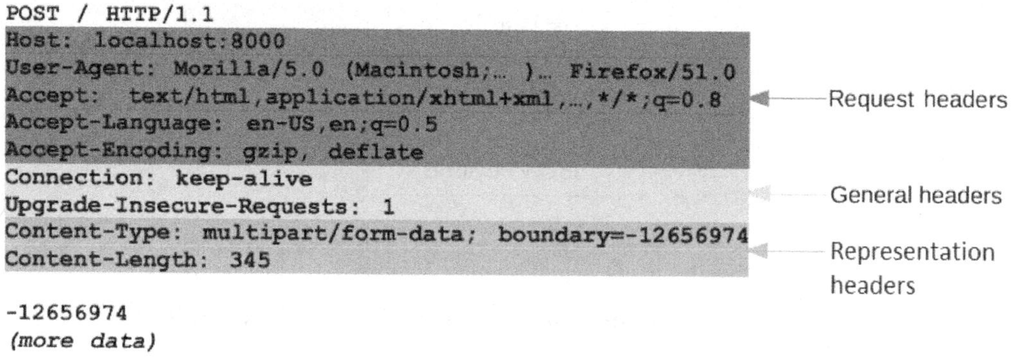

```
POST / HTTP/1.1
Host: localhost:8000
User-Agent: Mozilla/5.0 (Macintosh;... )... Firefox/51.0
Accept:   text/html,application/xhtml+xml,...,*/*;q=0.8         ◄──────Request headers
Accept-Language:  en-US,en;q=0.5
Accept-Encoding: gzip, deflate
Connection: keep-alive
Upgrade-Insecure-Requests: 1                                    ◄───────General headers
Content-Type: multipart/form-data; boundary=-12656974
Content-Length: 345                                            ◄───────Representation
                                                                        headers
-12656974
(more data)
```

Figure 9.6 – Attributions and copyright licensing by Mozilla Contributors is licensed under CC-BY-SA 2.5

Let's group the different header properties:

- Representation headers: content-type and content-length
- General headers: keep-alive and upgrade-insecure-requests
- Request headers: accept, accept-encoding, accept-language, host, and user-agent

Just by looking at the headers, we can understand many things about a request, such as the type of content the client is expecting, the language, and the browser used. The server can use this information to provide a better response to the client.

> **Important info**
>
> This is just a small list of the possible headers. There are many more headers that we can use to provide more information about the request or response. We can even create our own key-value pairs. You can find the list of the HTTP headers here: https://developer.mozilla.org/en-US/docs/Web/HTTP/Headers.

Response headers

We will finish by analyzing in the *Figure 9.7* what is included in the response header

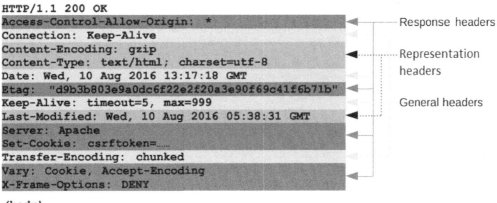

(body)

Figure 9.7 – Attributions and copyright licensing by Mozilla Contributors is licensed under CC-BY-SA 2.5

The response headers are very similar to the request headers, but they are not the same. They can be grouped as follows:

- Representation headers: `content-type`, `content-encoding`, and `last-modified`
- General headers: `connection`, `date`, `keep-alive`, and `transfer-encoding`
- Response headers: `access-control-allow-origin`, `etag`, `server`, `set-cookie`, `vary`, and `x-frame-options`

With the response headers, we can also provide additional information that will help the browsers and the web applications to digest and render the information properly.

The response headers are very important for the security of the application, as there are many headers that can prevent certain attacks in the web browser environment. For example, we can use `x-frame-options` to prevent the application from being loaded in an `iframe`, or use `feature-policy` to prevent the application from using features such as the camera or microphone. We will explore this in *Chapter 15*.

Status codes

Overall, one of the most important pieces of information that we can find in the response is the status code.

The status code allows us to understand whether the request was successful or not and can even provide more granular feedback. We can classify status codes into the following groups:

- 1xx: Informational
- 2xx: Success
- 3xx: Redirection
- 4xx: Client Error
- 5xx: Server Error

The most common status codes are `200 OK`, `201 Created`, `301 Moved Permanently`, `400 Bad Request`, `401 Unauthorized`, `403 Forbidden`, `404 Not Found`, `429 Too Many Requests`, `500 Internal Server Error`, and `503 Service Unavailable`. You can find the complete list of the status codes here: `https://developer.mozilla.org/en-US/docs/Web/HTTP/Status`.

As you can see, if you know the given status code, you can understand what happened with your request. For example, a `429` error code occurs when the client has sent too many requests in a given amount of time ("rate limiting"), but if you receive a `401` then the error is related to your authentication. Finally, if in the same scenario you receive `403`, you are correctly authenticated but you don't have enough permission to perform the given operation, such as deleting another user account.

We all have experienced the `404` error code, which is very common when we try to access a resource that doesn't exist. For example, if we try to access the following URL, `https://www.google.com/invented-resource`, we will receive a `404` error code.

---

418 I'm a teapot

There is a strong culture on the internet to build fancy 404 pages. You can find a lot of examples online, but not many people know that there is a special error code `418` that RFC 2324 (`https://tools.ietf.org/html/rfc2324`) describes as follows:

"Any attempt to brew coffee with a teapot should result in the error code "418 I'm a teapot". The resulting entity body MAY be short and stout."

While this might seem just like a running joke, it is actually supported by many entities including Node (`https://github.com/nodejs/node/issues/14644`) and Google.

Figure 9.8 – Web browser screenshot of google.com/teapot

As Shane Brunswick said on the Save 418 Movement website (`https://save418.com/`):

> *"It's a reminder that the underlying processes of computers are still made by humans. It'd be a real shame to see 418 go."*

And I do agree with him: behind these complex systems there are humans, and we should not forget that, in the same way that we should not forget that the internet could not exist without the open source movement and the hacker culture.

Request methods

Just as status codes are very important to understand responses, the request methods are essential to understand requests.

There are many request methods, but the most common are the following: GET, POST, PUT, PATCH, and DELETE. You can find the complete list of the request methods here: `https://developer.mozilla.org/en-US/docs/Web/HTTP/Methods`.

The way that we backend developers use them can differ a bit, but the most common way is the following:

- GET: Retrieve a resource

- POST: Create a resource

- PUT: Update a resource

- PATCH: Partially update a resource

- DELETE: Delete a resource

We will explore them in detail in *Chapter 11*, when we create an actual REST API with all the endpoints.

In the early days of the internet, we used forms to send data to the server and specified the given method in the form. See the following, for example:

```
<form action="/user" method="POST">
  <input type="text" name="username" />
  <input type="password" name="password" />
  <input type="submit" value="Submit" />
</form>
```

The preceding code was a common way to send data to a server in order to create a new user, but nowadays we use JavaScript to send data to the server. For example, we can use the fetch API to send data to the server as follows:

```
fetch('/user', {
  method: 'POST',
  headers: {
    'Content-Type': 'application/json'
  },
  body: JSON.stringify({
    username: 'john',
    password: '1234'
  })
})
```

And then we would use the response to inform the user whether the request was successful or not. While using JavaScript to send data to the server is more complex, it gives us more flexibility and control over the request.

> **Important note**
> When you enter a URL in the browser, the browser sends a GET request to the server. This is the default method that the browser uses. You have been using HTTP methods for a long time without knowing it.

HTTP payloads

HTTP messages can carry a payload, which means that we can send data to the server, and servers likewise can send data to their clients. This is often done with POST requests.

Payloads can be in many formats, but the most common are the following:

- `application/json`: Used when sharing JSON data
- `application/x-www-form-urlencoded`: Used when sending simple texts in ASCII, sending data in the URL
- `multipart/form-data`: Used when sending binary data (such as files) or non-ASCII texts
- `text/plain`: Used when sending plain text, such as a log file
- You can find the complete list of the content types here: `https://developer.mozilla.org/en-US/docs/Web/HTTP/Basics_of_HTTP/MIME_types`.

HTTP versions

HTTP has evolved over the years, and we have different versions of the protocol:

Version	Year	Status
HTTP/0.9	1991	Obsolete
HTTP/1.0	1996	Obsolete
HTTP/1.1	1997	Standard
HTTP/2	2015	Standard
HTTP/3	2022	Standard

Currently, the most used version of the protocol is the HTTP/1.1 version, but the HTTP/2 version is gaining popularity. The HTTP/3 version is quite new and not widely supported yet.

Nowadays, Node supports the HTTP/1.1 and HTTP/2 versions, but it doesn't support the HTTP/3 version yet. There is an ongoing strategic initiative to support it: `https://github.com/nodejs/node/issues/38478`.

In the next section, we will learn how important **Uniform Resource Locators** (**URLs**) are and how we can use them to structure access to resources in our web applications.

Using URLs in web applications

Let's take a look at the following table, made by Node.js, that describes the different parts of a URL:

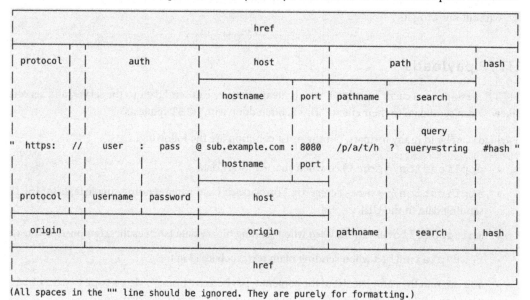

Figure 9.9 – URL structure from the Node.js Official Documentation. Attributions
and copyright licensing by Node.js Contributors is licensed under MIT

In the following chapters, we will use the URL parts a lot, so keep this table handy. There are many ways to parse a URL, but the most common way is to use the URL class:

```
import { URL } from 'node:url';

const myUrl = new URL('https://user:pass@sub.example.com:8080/p/a/t/
h?query=string#hash');

console.log(myUrl.hash); // #hash
console.log(myUrl.host); // sub.example.com:8080
console.log(myUrl.hostname); // sub.example.com
```

This class is available in Node.js and in the browser.

> **Important info**
>
> Node.js 20 introduced one of the most performant URL parsers available, called Ada 2.0: `https://www.yagiz.co/announcing-ada-url-parser-v2-0`.

Now that we know how flexible URLs are, let's explore in the next section how we can build a standard layer on top of our web services. This layer is the foundation of many online services and SaaS products. We will learn the basics of creating web application interfaces (APIs).

REST APIs in a nutshell

REST stands for **Representational State Transfer**, and is an architectural style for building APIs. It was introduced by Roy Fielding in his PhD dissertation (`https://www.ics.uci.edu/~fielding/pubs/dissertation/rest_arch_style.htm`) in 2000.

In practical terms, the idea is to define a set of resources that can be accessed by the client using HTTP, as we explored in the previous section.

Each resource is identified by a unique URL, and the client can perform operations on it using the HTTP methods. The server will respond with a status code and a payload when necessary.

For example, let's say that we have a REST API to manage a database of movies. We can define the following resources:

- `/movies`: This resource represents the collection of movies
- `/movies/:id`: This resource represents a single movie

> **Important tip**
> The `:id` part of the URL is a placeholder for the user ID. This is called a URL parameter, and takes the form of `/movies/1` or `/movies/12345`, and so on.

The client can perform the following operations on these resources using the aforementioned HTTP methods:

- `GET /movies`: Get all the movies
- `GET /movies/:id`: Get a single movie
- `POST /movies`: Create a new movie
- `PUT /movies/:id`: Update a movie
- `DELETE /movies/:id`: Delete a movie

Most of the time, the server will respond with a JSON payload, but it can also respond with other formats such as XML or HTML.

Let's see an example of a REST API in action. We will use simple-api (`https://www.npmjs.com/package/@ulisesgascon/simple-api`), which is a very simple HTTP API to build fast prototypes. This API includes Swagger documentation that can be used to explore the API.

Figure 9.10 – Web browser screenshot of the API documentation generated with Swagger

As you can see, the API is quite intuitive and easy to use because it follows the REST principles. So, you intuitively know how to use it. We can use Swagger to explore more details of the payload expected by the API when we create a new todo:

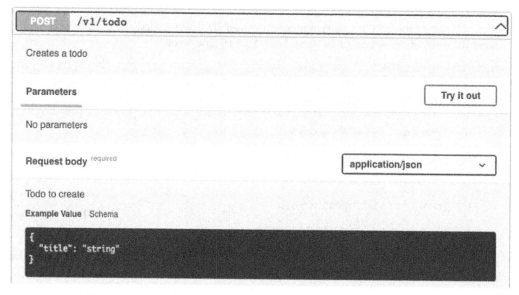

Figure 9.11 – Web browser screenshot of the API documentation generated with Swagger

It is also possible to explore the potential responses that the API can return for any specific endpoint that is available:

Figure 9.12 – Web browser screenshot of the API documentation generated with Swagger

If you understand how RESTful APIs work, you will be able to use any API based on HTTP. For example, the GitHub API `https://docs.github.com/en/rest` is a REST API that uses HTTP to expose its services.

There is a world full of APIs out there, waiting for you to use them to build amazing projects. Here is a great list of public APIs: `https://apilist.fun/`

Throughout the previous chapters, we have mentioned JSON, but we haven't explained it in detail, so in the next section we will deep dive into it, as it is the most common format to exchange data in modern APIs.

Exploring the JSON specification

JSON stands for **JavaScript Object Notation**, and is a lightweight data-interchange format. It is easy for humans to read and write, and it is easy for machines to parse and generate.

We can easily convert a JavaScript object to a JSON string using the `JSON.stringify()` method:

```
const user = {
  name: 'John',
  age: 30
};

const json = JSON.stringify(user);
```

And we can convert a JSON string to a JavaScript object using the `JSON.parse()` method:

```
const json = '{"name":"John","age":30}';
const user = JSON.parse(json);
```

While the JSON name includes the world JavaScript, it is a language-independent data format. Many programming languages have libraries to parse and generate JSON.

JSON is the most common format used to exchange data between clients and servers, such as when we use or build a REST API.

> **Important note**
>
> The JSON specification is quite simple, and I strongly suggest you read it. You can find it at `https://www.ecma-international.org/wp-content/uploads/ECMA-404_2nd_edition_december_2017.pdf`

In the next section, we will explore how to debug HTTP requests so that we can build complex projects easily.

Debugging HTTP requests

There are many ways to debug HTTP requests. The most common way is to use the developer tools, as these are easily accessible in most web browsers. It is also quite helpful when you are developing a website to keep these tools open and navigate between the tabs to debug UI components and network requests.

But there are also other tools that you can use, such as Postman (`https://www.postman.com/`) or Insomnia (`https://insomnia.rest/`), which were designed specifically for this purpose and offer many features out of the box (collections, authentication, etc.). These tools are the best option if you don't have a website and you are just testing API endpoints directly.

In the next chapters, we will use the developer tools of the browser to debug our HTTP transactions and will use Jest to test and debug our HTTP requests.

Other developers use more advanced tools such as Charles (`https://www.charlesproxy.com/`) or Wireshark (`https://www.wireshark.org/`), but they are not necessary for the scope of this book.

If you are not familiar with the developer tools of your browser, you can read more about it in *Chapter 2*.

Summary

In this chapter, we have learned a lot about the technologies that we will use to build our applications and that constitute the foundation of the modern internet.

Additionally, we have learned how RFC documents are used to define the standards of the internet and how we can use them to learn more about the technologies that we use.

Later on, we learned how the server-client architecture works and how HTTP is used to exchange data between the client and the server in detail, including HTTP methods and status codes.

Finally, we explored the URL parts and learned how to use them to build RESTful APIs. We also learned about the JSON specification in more detail and how to debug HTTP requests.

In the next chapter, we will explore how we can use databases to store data and how we can interact with them. This is the last piece of the puzzle before we can start building our final web application.

Further reading

- *Wikipedia | IP over Avian Carriers*: `https://en.wikipedia.org/wiki/IP_over_Avian_Carriers`

- *Wikipedia | HTTP*: `https://en.wikipedia.org/wiki/HTTP`

- *History of the Internet*: `https://www.youtube.com/watch?v=9hIQjrMHTv4`

- *How the Internet Works in 5 Minutes*: `https://www.youtube.com/watch?v=7_LPdttKXPc`

- An overview of HTTP: `https://developer.mozilla.org/en-US/docs/Web/HTTP/Overview`

- *Project Code Rush - The Beginnings of Netscape / Mozilla Documentary*: `https://www.youtube.com/watch?v=4Q7FTjhvZ7Y`

- *How The Internet Travels Across Oceans*: `https://www.youtube.com/watch?v=yd1JhZzoS6A`

- *There is a Reason Why Underwater Power Cables are So Expensive*: `https://www.youtube.com/watch?v=bkgvqC3M1Tw`

- *Jeff Geerling | Testing one of the oldest internet myths*: `https://www.youtube.com/watch?v=4pz2kMxCu8I`

10

Building Web Applications with Express

Express is the most popular web framework for JavaScript and has been the de-facto standard for many years. It is a very minimalistic framework, very easy to learn, and provides a lot of flexibility to build web applications.

In this chapter, we will start with the most basic "hello world" application to build a solid and well-tested REST API application. We will explore in detail all the critical components of Express, including request and response, middleware, and routing. We will also learn how to use the most common Express middleware and how to build our own middleware.

To sum up, here are the main topics that we will explore in this chapter:

- Serving static files for your project
- Building a server-rendered landing page using template engines
- Building a typical CRUD REST API application with Express
- Using the most common Express middleware, including third-party libraries
- Building your own middleware

Technical requirements

The code files for the chapter can be found at `https://github.com/PacktPublishing/NodeJS-for-Beginners`

Check out the code in action video for this chapter on `https://youtu.be/8QyDZVa7CNg`

Getting familiar with the Express library

Express is defined on its own website (`https://expressjs.com/`) as follows:

Fast, unopinionated, minimalist web framework for Node.js

So, the good news is that we have a lot of freedom to build our application. The bad news is that we must make a lot of decisions, and we must be careful to not make mistakes.

Express is very minimalistic in comparison with other web frameworks, so we have to add third-party libraries or build our own abstractions when needed. Express has a very active community, so we can find a lot of libraries to solve common problems.

Additionally, the official documentation is of great quality and there are plenty of resources to learn more about Express, which makes Express a great choice for beginners.

As Express is an unopinionated framework, when you follow a tutorial or a course you will find that sometimes the code is not consistent and doesn't follow the same patterns. This is because you have a lot of freedom in Express, and over time you will develop your own patterns and your own way of building applications that best fits you.

In this book, we will use Express version 4.18.3, but any Express 4.x version should be fine as well. We will use Node.js version 20.11.0. Both are the latest versions available at the time of writing.

Installing Express

To install Express, we must run the following command in a new Node.js project:

```
npm install express@4
```

You don't need any additional configuration; just install it and you are ready to go.

Hello World

Let's start with a simple example, a Hello World application. Create a new file called `helloWorld.js` and add the following code:

```
import express from 'express'

const app = express()
const port = 3000

app.get('/', (req, res) => {
  res.send('Hello World from Express!')
})
```

```
app.listen(port, () => {
  console.log(`Hello World app listening on port ${port}`)
})
```

Very simple, right? Let's break it down:

1. We import the Express library and create an instance of the Express application.

2. We define a route for the / root path and we send a response with the text `Hello World from Express!`.

3. We start the server and listen on port `3000`.

To run the application, we use the following command:

```
node helloWorld.js
```

If everything is OK, you should see the following output:

```
Hello World app listening on port 3000
```

Now, if you open your browser and go to `http://localhost:3000`, you should see the text **Hello World from Express!**, as shown in the following screenshot:

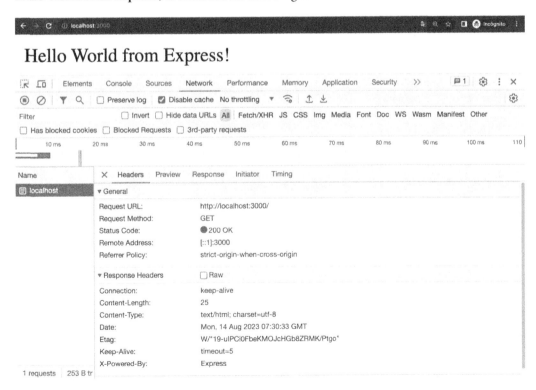

Figure 10.1 – Web browser screenshot showing a simple Express project

Using the generator

Express has a command-line tool to generate a basic application. To use it, we must run the following command:

```
npx express-generator@4
```

This will generate a new application with many files and folders. I recommend you create a new folder and run the command there, so you don't mess up your current project.

The output on execution should be something like the following:

```
create : public/
create : public/javascripts/
create : public/images/
create : public/stylesheets/
create : public/stylesheets/style.css
create : routes/
create : routes/index.js
create : routes/users.js
create : views/
create : views/error.jade
create : views/index.jade
create : views/layout.jade
create : app.js
create : package.json
create : bin/
create : bin/www

install dependencies:
  $ npm install

run the app:
  $ DEBUG=generated:* npm start
```

Then the next step is to install the dependencies:

```
npm install
```

Finally, we can start the application:

```
npm start
```

If everything is OK, you should see the following output:

```
> generated@0.0.0 start
> node ./bin/www
GET / 304 125.395 ms - -
GET /stylesheets/style.css 304 1.265 ms - -
GET / 304 11.043 ms - -
GET /stylesheets/style.css 304 0.396 ms - -
GET /ws 404 11.822 ms - 1322
```

If you access `http://localhost:3000` in the browser, you should see the following page:

Figure 10.2 – Web browser screenshot showing the Express app
generated using the `express-generator`

Feel free to explore the generated code, but don't worry if you don't understand everything as we will cover all the important parts in the following sections. Note that also the route `http://localhost:3000/users` is working and if you try any other route, you will get a 404 error, as with `http://localhost:3000/invented` for example.

Debugging

Now, let me show another cool thing that the Express generator includes and that we will use in our project later. If you start the application with the command `DEBUG=* npm start` or `set DEBUG=* && npm start` (if you use Windows) in the terminal output will be more verbose and you will see a lot of information about the requests and responses:

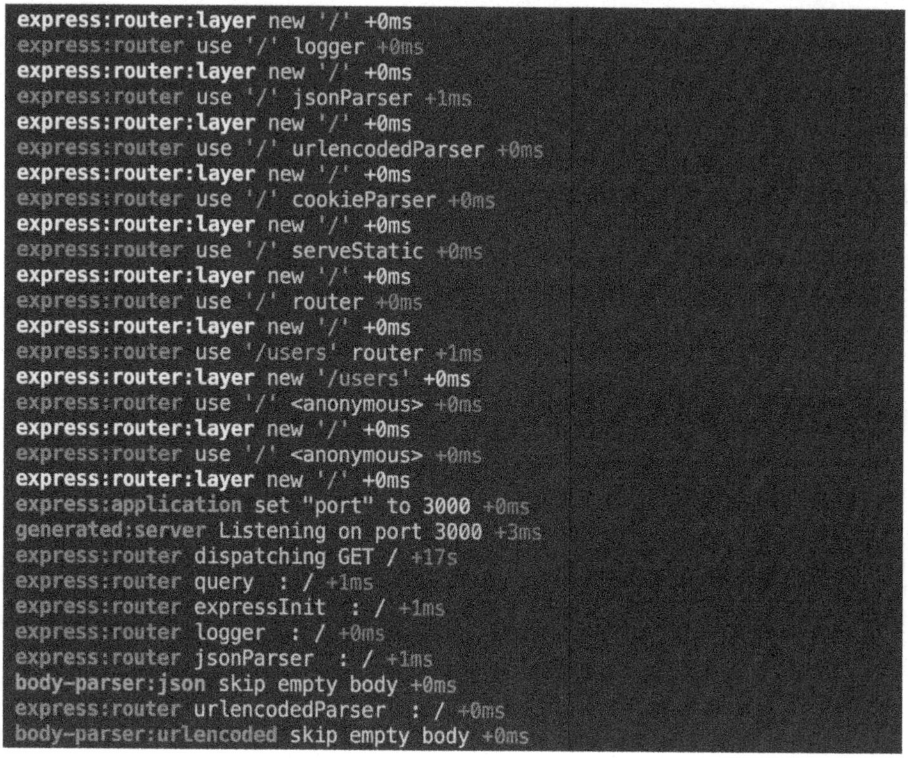

```
express:router:layer new '/' +0ms
express:router use '/' logger +0ms
express:router:layer new '/' +0ms
express:router use '/' jsonParser +1ms
express:router:layer new '/' +0ms
express:router use '/' urlencodedParser +0ms
express:router:layer new '/' +0ms
express:router use '/' cookieParser +0ms
express:router:layer new '/' +0ms
express:router use '/' serveStatic +0ms
express:router:layer new '/' +0ms
express:router use '/' router +0ms
express:router:layer new '/' +0ms
express:router use '/users' router +1ms
express:router:layer new '/users' +0ms
express:router use '/' <anonymous> +0ms
express:router:layer new '/' +0ms
express:router use '/' <anonymous> +0ms
express:router:layer new '/' +0ms
express:application set "port" to 3000 +0ms
generated:server Listening on port 3000 +3ms
express:router dispatching GET / +17s
express:router query  : / +1ms
express:router expressInit  : / +1ms
express:router logger  : / +0ms
express:router jsonParser  : / +1ms
body-parser:json skip empty body +0ms
express:router urlencodedParser  : / +0ms
body-parser:urlencoded skip empty body +0ms
```

Figure 10.3 – Terminal screenshot

This is because Express and many other dependencies use the debug library (https://www.npmjs.com/package/debug) to log information. By using the DEBUG=* environment variable, we are telling to debug library to print the information related to all the namespaces. But we can be more selective and limit the scope for Express, for example, by using the DEBUG=express:* npm start environment variable.

Now, that we have a basic understanding of Express, it is time to explore how we can use template engines to render the HTML pages that will be sent to the browser.

Understanding template engines

In *Chapter 9*, we learned the difference between **single-page applications** (**SPAs**) and server-side rendering.

Express provides a way to render HTML pages using template engines. This is the key feature to build server-side rendered applications with Express.

Choosing a template engine

The first thing that we must do is to choose a template engine. There are many options available. The most popular option historically was Jade (`https://www.npmjs.com/package/jade`), but it was renamed to Pug (`https://www.npmjs.com/package/pug`). You can find many tutorials and examples by searching using both names.

I personally prefer **Embedded JavaScript templating** (**ejs**) (`https://www.npmjs.com/package/ejs`) for its simplicity and because it is well documented. Over time, you will get more familiar with the template engines and will be able to choose the one that better fits your needs.

Rendering a template

So, going back to our hello world example, let's create a new file called `helloWorldTemplate.js` and add the following code:

```
import express from ('express')
const app = express()
const port = 3000

app.set('view engine', 'ejs')

app.get('/', (req, res) => {
  res.render('index', {
    title: 'This is an Express app',
    subtitle: 'using EJS as template engine'})
})

app.listen(port, () => {
  console.log(`Application running in http://localhost:${port}`)
})
```

Now, we have to create a new folder called `views`, inside of which we create a new file called `index.ejs` with the following content:

```
<!DOCTYPE html>
<html lang="en">
<head>
  <meta charset="UTF-8">
  <title><%= title %></title>
</head>
<body>
  <h1><%= title %></h1>
  <h2><%= subtitle %></h2>
```

```
</body>
</html>
```

As you can see, the template engine uses the `<%=` and `%>` tags to interpolate the values. In this case, we are passing the `title` variable to the template.

Finally, we have to install the `ejs` dependency:

```
npm install ejs@3
```

Then we start the application as follows:

```
node helloWorldTemplate.js
```

If you access `http://localhost:3000` in the browser, you should see the following displayed:

This is an Express app

using EJS as template engine

Figure 10.4 – Web browser screenshot showing the templeate rendered for the end user.

Additionally, if you access `view-source:http://localhost:3000/`, you will see the raw HTML that Express is sending to the browser:

```
<!DOCTYPE html>
<html lang="en">
<head>
  <meta charset="UTF-8">
  <title>This is an Express app</title>
</head>
<body>
  <h1>This is an Express app</h1>
  <h2>using EJS as template engine</h2>
</body>
</html>
```

As you can see the template engine is interpolating the values and generating the HTML for us.

Understanding the process

Now, let's understand what is actually happening in the code:

```
app.set('view engine', 'ejs')
```

The preceding line tells Express that we are going to use `ejs` as our template engine, so now we can use `res.render` to render the template.

```
res.render('index', {
    title: 'This is an Express app',
    subtitle: 'using EJS as template engine'
})
```

In the preceding code, the `res.render` method receives two parameters. The first one is the name of the template, in this case, `index` (`views/index.ejs`), and the second one is the data that we want to interpolate in the template.

Then the template engine will replace the `<%= title %>` and `<%= subtitle %>` tags with the values that we are passing in the second parameter of the `res.render` method.

In real-world applications, the data that we pass to the template will be dynamic; for example, the data that we get from a database or an external API. But for now, we are going to use static data to keep the example simple.

In the next section, we will learn how we can take advantage of the request object to build more rich and powerful applications.

Mastering requests

In *Chapter 9*, we learned all the theory around HTTP requests and responses. Here, we will cover how to handle these with Express.

In this section, we are going to focus on this snippet of pseudo-code:

```
import express from ('express')
const app = express()
app.method(route, handler)
```

We have three elements here to understand:

- `method`, that is, the HTTP method that we want to handle, for example, GET, POST, PUT, DELETE, and so on

- `route`, that is, the path that we want to handle, for example, /, /users, or /users/:id

- `handler`, that is, the callback function that will be executed when `method` and `route` match

HTTP methods

Express provides a method for each HTTP method. There are many out there (get, post, put, head, delete, options, trace, copy, lock, mkcol, move, purge, propfind, proppatch, unlock, report, mkactivity, checkout, merge, m-search, notify, subscribe, unsubscribe, patch, search, and connect).

The most common are get, post, put, and delete, so we are going to focus on them:

```
app.get ('/', () => {})
app.post('/', () => {})
app.put('/', () => {})
app.delete('/', () => {})
```

If you want to manage all the HTTP methods in the same route, you can use the all method:

```
app.all('/', () => {})
```

Routes

The routes are very flexible and can be dynamic. We can define them in different ways, including regular expressions.

Static paths

Static paths are the most common way of defining routes. They are used to handle requests to a specific path, for example, /, /users, or /user/me:

```
app.get('/', () => {})
app.get('/users', () => {})
app.get('/user/me', () => {})
```

Dynamic parameters

Dynamic parameters are used to handle the requests to a specific path. We can use the : character to define a dynamic parameter, such as /users/:id or /users/:id/profile:

```
app.get('/users/:id', () => {})
```

In this case, :id is a dynamic parameter, so it will match with any value, including /users/1, /users/peter, /users/jane-doe, and so on.

You can even combine static and dynamic parameters, such as /users/:id/profile:

```
app.get('/users/:id/profile', () => {})
```

The preceding example will resolve requests to `/users/1/profile`, `/users/peter/profile`, `/users/jane-doe/profile`, and so on.

This pattern is quite common in transportation apps, for example, where you can have a route such as `/users/:id/rides/:rideId` to get the details of a specific ride, or when you book tickets for a flight using a route such as `/flights/from/:originCity/to/:destinationCity`. Express will provide the values of the dynamic parameters in the `req.params` object:

```
app.get('/users/:id', (req, res) => {
    const { originCity, destinationCity } = req.params
    res.send(`You are flying from ${originCity} to
${destinationCity}`)
})
```

Optional parameters

The optional parameters are used to handle the requests to a specific path, but the parameter is optional. This can be done with the ? character, such as `/invoice/:id?`:

```
app.get('/invoice/:id?', (req, res) => {
    const id = parseInt(req.params.id)
    if (id) {
        res.send(`You are looking for the invoice with id ${id}`)
    } else {
        res.send(`You are looking for all the invoices`)
    }
})
```

In this case the `:id` parameter is optional, so it will match with `/invoice`, `/invoice/167`, `/invoice/G123S8123SD123MJ`, and so on.

Regular expressions

We can use regular expressions to define routes. This is quite useful when we want to match the route using predictable patterns – for example, `/.*fly$/` will identify any text that ends with `fly`:

```
app.get(/.*fly$/, (req, res) => {
  res.send(`Match with any route that ends with fly`)
})
```

The preceding route will match with `/butterfly`, `/dragonfly`, `/fly`, `/mcfly`, and so on. Let's create a less exotic example:

```
app.get('/msg/:id/:action(edit|delete)', (req, res, next) => {
  res.send(`You request the action ${req.params.action} for the
message ${req.params.id}`);
});
```

In this case, the route will match with /msg/1/edit, /msg/1/delete, and so on.

> **Note**
>
> If you're unfamiliar with regular expressions, don't worry: you can use the other options to define your routes. But if you want to explore regular expressions more deeply, I recommend you to try *Regular Expressions 101* (https://regex101.com/).

Query params

In *Chapter 9*, we learned about the different parts of the URL and saw that the query params are those parts that start with ?. These are used to send extra information to the server. For example, in the URL /films?category=scifi&director=George+Lucas we are sending two query params, category and the director.

We can capture the query params in the req.query object to use them in our routes:

```
app.get('/films', (req, res) => {
    const { category, director } = req.query
    res.send(`You are looking for films with category ${category} and
director ${director}`)
})
```

It is important to note that query params are optional, meaning that requests might not have any query param at all. In that case, the req.query object would be empty.

> **Note**
>
> URL fragments (i.e., /mypath#fragment) are not part of requests and will not be included as such by the browser, so we can't capture them. See https://github.com/expressjs/express/issues/1083 for more info.

The importance of order

The routes are registered in the order that you defined them, which allows Express to avoid conflicts between routes. Let's see an example:

```
app.get('/users/:id', () => {
    res.send(`You are looking for the user with id ${req.params.id}`)
})
app.get('/users/me', () => {
```

```
        res.send(`You are looking for the current user`)
})
```

If you try to access /users/me, you will get the message You are looking for the user with id me because the /users/:id route is registered first, so it will match with /users/me and the me value will be stored in the req.params.id property.

You can solve this issue by shifting the order of the routes:

```
app.get('/users/me', () => {})
app.get('/users/:id', () => {})
```

In big projects, this can become a problem if you don't have a good strategy to define the routes. This is also a good reason to include automated tests in your project to avoid accidental misconfigurations of routes.

Handlers

Handlers are the functions that are executed when a request matches with a route. While a handler is a simple function with three parameters (req, res, and next), it has the big responsibility of handling the response to the request or delegating the request to other handlers:

```
app.get('/', (req, res, next) => {
    res.send("Hello World")
})
```

Let's see the parameters of the handler in more detail.

request

The request object (req) contains all the information about the request, including the parameters, IP, headers, body, and so on. If you use other libraries that extend the capabilities of Express, very often you will find more properties in this object.

You can find more information about the request object in the Express documentation (https://expressjs.com/en/4x/api.html#req).

response

The response object (res) contains all the methods to handle the response of the request, including simple methods like send or json to more complex methods like download or redirect.

In the following section, we will learn more about the response object capabilities.

next

The next function (next) is used to delegate the request to the next handler. This is useful when you want to split the logic of the handler into multiple functions or delegate error management.

We will learn both strategies in the next two sections, when we will discuss the middleware pattern and mastering responses.

In the next section, we will learn how we can take advantage of the response object and how to customize the responses based on many different scenarios, such as HTTP redirection, HTTP header customization, and more.

Mastering responses

Responses are the way by which the server communicates back to the client after a request, so it is crucial to understand how to manage them. In this section, we will learn about adding headers, status codes, redirects, sending data, and sending files.

You will discover the available methods when you start to build more complex applications. You can find more information about the response object in the Express documentation (https://expressjs.com/en/4x/api.html#res).

Header management

Headers are used to send extra information about the response. Express handles headers by using the set method, which receives two parameters, the name of the header and the value of the header:

```
app.get('/', (req, res, next) => {
    res.set('Content-Type', 'text/html')
    res.send("<h1>Hello World</h1>")
})
```

In the preceding example, we are setting the Content-Type header to text/html so the browser will know that the response is an HTML document and will render it as HTML.

Multiple headers

You can also use the set method to set multiple headers at the same time by passing an object as the first parameter:

```
app.get('/', (req, res, next) => {
    res.set({
        'Content-Type': 'text/html',
        'x-powered-by': 'Unicorns and rainbows'
    })
```

```
        res.send("<h1>Hello World</h1>")
    })
```

In the preceding code, we are setting two headers, Content-Type and x-powered-by.

Removing headers

You can remove a header by using the removeHeader method, which receives the name of the header as the first parameter:

```
app.get('/', (req, res, next) => {
    res.set({
        'Content-Type': 'text/html',
        'x-powered-by': 'Unicorns and rainbows'
    })
    res.removeHeader('x-powered-by')
    res.send("<h1>Hello World</h1>")
})
```

In the preceding example, we are removing the x-powered-by header that we just added in the previous statement.

Status codes

A status code is a number that represents the status of the response. It is used to communicate the status of the request to the client. It is important to use the correct status code, as it is part of the HTTP protocol that we discussed in *Chapter 9*.

You can manage status codes using the status method, which receives the status code as the first parameter:

```
app.get('/', (req, res, next) => {
    res.status(200)
    res.send("<h1>Hello World</h1>")
})
```

In the preceding example, we are setting the status code to 200, which means that the request was successful, By default, Express will set the status code to 200 if you don't set it.

Chaining methods

You can chain the status method with other methods, such as set or send:

```
app.get('/', (req, res, next) => {
    res.status(200).set('Content-Type', 'text/html').send("<h1>Hello
World</h1>")
})
```

Sending status codes only

If you want to send only the status code, you can use the `sendStatus` method, which receives the status code as the first parameter:

```
app.get('/', (req, res, next) => {
    res.sendStatus(500)
})
```

In the preceding example, we are sending the 500 status code, which means that the request was not successful.

Redirects

You can redirect the request to another URL by using the `redirect` method, which receives the URL as the first parameter:

```
app.get('/', (req, res, next) => {
    res.redirect('https://ulisesgascon.com/')
})
```

In the preceding example, we are redirecting the request to `https://ulisesgascon.com`.

The default status code for redirects is 302, but you can change this by specifying the status code as the first parameter:

```
app.get('/', (req, res, next) => {
    res.redirect(301, 'https://ulisesgascon.com/')
})
```

The `redirect` method also accepts relative URLs, so you can redirect to another route in your application:

```
app.get('/', (req, res, next) => {
    res.redirect('/about')
})
```

You can even redirect to a higher level in the URL:

```
app.get('/about/me', (req, res, next) => {
    res.redirect('..')
})
```

In this case, the request will be redirected to `/about`, similar to when you do `cd ..` in the terminal.

It is also possible to redirect to the referrer URL using the `back` method. If the referrer header is not present in the request, then the request will be redirected to `/`:

```
app.get('/', (req, res, next) => {
    res.redirect('back')
})
```

Sending data

At the beginning of the chapter, we saw how to use `res.render` to render a template, but there are other ways to send data to the client. The most common way to send data is by using the `send` method, which receives the data as a parameter. This can be any type of data, including buffers:

```
app.get('/', (req, res, next) => {
    res.send("Hello World")
})
```

Using res.send()

Under the hood, the `send` method will convert the data to a string and will set the `Content-Type` header to `text/html` unless you specify otherwise using `res.set()`. It will also include `Content-Length`.

If you use buffers, the `Content-Type` will be set to `application/octet-stream` and `Content-Length` will be set to the length of the buffer, but you can change this by using `res.set()`:

```
app.get('/', (req, res, next) => {
    res.set('Content-Type', 'text/html')
    res.send(Buffer.from('<p>Hello World</p>'))
})
```

Using res.json()

If you want to send JSON data, you can use the `json` method directly, which receives the data as the first parameter. It will set the `Content-Type` header to `application/json` and perform the serialization of the data for you:

```
app.get('/', (req, res, next) => {
    res.json({message: 'Hello World'})
})
```

This is the most common way to send JSON data, but you can also use the send method and set the Content-Type header to application/json, performing the serialization of the data yourself:

```
app.get('/', (req, res, next) => {
    res.set('Content-Type', 'application/json')
    res.send(JSON.stringify({message: 'Hello World'}))
})
```

This can be very useful if you want to use a different stringification library, such as fast-json-stringify (https://www.npmjs.com/package/fast-json-stringify).

Sending files

You can send files to the client by using the sendFile method, which receives the path to the file as the first parameter:

```
app.get('/report', (req, res, next) => {
    res.sendFile('/path/to/file.txt')
})
```

In the preceding example, we are sending the /path/to/file.txt file to the client. This method allows for huge flexibility including a callback to manage possible errors. Consult the documentation (http://expressjs.com/en/4x/api.html#res.sendFile) for more information.

Another way to send files is by using the res.download() method, which receives the path to the file as the first parameter:

```
app.get('/report', (req, res, next) => {
    res.attachment('/path/to/file.txt')
})
```

This method will set the Content-Disposition header to attachment and the Content-Type header to application/octet-stream unless you specify otherwise using res.set(). This method allows huge flexibility, including a callback to manage possible errors. You can check the documentation (http://expressjs.com/en/4x/api.html#res.download) for more information.

In the next section, we will learn just how powerful the middleware pattern is and how we can use it to build more complex applications.Express is based on the middleware pattern, so it is important to understand it because it will allow us to extend the capabilities of Express easily.

Using the middleware pattern

The heart of Express is the middleware pattern, which allows you to extend the functionality of the framework by adding functions that will be executed in the request-response cycle. The middleware functions are executed in the order that they are added to the application, and they can be added to the application or alternatively to a route.

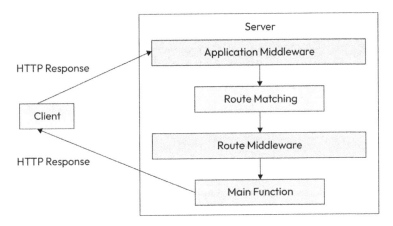

Figure 10.5 – Middleware pattern full process from application middleware to main function

We can understand the middleware pattern as a pipeline, where the request is passed through the pipeline, and each middleware function can modify the request and the response, and pass the request to the next middleware function in the pipeline. The middleware functions can also end the request-response cycle by sending a response to the client.

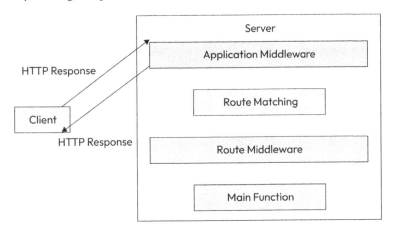

Figure 10.6 – Middleware pattern limited to Application Middleware

We can add a global middleware to the application, which will validate whether the request is authenticated. When the user is properly authenticated, we can pass the request to the next middleware function in the pipeline, and if the user is not authenticated, we can end the request-response cycle by sending a response to the client with an error message.

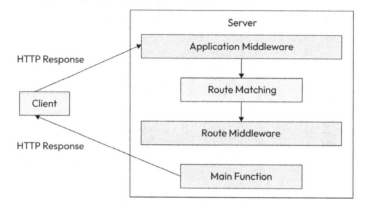

Figure 10.7 – Middleware pattern from Application Middleware to Route Middleware

We can also add a middleware function to a route, to validate (for example) that the user has the proper permissions to access the route, and if so then we can pass the request to the next middleware function in the pipeline, and if the user doesn't have the proper permissions we can end the request-response cycle by sending a response to the client with an error message.

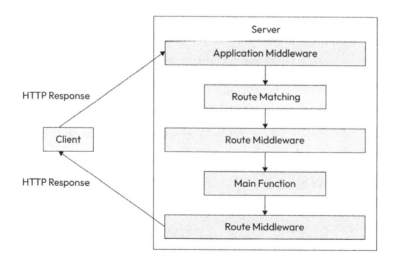

Figure 10.8 – Middleware pattern full process from application middleware to main function

When the main function of the middleware has any kind of problem, such as an exception, that doesn't allow the middleware to continue with the request-response cycle, then the error middleware can take control and respond to the client with the error message.

As you can see, the middleware pattern is quite complex to get familiar with, but at the same time is very powerful, because it allows us to abstract and reuse code easily. We can resolve the requests as sequence of functions where each function can take ownership when needed so we can isolate the proper business logic quite well.

Understanding the scope

So, we have three possible scopes for the middleware functions:

- **Global middleware**: This will be executed for all the requests that are received by the application.
- **Route middleware**: This will be executed for all the requests that are received by the route.
- **Error middleware**: This will be executed when an error is thrown by a middleware function.

Middleware anatomy

So, let's see the anatomy of a middleware function:

```
const middleware(req, res, next) {}
```

Basically, a middleware function receives three parameters: the request object, the response object, and the next function.

Now let's see what we can do with a middleware function in detail.

Adding context to the request

One very common use case for middleware functions is to add context to the request object. The idea is to extend the request object with additional properties that will be used by the next middleware functions in the pipeline. Let's see an example:

```
const detectLangMiddleware(req, res, next) {
    req.lang = req.headers['accept-language'] || 'en'
    next()
}
```

In the preceding example, we are adding a new property to the request object called `lang`. This property can be consumed by the next middleware functions in the pipeline as `req.lang`.

This is a very simple example but is quite commonly deployed to create simple and focused middleware functions that can be composed easily.

As you can see, `detectLangMiddleware` is using `next()` to let Express know that the middleware has finished and there were no errors. In this case, if we don't call `next()`, the application will hang forever.

Managing responses

Another common use case for middleware functions is to manage the response. For example, we can add a middleware function that will redirect the user to `https://updatemybrowser.org/` if the user is using Internet Explorer:

```
const legacyBrowsersMiddleware(req, res, next) {
    if (req.headers['user-agent'].includes('MSIE')) {
        res.redirect('https://updatemybrowser.org/')
    } else {
        next()
    }
}
```

As you can see, if the user is using Internet Explorer, they will be redirected to `https://updatemybrowser.org/`. We do not call `next()` because we don't want to continue with the request-response cycle as we have already sent a response to the client with `res.redirect()`.

If the user is not using Internet Explorer, we call `next()` to continue with the request-response cycle as usual.

Additional configuration

In *Chapter 3*, we learned how closures work. It is quite common to use closures to add additional configuration to the middleware functions. Let's see an example:

```
const detectLangMiddleware = defaultLang => (req, res, next) => {
    req.lang = req.headers['accept-language'] || defaultLang
    next()
}
```

In the preceding code, we have changed the middleware function from before to use a closure to receive the default language as a parameter, so we don't need to use en by default.

So now this middleware function will be executed as follows:

```
import { detectLangMiddleware } from './utils'

// With the closure
app.use(detectLangMiddleware('es'))
// without the closure
app.use(detectLangMiddleware)
```

This is a common pattern for middleware functions that require additional configuration, such as the default language in this case, or tokens, and so on.

Testing

An additional advantage of this middleware pattern is that we can unit test the middleware functions easily because they are just functions that receive a request, a response, and a next function as parameters, and then execute them. We can mock the request and the response, and we can mock the next function to check that the middleware is working properly.

We will see this in more detail later this chapter, but in the meantime, you can check my library called `user-language-middleware` (https://www.npmjs.com/package/user-language-middleware). The full test suite can be found at https://github.com/UlisesGascon/user-language-middleware/blob/main/__tests__/userLanguageMiddleware.test.js to get more familiar with the testing of middleware functions.

Adding middleware to the application

You can add middleware to the application using the `app.use()` method. This method receives a middleware function as a parameter and will be executed for all the requests received by the application:

```
app.use(legacyBrowsersMiddleware)
```

Note that the order of the middleware functions is important because they will be executed in the same order that they are added to the application.

Adding middleware to a route

You can add the middleware to a route the same way that you add it to an application, only using the `app.METHOD()` method instead of `app.use()`:

```
app.get('/users', legacyBrowsersMiddleware, (req, res) => {
    res.send('Hello world')
})
```

So, `legacyBrowsersMiddleware` will be executed only for the GET /users route, and if `legacyBrowsersMiddleware` calls `next()` the next middleware function in the pipeline will be executed, whichi in this case is `(req, res) => { res.send('Hello world') }`.

Yes, we have been using this pattern since the beginning of the chapter! It is indeed fair to say *all the routes are middleware functions in Express.*

Chaining middleware

You can chain middleware functions in the same `app.METHOD()` method, simply by adding the following:

```
app.get('/users', legacyBrowsersMiddleware, detectLangMiddleware,
(req, res) => {
```

```
        res.send('Hello world')
    })
```

This is very common in large applications where you have a lot of middleware functions that are executed in a specific order. It is a good practice to review the order of the middleware functions to avoid unexpected behaviors and to migrate them to the application level if they are used in multiple routes, adapting the business logic if needed.

Common middleware used in Express

Historically, the Express team has included some middleware functions in the framework, but most of them have been moved to external packages since Express 4. However, there are still a few middleware functions included in the framework.

Static files

Express includes a middleware function to serve static files from a directory. This is very useful to serve the static assets of a web application, such as images, CSS files, or JavaScript files:

```
app.use(express.static('public'))
```

You can also use multiple directories to serve static files:

```
app.use(express.static('public'))
app.use(express.static('files'))
```

Error handling

Express includes a middleware function to handle errors. This middleware function must be the last one in the pipeline, and it must receive four parameters instead of three. The first parameter is the error, the second is the request, third is the response, and the fourth one is the next function:

```
app.use((err, req, res, next) => {
    console.error(err.stack)
    res.status(500).send('Ohh! The Server needs some love')
})
```

If you have an error in any middleware function, you can call `next(err)` and this middleware function will be executed, as it also will if you throw an error in a route handler. Let's see it in action:

```
import express from 'express'
const app = express()
const port = 3000
```

```
app.get('/next-error', (req, res, next) => {
    next(new Error('Ohh! Something went wrong'))
})

app.get('/throw-error', (req, res) => {
    throw new Error('Ohh! Something went wrong')
})

app.use((err, req, res, next) => {
    console.error(err.stack)
    res.status(500).send('Ohh! The Server needs some love')
})

app.listen(port, () => {
  console.log(`running at http://localhost:${port}`)
})
```

If you now go to `http://localhost:3000/next-error` or `http://localhost:3000/throw-error`, you will see that the error handler middleware function is taking control.

In the next section, we will continue learning about the middleware pattern, but we will focus on the third-party middleware functions available in the ecosystem. Currently, there is huge amount of middleware functions that you can use in your Express applications, so it is important to know how to use them properly. While using third-party middleware functions you can save a lot of time and effort, you need to be careful because it means adding more dependencies to your project.

Using third-party middleware

There are a lot of third-party middleware functions that you can use in your Express applications. Let's see how to install and use them.

One of the most popular middleware functions is `body-parser` (`https://www.npmjs.com/package/body-parser`). Basically, it will parse the HTTP body of the incoming request and make it available under the `req.body` property.

Install it using npm as follows:

```
npm install body-parser@1
```

Then you can import it and use it in your application. Create a new file called `echo_payload.js` with the following content:

```
import express from 'express'
import bodyParser from 'body-parser'
```

```
const app = express()
const port = 3000

app.use(bodyParser.json())

app.post('/echo', (req, res) => {
    // Echo the request body
    res.json(req.body)
})

app.listen(port, () => {
  console.log(`running at http://localhost:${port}`)
})
```

Now run the application with `node echo_payload.js` and then use `curl` or a similar tool to send a POST request to the `/echo` route:

```
curl -X POST -H "Content-Type: application/json" -d '{"name":"John"}' http://localhost:3000/echo
```

You will see that the response is the same JSON that you sent in the request body.

Summary

In this chapter, we learned about the many uses of Express, including how to create a basic server, how to add routes, how to add static files, and how to use templates.

Additionally, we learned how the middleware pattern works and how we can create our own middleware and use it at different levels in our application. We also checked out some third-party middleware including `body-parser`.

In the next chapter, we will learn how to use a super test to test our first API in depth. We will cover how to test the routes and the stores and will create a solid API that we will develop in the coming chapters.

Further reading

- Express documentation: `https://expressjs.com/`

- *Express, State of the Union* by Doug Wilson: `https://www.youtube.com/watch?v=HxGt_3F0ULg`

- *Node.js Foundation to Add Express as an Incubator Project*: `https://nodejs.medium.com/node-js-foundation-to-add-express-as-an-incubator-project-225fa3008f70`

Part 4:
Building Solid Web
Applications with Node.js

In *Part 4*, we will build a web application together using Express and MongoDB as the main stack. You will learn advanced topics such as error handling or security by implementing them in the project while learning all the theories and best practices to secure your web application.

This part includes the following chapters:

- *Chapter 11, Building a Web Application Project from Scratch*

- *Chapter 12, Data Persistence with MongoDB*

- *Chapter 13, User Authentication and Authorization with Passport.js*

- *Chapter 14, Error handling in Node.js*

- *Chapter 15, Securing Web Applications*

11

Building a Web Application Project from Scratch

In this chapter, we will start a new project that will be the base for the next chapters. We will apply all the lessons learned from the previous chapters and we will put into practice asynchronous programming, Node.js core libraries, external modules, testing, and all the concepts that we learned about regarding REST APIs.

This project will evolve, so we will iterate over the project, adding new features and new tests, so you can experience the full development cycle of a real-world application using Node.js.

In this chapter, we will use the file system library to store the changes we produce in the project while managing operations from the REST API we create. In the next chapter, we will learn how to connect the web application to MongoDB, but we will do a migration using the tests that we built in this chapter.

At the end of the book, we will deploy this project in several ways, and we will expose our application to the internet and to real users.

To sum up, here are the main topics that we will explore in this chapter:

- How to start an Express application including UI and API REST
- How to test an Express application using Supertest and Jest
- How to include data stores in our projects

Technical requirements

The coode files for the chapter can be found at https://github.com/PacktPublishing/NodeJS-for-Beginners

Check out the code in action video for this chapter on https://youtu.be/JYWmvQrGu78

The project Kickoff

This is so exciting! We are going to apply all the knowledge that we have learned in the previous chapters to build a CRUD REST API with Express. We will use the file system to store the data, and we will use the most common Express middleware to build a robust API.

The project goal

We are going to build a microblogging platform called "Whispering," where users can create, read, update, and delete whispers (short posts).

Preview

While we will focus on the backend, we will have a basic frontend included to test the API. So, we will start working with a simple app skeleton that we will evolve over the next chapters.

Welcome to Whispering!

Photo by Brooke Cagle from Unsplash

What is Whispering?

Whispering is a microblogging platform that allows you to share your thoughts with the world and learn Node.js on the way.

Community live

Currently there are 3 whispers available

Figure 11.1 – Preview of the home page from the project in the web browser

Requirements

The requirements will evolve over the next chapters, but for now, we will focus on the following:

- Adding a welcome landing page using a template engine

- Serving static files

- Adding a CRUD REST API with Express

- Using the file system to store the data in JSON format

- Adding tests to ensure that the API is working as expected

Starting with the first step

To start working on the project, we need to download the project from `https://github.com/PacktPublishing/NodeJS-for-Beginners/archive/refs/heads/main.zip` and access the `step0` folder. Now, enter the folder and feel free to explore the code. You will see that we have a basic skeleton with the following structure:

```
|_____.babelrc
|_____db.json
|_____server.js
|_____store.js
|_____jest.config.js
|_____tests
| |_____server.test.js
| |_____fixtures.js
| |_____store.test.js
| |_____utils.js
|_____index.js
|_____public
| |_____index.html
| |_____styles.css
| |_____app.js
| |_____people.jpg
|_____package-lock.json
|_____package.json
|_____.nvmrc
|_____views
| |_____about.ejs
```

Now that we are clear about the project objective, let's start building the application. In the next section, we will start building the application by adding the dependencies, the basic structure, the stores, and other things in order to build a solid REST API that can be used in the next chapters.

Building a REST API

Now that we have a basic understanding of Express, let's build a REST API for the microblogging platform. We will start with the basic CRUD operations and then we will add more features.

In *Chapter 9*, we learned about the principles of building RESTful APIs. We will apply them now. As the platform is called "whispering" and the users will be able to create, read, update, and delete whispers, we will have the following endpoints:

- `GET /api/v1/whisper`: Get all the whispers
- `GET /api/v1/whisper/:id`: Get a whisper by ID
- `POST /api/v1/whisper`: Create a new whisper
- `PUT /api/v1/whisper/:id`: Update a whisper by ID
- `DELETE /api/v1/whisper/:id`: Delete a whisper by ID

In this case, we used the prefix `/api/v1/` because we are building the first version of the API. It is a good practice to version the API in the URL because, in the future, you may want to introduce breaking changes, and it will be hard for your consumers to adapt to the new changes if you don't version the API.

Adding the routes

As the first step, let's add the dependencies:

```
npm install express@4 body-parser@1
```

Let's start by adding the routes to the `server.js` file and configure Express:

```
import express from 'express'
import bodyParser from 'body-parser'

const app = express()

app.use(bodyParser.json())

app.get('/api/v1/whisper', (req, res) => {
    res.json([])
```

```
})

app.get('/api/v1/whisper/:id', (req, res) => {
    const id = parseInt(req.params.id)
    res.json({ id })
})

app.post('/api/v1/whisper', (req, res) => {
    res.status(201).json(req.body)
})

app.put('/api/v1/whisper/:id', (req, res) => {
  //const id = parseInt(req.params.id)
  res.sendStatus(200)
})

app.delete('/api/v1/whisper/:id', (req, res) => {
    res.sendStatus(200)
})

export { app }
```

We created the basic routes for the CRUD operations, and we are returning a JSON response with the data that we received in the request. This time, we made a little change, and we will export the app object so we can use it in the tests later. Now, let's initialize the server in the index.js file:

```
import { app } from "./server.js";

const port = 3000

app.listen(port, () => {
    console.log(`Running in http://localhost:${port}`)
})
```

Now let's add the npm scripts to run the application in the package.json file:

```
{
    "scripts": {
        "start": "node index.js"
    }
}
```

Adding the stores

As this is a simple application, we will use the file system to store the data. We will create a `store.js` file and we will add the following functions:

```
import fs from 'node:fs/promises'
import path from 'node:path'

const filename = path.join(process.cwd(), 'db.json')

const saveChanges = data => fs.writeFile(filename, JSON.
stringify(data))

const readData = async () => {
    const data = await fs.readFile(filename, 'utf-8')
    return JSON.parse(data)
}

const getAll = readData

const getById = async (id) => {
    const data = await readData()
    return data.find(item => item.id === id)
}

const create = async (message) => {
    const data = await readData()
    const newItem = { message, id: data.length +1}
    await saveChanges(data.concat([newItem]))
    return newItem
}

const updateById = async (id, message) => {
    const data = await readData()
    const newData = data.map(current => {
        if (current.id === id) {
            return { ...current, message }
        }
        return current
    })
    await saveChanges(newData)

}
```

```
const deleteById = async id => {
    const data = await readData()
    await saveChanges(data
.filter(current => current.id !== id)
    )
}
```

```
export { getAll, getById, create, updateById, deleteById }
```

Basically, we are using the file system to store the data in a JSON file. We are using saveChanges to save the data and readData to read the data.

Then we have the basic CRUD operations defined in the functions getAll, getById, create, and updateById.

Now, let's add the tests for the store. As the first step, let's add the dependencies, npm install -D jest@29 @babel/preset-env@7, and then let's add the skeleton for the tests to the tests/ store.test.js file:

```
import { getAll, getById, create, updateById, deleteById } from '../
store.js'
import { writeFileSync } from 'node:fs'
import { join } from 'node:path'

const dbPath = join(process.cwd(), 'db.json')
const restoreDb = () => writeFileSync(dbPath, JSON.stringify([]))
const populateDb = (data) => writeFileSync(dbPath, JSON.
stringify(data))
const fixtures = [{ id: 1, message: 'test' }, { id: 2, message: 'hello
world' }]
const inventedId = 12345
const existingId = fixtures[0].id

describe('store', () => {
    beforeEach(() => populateDb(fixtures))
    afterAll(restoreDb)
    // Here we will be the tests
})
```

In *Chapter 8*, we learned the principles of testing. One of the principles is that the tests should be independent, and that means that the tests should not depend on the state of previous tests and that we can run them as many times as we want and the result should not change.

As we are using an external file to store the data, we need to make sure that the data is in the initial state before each test. So, we are using the beforeEach function to populate the database with the fixtures and the `afterAll` function to restore the database to the initial state. This way, we can make sure that the tests always start from the same state.

Also, we added some fixtures and variables that we will use in the tests when we need to create, update, or delete data. This will help us to avoid hardcoding values and make the tests more readable.

Now, let's add the tests for the `getAll` function:

```
describe('getAll', () => {
    it("Should return an empty array when there's no data", async ()
=> {
        restoreDb()
        const data = await getAll()
        expect(data).toEqual([])
    })
    it('Should return an array with one item when there is one item',
async () => {
        const data = await getAll()
        expect(data).toEqual(fixtures)
    })
})
```

We have two test cases only – when the database is empty and when the database has data. In both cases, we are expecting an array.

Now, let's add the tests for the `getById` function:

```
describe('getById', () => {
    it('Should return undefined when there is no item with the given
id', async () => {
        const item = await getById(inventedId)
        expect(item).toBeUndefined()
    })
    it('Should return the item with the given id', async () => {
        const item = await getById(fixtures[0].id)
        expect(item).toEqual(fixtures[0])
    })
})
```

We have two test cases only – when we match an item and when we don't match an item.

Now, let's add the tests for the `create` function:

```
describe('create', () => {
    it('Should return the created item', async () => {
        const newItem = { id: fixtures.length + 1, message: 'test 3' }
        const item = await create(newItem.message)
```

```
                expect(item).toEqual(newItem)
        })
        it('Should add the item to the db', async () => {
            const newItem = { id: fixtures.length + 1, message: 'test 3' }
            const { id } = await create(newItem.message)
            const item = await getById(id)
            expect(item).toEqual(newItem)
        })
    })
})
```

In this case, we expect the item to be returned including the ID when it is returned from the function, and we expect the item to be added to the database.

Let's add the tests for the `updateById` function:

```
describe('updateById', () => {
    it('Should return undefined when there is no item with the given
id', async() => {
        const item = await updateById(inventedId)
        expect(item).toBeUndefined()
    })
    it('Should not return the updated item', async () => {
        const updatedItem = { id: existingId, message: 'updated' }
        const item = await updateById(updatedItem.id, updatedItem.
message)
        expect(item).toBeUndefined()
    })
    it('Should update the item in the db', async () => {
        const updatedItem = { id: existingId, message: 'updated' }
        await updateById(updatedItem.id, updatedItem.message)
        const item = await getById(existingId)
        expect(item).toEqual(updatedItem)
    })
})
```

In this case, we expect the item to be updated in the database only if it exists, but not to be returned from the function at all.

Let's add the last tests for the `deleteById` function:

```
describe('deleteById', () => {
    it('Should return undefined when there is no item with the given
id', async () => {
        const item = await deleteById(inventedId)
        expect(item).toBeUndefined()
    })
```

```
    it('Should not return the deleted item', async () => {
        const item = await deleteById(existingId)
        expect(item).toBeUndefined()
    })
    it('Should delete the item from the db', async () => {
        await deleteById(existingId)
        const items = await getAll()
        expect(items).toEqual(fixtures.filter(item => item.id !==
existingId))
    })
})
```

We expect a similar behavior as in the updateById function. The item should be deleted from the database only if it exists, and the item is not returned. Now, let's include the test scripts in the package.json file:

```
{
    "scripts": {
        "start": "node index.js",
        "test": "jest",
        "test:coverage": "jest --coverage"
    }
}
```

Run the tests with npm run test. Your output should be similar to this:

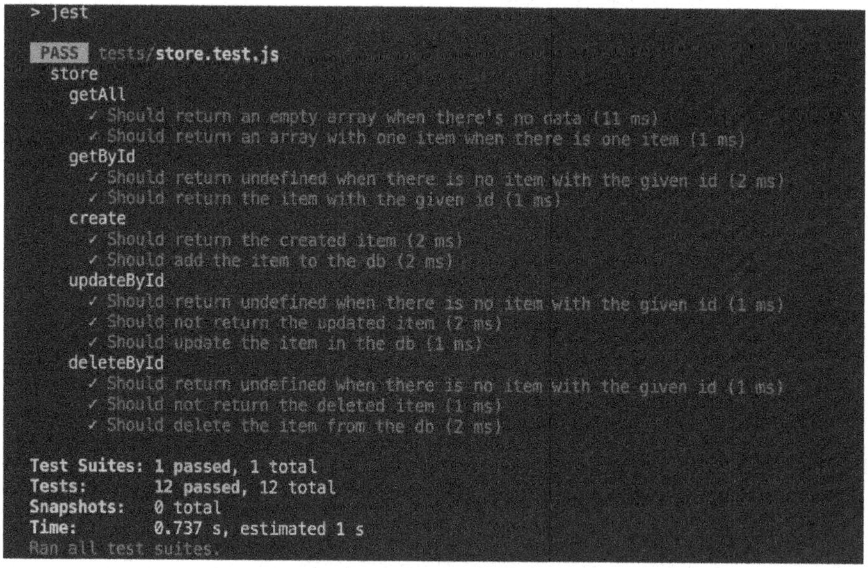

Figure 11.2 – Terminal screenshot

Our first storage is working, and fully tested. Now, let's just finish by adding a linter to the project. First, install the linter with npm i -D standard@17 and then update the package.json scripts:

```
{
    "scripts": {
        "start": "node index.js",
        "test": "jest",
        "test:coverage": "jest --coverage",
        "lint": "standard",
        "lint:fix": "standard --fix"
    }
}
```

Now, you can run the linter with npm run lint and fix the errors with npm run lint:fix. Sometimes you might need to fix the errors manually, but most of the time the linter will fix them for you.

Adding the static files

Now, let's add the static files to the application. Basically, in the public folder, we have several files that we want to serve to the client, such as the index.html, style.css, and app.js files. So, let's add the following code to the server.js file:

```
const app = express()
app.use(express.static('public'))
app.use(bodyParser.json())
```

Now if we start the server with npm run start, and you go to http://localhost:3000/styles.css, you will see the content of the styles.css file.

> **Note**
>
> Until we finish this chapter, the URL http://localhost:3000 might not work as expected, as the backend is not finished yet.

Adding the templates

In this project we will use the server render approach to handle certain parts of the application. So we will install the ejs template engine:

```
npm i ejs@3
```

Let's import the store functions in the `server.js` file:

```
import express from 'express'
import bodyParser from 'body-parser'
import { getAll, getById, create, updateById, deleteById } from './
store.js'

const app = express()
```

Then, register the template engine in the `server.js` file:

```
app.use(bodyParser.json())
app.set('view engine', 'ejs')

app.get('/api/v1/whisper', async (req, res) => {
    const whispers = await getAll()
    res.json(whispers)
})
```

Finally, we will create a route, `about`, that will render the `views/about.ejs` template and we will provide the whispers to the template:

```
app.set('view engine', 'ejs')

app.get('/about', async (req, res) => {
    const whispers = await getAll()
    res.render('about', { whispers })
})

app.get('/api/v1/whisper', async (req, res) => {/*...*/})
```

Now, let's start the server with `npm run start` and go to `http://localhost:3000/about` and you will see the template rendered.

Information

If you are having issues running the project in this chapter while following the steps, or you tried an alternative approach, you can use the `step1` folder from the source code that you downloaded at the beginning of the chapter to compare and fix possible bugs more easily.

In the next section, we will continue building the REST API by adding tests. Adding tests to the REST API is very important because it will allow us to make sure that the API is working as expected and it will allow us to iterate over it in the next chapters more easily.

Testing with supertest

Now, it is time to make sure that our REST API is working as expected. We will learn in this section how to build solid tests while using Express.

Adding stores to the server

We will refactor each route to use the store functions. Let's start with the GET `/api/v1/whisper` route:

```
app.get('/api/v1/whisper', async (req, res) => {
    const whispers = await getAll()
    res.json(whispers)
})
```

Basically, we are using the `getAll` function to get all the whispers and we are returning them in the response. Now, let's refactor the GET `/api/v1/whisper/:id` route:

```
app.get('/api/v1/whisper/:id', async (req, res) => {
    const id = parseInt(req.params.id)
    const whisper = await getById(id)
    if (!whisper) {
        res.sendStatus(404)
    } else {
        res.json(whisper)
    }
})
```

In this case, we will return a 404 status code if the whisper doesn't exist, and we will return the whisper if it exists. Now, let's refactor the POST `/api/v1/whisper` route:

```
app.post("/api/v1/whisper", async (req, res) => {
  const { message } = req.body;
  if (!message) {
    res.sendStatus(400);
  } else {
    const whisper = await create(message);
    res.status(201).json(whisper);
  }
});
```

In this case, we are validating that the message is not empty in the request body, returning a 400 status code in those cases. If the creation was successful, we return the whisper details. Now, let's refactor the PUT /api/v1/whisper/:id route:

```
app.put('/api/v1/whisper/:id', async (req, res) => {
    const { message } = req.body
    const id = parseInt(req.params.id)
    if(!message) {
        res.sendStatus(400)
    } else {
        const whisper = await getById(id);
        if (!whisper) {
            res.sendStatus(404);
        } else {
            await updateById(id, message);
            res.sendStatus(200);
        }
    }
})
```

In this case, we do a payload validation as in POST /api/v1/whisper and we validate that the whisper exists before updating it. Now, let's refactor the DELETE /api/v1/whisper/:id route:

```
app.delete('/api/v1/whisper/:id', async (req, res) => {
    const id = parseInt(req.params.id)
    const whisper = await getById(id)
    if(!whisper) {
        res.sendStatus(404)
        return
    }
    await deleteById(id)
    res.sendStatus(200)
})
```

In this case, we validate that the whisper exists before deleting it. Now, let's add the tests for the routes.

Creating test utils

Before we start adding the tests, there is some code that we can reuse between the test files, such as the fixtures and the functions to populate and restore the database. So, let's do a little refactoring first.

As the first step, let's create a file called fixtures.js in the tests folder, and let's add the following content:

```
const whispers = [{ id: 1, message: 'test' }, { id: 2, message: 'hello
world' }]
const inventedId = 12345
const existingId = whispers[0].id

export {
    whispers,
    inventedId,
    existingId
}
```

Then, create a file called utils.js in the tests folder, and let's add the following content:

```
import { writeFileSync } from 'node:fs'
import { join } from 'node:path'

const dbPath = join(process.cwd(), 'db.json')
const restoreDb = () => writeFileSync(dbPath, JSON.stringify([]))
const populateDb = (data) => writeFileSync(dbPath, JSON.
stringify(data))

export { restoreDb, populateDb }
```

Now, let's refactor the store.test.js file to use the new files:

```
import { getAll, getById, create, updateById, deleteById } from '../
store.js'
import { restoreDb, populateDb } from './utils.js'
import { whispers, inventedId, existingId } from './fixtures.js'

describe('store', () => {
    //...
})
```

Also, find and replace the fixtures variable with whispers in the tests.

Now you can run the tests with `npm run test` and you will see that the tests are passing:

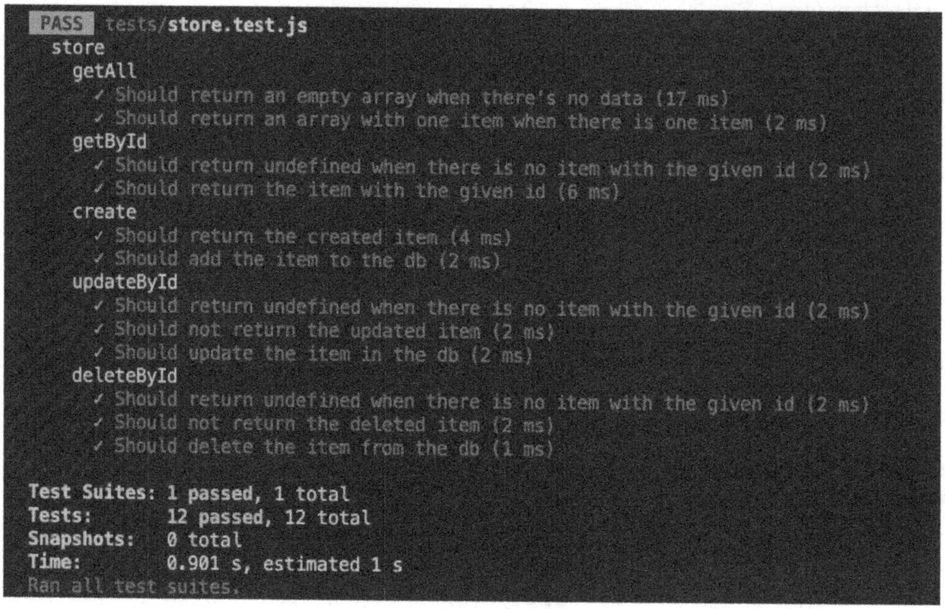

Figure 11.3 – Terminal screenshot

Adding server tests

Now, let's add the tests for the routes. In this case, we will use supertest (https://www.npmjs.com/package/supertest) to test the routes. As the first step, let's install the new dependency:

```
npm i -D supertest@6
```

Defining the tests

You can use `it.todo` to mark the tests that you need to add. This way, you can focus on the description of the tests and not on the implementation details. So, let's create the `tests/server.test.js` file with the following content:

```
import supertest from 'supertest'
import { app } from '../server'
import { restoreDb, populateDb } from './utils.js'
import { whispers, inventedId, existingId } from './fixtures.js'
import { getById } from '../store'

describe('Server', () => {
    beforeEach(() => populateDb(whispers))
    afterAll(restoreDb)
```

```
describe("GET /api/v1/whisper", () => {
    it.todo("Should return an empty array when there's no data")
    it.todo("Should return all the whispers")
})
describe("GET /api/v1/whisper/:id", () => {
    it.todo("Should return a 404 when the whisper doesn't exist")
    it.todo("Should return a whisper details")
})
describe("POST /api/v1/whisper", () => {
    it.todo("Should return a 400 when the body is empty")
    it.todo("Should return a 400 when the body is invalid")
    it.todo("Should return a 201 when the whisper is created")
})
describe("PUT /api/v1/whisper/:id", () => {
    it.todo("Should return a 400 when the body is empty")
    it.todo("Should return a 400 when the body is invalid")
    it.todo("Should return a 404 when the whisper doesn't exist")
    it.todo("Should return a 200 when the whisper is updated")

})
describe("DELETE /api/v1/whisper/:id", () => {
    it.todo("Should return a 404 when the whisper doesn't exist")
    it.todo("Should return a 200 when the whisper is deleted")
})
})
```

Run the tests with the npm run test command:

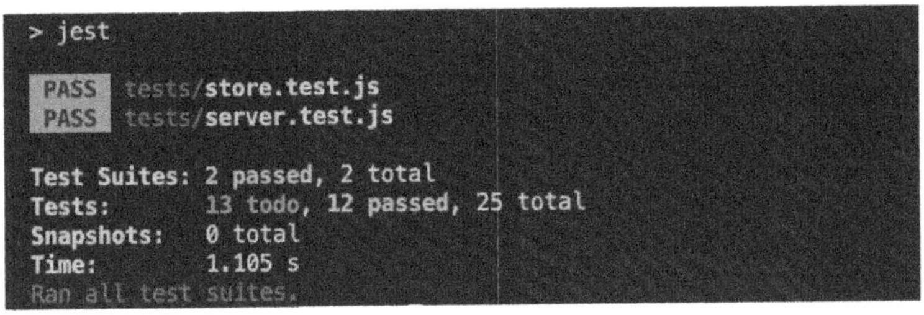

```
> jest

PASS  tests/store.test.js
PASS  tests/server.test.js

Test Suites: 2 passed, 2 total
Tests:       13 todo, 12 passed, 25 total
Snapshots:   0 total
Time:        1.105 s
Ran all test suites.
```

Figure 11.4 – Terminal screenshot

You will see that the previous tests pass, and the new tests are marked as *todo*. This is a good practice to keep track of the tests that you need to add, and it does not break the test suite.

Adding the tests with supertest

Basically, we will use supertest to make requests to the server and we will validate the response. Let's start with the GET /api/v1/whisper route. Let's replace the it.todo tests with the following code:

```
describe("GET /api/v1/whisper", () => {
    it("Should return an empty array when there's no data", async ()
=> {
        await restoreDb() // empty the db
        const response = await supertest(app).get("/api/v1/whisper")
        expect(response.status).toBe(200)
        expect(response.body).toEqual([])
    })
    it("Should return all the whispers", async () => {
        const response = await supertest(app).get("/api/v1/whisper")
        expect(response.status).toBe(200)
        expect(response.body).toEqual(whispers)
    })
})
```

In each request, we check that the status code and the response payload are correct. Now, let's add the tests for the GET /api/v1/whisper/:id route:

```
describe("GET /api/v1/whisper/:id", () => {
    it("Should return a 404 when the whisper doesn't exist", async ()
=> {
        const response = await supertest(app).get(`/api/v1/
whisper/${inventedId}`)
        expect(response.status).toBe(404)
    })
    it("Should return a whisper details", async () => {
        const response = await supertest(app).get(`/api/v1/
whisper/${existingId}`)
        expect(response.status).toBe(200)
        expect(response.body).toEqual(whispers.find(w => w.id ===
existingId))
    })
})
```

As you can see, the tests are very similar to the ones we did for storage.test.js. Now, let's add the tests for the POST /api/v1/whisper route.

We will start by adding the parent description for the route:

```
describe("POST /api/v1/whisper", () => {
    // it("....")
})
```

All the tests will be added inside the `describe` function. So, let's define all the scenarios that we want to cover in the tests:

We want to be sure that we return a 400 status code when the request does not include a body:

```
it("Should return a 400 when the body is empty",
async () => {
  const response = await supertest(app)
    .post("/api/v1/whisper")
    .send({})
  expect(response.status).toBe(400)
})
```

We want to be sure that we return a 400 status code when the request does not include a proper body, for example, when some required properties are missing:

```
it("Should return a 400 when the body is invalid",
async () => {
  const response = await supertest(app)
    .post("/api/v1/whisper")
    .send({invented: "This is a new whisper"})
  expect(response.status).toBe(400)
})
```

We want to be sure that we return a 201 status and the details of the new whisper when the payload in the request is correct. Also, we want to check that the whisper was properly stored in the database:

```
it("Should return a 201 when the whisper is created",
async () => {
  const newWhisper = {
id: whispers.length + 1,
message: "This is a new whisper"
  }
  const response = await supertest(app)
    .post("/api/v1/whisper")
    .send({message: newWhisper.message})
  // HTTP Response
  expect(response.status).toBe(201)
  expect(response.body).toEqual(newWhisper)
  // Database changes
  const storedWhisper = await getById(newWhisper.id)
  expect(storedWhisper).toStrictEqual(newWhisper)
})
```

As you can see, when we created a new whisper we also validated that the whisper was added to the database. This is because these tests are integration tests and we want to make sure that the changes are recorded in the *database* as well.

Now, let's add the tests for the `PUT /api/v1/whisper/:id` route. We will start by adding the parent description for the route:

```
describe("PUT /api/v1/whisper/:id", () => {
    // it("....")
})
```

All the tests will be added inside the `describe` function. So, let's define all the scenarios that we want to cover in the tests:

We want to be sure that we return a 400 status code when the request does not include a body:

```
it("Should return a 400 when the body is empty",
async () => {
  const response = await supertest(app)
    .put(`/api/v1/whisper/${existingId}`)
    .send({})
  expect(response.status).toBe(400)
})
```

We want to be sure that we return a 400 status code when the request does not include a proper body, for example, when some required properties are missing:

```
it("Should return a 400 when the body is invalid",
async () => {
  const response = await supertest(app)
    .put(`/api/v1/whisper/${existingId}`)
    .send({invented: "This a new field"})
  expect(response.status).toBe(400)
})
```

We want to be sure that we return a 404 status code when the request is targeting a non-existent whisper:

```
it("Should return a 404 when the whisper doesn't exist",
async () => {
  const response = await supertest(app)
    .put(`/api/v1/whisper/${inventedId}`)
    .send({message: "Whisper updated"})
  expect(response.status).toBe(404)
})
```

We want to be sure that we return a 200 status when the payload and the target are correct. Also, we want to check that the whisper was properly updated in the database:

```
it("Should return a 200 when the whisper is updated",
async () => {
  const response = await supertest(app)
    .put(`/api/v1/whisper/${existingId}`)
    .send({message: "Whisper updated"})
  expect(response.status).toBe(200)
  // Database changes
  const storedWhisper = await getById(existingId)
  expect(storedWhisper).toStrictEqual({id: existingId, message:
"Whisper updated"})
})
```

Finally, let's add the tests for the DELETE /api/v1/whisper/:id route. We will start by adding the parent description for the route:

```
describe(" DELETE /api/v1/whisper/:id", () => {
    // it("....")
})
```

All the tests will be added inside the describe function. So, let's define all the scenarios that we want to cover in the tests:

We want to be sure that we return a 404 status code when the request is targeting a non-existent whisper:

```
it("Should return a 404 when the whisper doesn't exist", async () => {
  const response = await supertest(app)
    .delete(`/api/v1/whisper/${inventedId}`)
  expect(response.status).toBe(404)
})
```

We want to be sure that we return a 200 status code when the request is targeting a valid whisper. Also, we want to check that the whisper was properly removed from the database:

```
it("Should return a 200 when the whisper is deleted", async () => {
  const response = await supertest(app)
    .delete(`/api/v1/whisper/${existingId}`)
  expect(response.status).toBe(200)
  // Database changes
  const storedWhisper = await getById(existingId)
  expect(storedWhisper).toBeUndefined()
})
```

Now, you can run the tests with `npm run test` and you will see that the tests are passing:

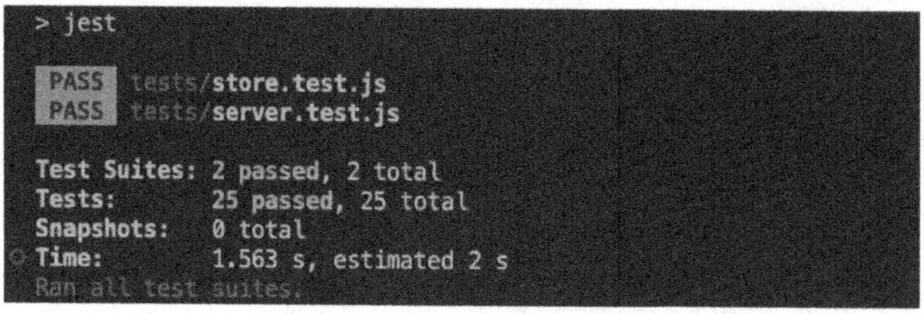

```
> jest

PASS  tests/store.test.js
PASS  tests/server.test.js

Test Suites: 2 passed, 2 total
Tests:       25 passed, 25 total
Snapshots:   0 total
Time:        1.563 s, estimated 2 s
Ran all test suites.
```

Figure 11.5 – Terminal screenshot

> **Information**
>
> If you are having issues running the project in this chapter while following the steps, or you tried an alternative approach, you can use the `step2` folder from the source code that you downloaded at the beginning of the chapter to compare and fix possible bugs more easily.

In the next section, we will review the final result and we will see how to use the application and what we are planning to do in the next chapters.

Reviewing the final result of the project

At this point, you should have a fully functional REST API with Express and if your tests are passing, you can start using the application.

The about page

If you go to `http://localhost:3000/about`, you will see the about page:

Welcome to Whispering!

Photo by Brooke Cagle from Unsplash

What is Whispering?

Whispering is a microblogging platform that allows you to share your thoughts with the world and learn Node.js on the way.

Community live

Currently there are 3 whispers available

Figure 11.6 – Web browser screenshot

This page was served using the server render approach, and we are using the EJS template engine to render the page. We are using the whispers data from the database to render the page. The text *Currently there are 3 whispers available* is dynamic text that will change depending on the number of whispers in the database.

You can see the reference in the `views/about.ejs` file:

```
<p>Currently there are <%= whispers.length %> whispers available</p>
```

Web interface

The web interface is a simple page where you can create, update, and delete whispers. You can access the web interface at `http://localhost:3000`. It will start with an empty list of whispers. In my case, I have three whispers in the database, so I will see the following page:

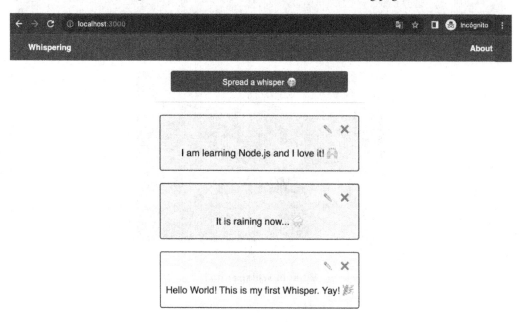

Figure 11.7 – Web browser screenshot

In order to make the frontend source code more readable, I used plain JavaScript to make the requests to the API and old browser APIs such as `prompts` and `confirms` to interact with the user. You can see the source code in the `public/app.js` file. For a production application, you should avoid these browser APIs as they are quite limited and implement a solution that works on all devices using UI elements that are properly integrated. Also, you will need to handle errors and loading states. For larger projects, it is quite common to use UI libraries such as tailwind (`https://tailwindcss.com/`) or frameworks such as Vue (`https://vuejs.org/`).

Adding whispers

It is possible to add whispers to the list. Just click on the **Spread a whisper** button and you will see a prompt asking for the message of the whisper:

Figure 11.8 – Web browser screenshot

Editing whispers

It is possible to edit whispers. Just click on the pencil button and you will see a prompt asking for the new message of the whisper:

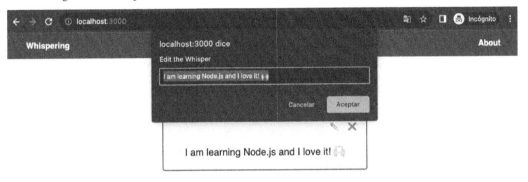

Figure 11.9 – Web browser screenshot

Deleting whispers

It is possible to delete whispers. Just click on the trash button and you will see a confirm dialog asking for the confirmation:

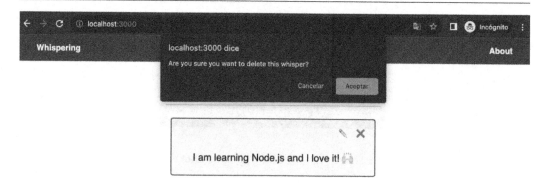

Figure 11.10 – Web browser screenshot

Your challenge

If you are familiar with frontend development, you can try to improve the web interface and make it more user-friendly or directly replace it with a modern frontend framework such as React, Vue, or Angular. If you are not familiar with front-end development, you can skip this challenge and continue with the next chapter.

Let's celebrate it!

Feel free to explore the code and play with it, you can start the application with npm run start and you can go to http://localhost:3000 and create a few whispers that you can later edit or remove from the web interface.

Next steps

Congratulations! You have created a solid REST API, but there are a lot of things that you can do to improve it. In the next chapter, we will see how to properly store the information in the database.

In *Chapter 13*, we will see how to add authentication to the API, so only authenticated users can create, update, or delete whispers and multiple users will be able to use our application.

Summary

In this chapter, we learned how to use supertest to test our API in depth. We learned how to test the routes and how to test the stores. We created a solid API that we will evolve in the next chapters.

In the next chapter, we will see how to properly store the information in the database, using MongoDB. We will take the opportunity to refactor our project and use a better software pattern to organize the code and a MongoDB database to store the data.

12

Data Persistence with MongoDB

In this chapter, we will explain how MongoDB works and why it is a great starting point for a web application. We will learn how to install MongoDB locally using containers with Docker and Docker Compose and also how to use external MongoDB instances.

We will explore how to use Mongoose to interact with MongoDB, and we will migrate our application to use MongoDB instead of a JSON file, we will use tests to grant that the migration was properly done and we didn't introduce any regression.

In summary, here are the main topics that we will explore in this chapter:

- How to set up MongoDB locally using containers with Docker and Docker Compose
- How to use an **Object–relational mapping** (**ORM**) library such as Mongoose to interact with MongoDB
- How to migrate our application to use MongoDB instead of a JSON file
- How to test any application using MongoDB
- How to use environment variables to store sensitive information and how to load them in Node.js

By the end of this chapter, you will be comfortable using MongoDB in your Node.js projects, and you will know how to use tests to plan more complicated features such as a database migration.

Technical requirements

The code files for the chapter can be found at `https://github.com/PacktPublishing/NodeJS-for-Beginners`.

Check out the code in action video for this chapter on `https://youtu.be/0CHOQ35c-_Y`

To start working on this chapter, we need to download the project from `https://github.com/PacktPublishing/NodeJS-for-Beginners/archive/refs/heads/main.zip` and access the `step2` folder.

What is MongoDB?

If you are familiar with relational databases, you will find MongoDB very different. MongoDB is a document-oriented database, which means that it stores data in documents instead of tables. A document is a set of key-value pairs, and it is the basic unit of data in MongoDB. Documents are similar to JSON objects, and they are stored in a collection. A collection is a group of documents that have the same structure. In MongoDB, documents are stored in **Binary JSON (BSON)**, a binary representation of JSON documents.

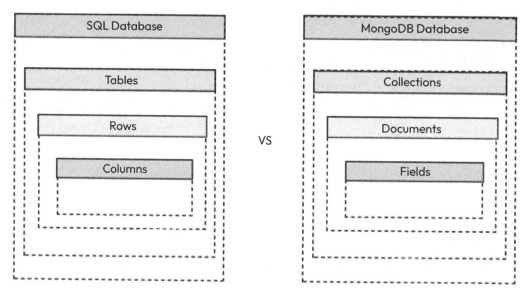

Figure 12.1 – A SQL data structure compared to a MongoDB data structure

In the preceding diagram, we can see the difference between a relational database and a document-oriented database more clearly.

Versions

There are several versions of MongoDB, but the most popular is MongoDB Community Server. In our project, we will also use MongoDB Community Server as well, at no extra cost to us.

In *Chapter 16*, we will explore more versions of MongoDB when we deploy our application to the cloud.

If you want to know more about the different versions of MongoDB, you can check out the following link: `https://www.mongodb.com/try/download/community`

In the next section, we will explain how to install MongoDB locally using containers with Docker and Docker Compose, as well as how to use external MongoDB instances.

Setting up MongoDB

There are several ways to install MongoDB, but we will use Docker Compose to install it locally. Docker Compose is a tool for defining and running multi-container Docker applications. With Docker Compose, we will be able to run MongoDB and our web application in different containers. If you are not familiar with Docker, there is a fantastic guide from MongoDB (`https://www.mongodb.com/compatibility/docker`) that can help you get a deeper understanding.

Installing Docker

If you don't have Docker installed, you can follow the instructions at `https://docs.docker.com/get-docker/`, depending on your operating system.

Checking the installation

Let's check that Docker is installed correctly. Open a terminal and run the following command:

```
docker --version
```

You should see the version installed – in my case, 24.0.2:

```
Docker version 24.0.2, build cb74dfc
```

We can also check that Docker Compose is installed correctly. Open a terminal and run the following command:

```
docker-compose --version
```

You should see something like this:

```
Docker Compose version v2.19.1
```

Running MongoDB with a container

The beauty of Docker is that we can run MongoDB in a container. A container is a standard unit of software that packages up code and all its dependencies. That way, we can create a MongoDB container and run it on our local machine, and we don't have to install MongoDB locally. When we don't need the container anymore, we can stop it and remove it.

In our case, we will use Mongo 7.0.0, which is the latest version of MongoDB. We will use the official image of MongoDB, which is available on Docker Hub. You can find more information about this image at the following link: `https://hub.docker.com/_/mongo`.

To run MongoDB in a container, we will use the following command:

```
docker run --name whispering-database -p 27017:27017 -d mongo:7.0.0
```

This command will create a container with the name `whispering-database`, and it will map port `27017` of the container to port `27017` of the host machine. The `-d` flag means that the container will run in the background.

The output should be something like this:

```
Unable to find image 'mongo:7.0.0' locally
7.0.0: Pulling from library/mongo
99de9192b4af: Pull complete
18b9e63943e7: Pull complete
ccf1fde52048: Pull complete
8317989437cb: Pull complete
1bde6bf8acc1: Pull complete
11fb005be9eb: Pull complete
81a254c162fc: Pull complete
2a574922bf90: Pull complete
22659e13b0a2: Pull complete
Digest: sha256:a89d79ddc5187f57b1270f87ec581b7cc6fd697efa12b8
f1af72f3c4888d72b5
Status: Downloaded newer image for mongo:7.0.0
27ead2313a72c0cb0d2d1bf18ef2a37062a63851ebc9355359dbc1a4741ac168
```

As shown in the output, the image was not found locally, so it was downloaded from Docker Hub. You might get an error, if the port 2701 is already in use, as the container can't take control over. You can easily check this by following these steps (`https://kb.vmware.com/s/article/1003971`). If everything goes well, the container is running in the background, so we can check that it is running with the following command:

```
docker ps
```

The output should be something like this:

```
CONTAINER ID    IMAGE         COMMAND                 CREATED
STATUS          PORTS                    NAMES
7d28f8c555b9    mongo:7.0.0   "docker-entrypoint.s…"  7 seconds ago
Up 6 seconds    0.0.0.0:27017->27017/tcp    whispering-database
```

You can stop the container with the following command:

```
docker stop whispering-database
```

And you can remove the container with the following command:

```
docker rm whispering-database
```

If you removed the container, you can always create a new container again with the following command:

```
docker run --name whispering-database -p 27017:27017 -d mongo:7.0.0
```

Running MongoDB with Docker Compose

An alternative to running MongoDB with a container is to use Docker Compose. Docker Compose is a tool to define and run multi-container Docker applications using a YAML file. One of the advantages of using Docker Compose is that we can define the configuration of the container in a YAML file, so we don't have to remember the commands to run the container.

Let's create a `docker-compose.yml` file with the following content for our project:

```
version: '3.8'
services:
  database:
    container_name: whispering-database
    image: mongo:7.0
    ports:
      - '27017:27017'
    volumes:
      - db-storage:/data/db
volumes:
  db-storage:
```

In this file, we define a service called `database` that uses the `mongo:7.0` image. We also map port `27017` of the container to port `27017` of the host machine. Finally, we define a volume called `db-storage` that will be used to store the data of the database, so we don't lose it when we stop the container.

In order to run the container in the background, we have to run the following command:

```
docker-compose up -d
```

The output should be something like this:

```
[+] Running 1/1
✓ database Pulled                          1.8s
```

```
[+] Running 3/3
✓ Network app_default        Created      0.1s
✓ Volume "app_db-storage"    Created      0.0s
✓ Container app-database-1    Started      0.5s
```

Your containers are now ready to use, but you can stop them by running the following command in the same folder:

```
docker-compose down
```

In the next section, we will learn how to include the Docker-related commands to the `package.json` as npm scripts.

Adding Docker commands to package.json

Sometimes, it is hard to remember the docker compose commands, so we can add them to the `package.json` file. Add the following scripts:

```
"scripts": {
    "start": "node index.js",
    "test": "jest",
    "test:coverage": "jest --coverage",
    "lint": "standard",
    "lint:fix": "standard --fix",
    "infra:start": "docker-compose up -d --build",
    "infra:stop": "docker-compose down --remove-orphans"
}
```

Then, we can use `npm run infra:start` and `npm run infra:stop` to manage the project database on our local machine.

Connecting to MongoDB

There are two ways to connect to MongoDB – using the `mongo` shell or port `27017`. In this section, we will explain how to connect to MongoDB using both ways.

We can connect to MongoDB using the `mongo` shell with the following command if we use Docker:

```
npm run infra:start
docker exec -it whispering-database /bin/bash
```

You can see now that we are inside the container, as an alternative you can use directly the docker compose command to access the container `docker-compose exec database /bin/bash`. Now, we can connect to MongoDB with the following command:

```
mongod
```

You should see something like this:

```
root@7d515e1c8f85:/# mongod
{"t":{"$date":"2023-08-19T13:45:08.554+00:00"},"s":"I",  "c":"CONTROL",
  "id":23285,    "ctx":"main","msg":"Automatically disabling TLS 1.0,
to force-enable TLS 1.0 specify --sslDisabledProtocols 'none'"}
{"t":{"$date":"2023-08-19T13:45:08.556+00:00"},"s":"I",  "c":"NETWORK",
  "id":4915701, "ctx":"main","msg":"Initialized wire specification",
"attr":{"spec":{"incomingExternalClient":{"minWire
Version":0,"maxWireVersion":21},"incomingInternalClient":{"minWire
Version":0,"maxWireVersion":21},"outgoing":{"minWireVersion":6,"maxWire
Version":21},"isInternalClient":true}}}
```

This way, we can access a mongo shell directly if needed. In the following sections, we will explain how to connect to MongoDB using port 27017.

Other ways to install MongoDB

If you don't want to use Docker Compose, you can install MongoDB locally. You can find the instructions for your operating system at the following link: `https://docs.mongodb.com/manual/administration/install-community/`.

Remember that you can also use MongoDB Atlas (`https://www.mongodb.com/atlas`) or any other cloud provider that offers MongoDB as a service.

Now that we have MongoDB running, we can start using it, but first, we need to understand how to use secrets in Node.js so that we can pass the connection string to the application in a safe mode. So, in the next section, we will explain how to load secrets in Node.js.

How to load secrets in Node.js

Our application will need to connect to MongoDB, so we need to store the connection string in a safe place. You should never store secrets in your code; a very common practice is to store them in environment variables. In this section, we will explain how to load secrets from environment variables in Node.js.

Environment variables

Environment variables are variables that are set in the environment in which the process runs. They are usually set in the operating system, but we can also set them in the terminal. We can access the environment variables in Node.js using the `process.env` object:

```
console.log(process.env.MY_SECRET)
```

You can set an environment variable in the terminal with the following command:

```
export MY_SECRET=secret
```

Then, you can run your application with the following command:

```
node index.js
```

Alternatively, you can set the environment variable in the same command:

```
MY_SECRET=secret node index.js
```

> **Important note**
>
> If you are using Windows you might need to use a different approach to handle environmental variables in the terminal. Read (`https://www3.ntu.edu.sg/home/ehchua/programming/howto/Environment_Variables.html`) for additional information.

In the next section, we will learn how to use a `.env` file to manage the secrets in a more ergonomic way.

The .env file

While using environmental variables directly in the terminal is a very common practice, it is not very convenient. We can use a file called `.env` to store our environment variables. We can create a `.env` file with the following content:

```
MY_SECRET=secret
```

Then, we can use the `dotenv` package (`https://www.npmjs.com/package/dotenv`) to load the environment variables from the `.env` file, but it's worth mentioning that Node.js 20.6.0 introduced support for loading environment variables from a `.env` file, so we don't need to use third-party packages anymore (`https://github.com/nodejs/node/releases/tag/v20.6.0`).

> **Warning**
>
> We should never commit the `.env` file to the repository because it contains secrets. You can include the `.env` file into the `.gitignore` file to avoid commit the .env file along the project source code.

dotenv

The most common way to load environment variables from a `.env` file is to use the `dotenv` package (https://www.npmjs.com/package/dotenv). We can install it with the following command:

```
npm install dotenv@16
```

Then, we can load the environment variables from the `.env` file with the following code:

```
import 'dotenv/config'
```

Alternatively, we can do it directly using the `--require` flag:

```
node --require dotenv/config index.js
```

In the next section, we will explain how to use **Object-Relational Mapping** (**ORM**) to interact with MongoDB and how this can make our life easier when building a web application for the first time.

Using an ORM – Mongoose

We can use MongoDB directly, but it will require a bigger understanding and more code to interact with the database. As the objective of this book is to learn Node.js, we will use an ORM to interact with MongoDB. An ORM is a library that allows us to interact with a database using objects instead of SQL queries. In this section, we will use Mongoose (https://mongoosejs.com/). Alternatively, you can use MongoDB Node.js Driver, which is the official MongoDB driver (https://docs.mongodb.com/drivers/node/) for Node.js. The official documentation can be found at https://mongoosejs.com/docs/guide.html.

Mongoose offers several features that are quite convenient for a web application:

- **Schema validation**: We can define the schema of the documents, and Mongoose will validate the data before saving it to the database

- **Model**: We can define a model for each collection, and we can use it to interact with the database

- **Middleware**: We can define middleware functions that will be executed before or after certain events – for example, we can define a middleware function that will be executed before saving a document to the database

- **Plugins**: We can use plugins to extend the functionality of Mongoose

Also, if you are new to Node.js or MongoDB, you will find Mongoose easier to use than MongoDB directly, and there are plenty of tutorials and resources that you can use to get used to it quickly.

> **Info**
>
> Mongo has a huge ecosystem, and it might be a bit overwhelming at the beginning, but you can find a curated list of awesome MongoDB resources at `https://github.com/ramnes/awesome-mongodb`.

Now that we have MongoDB running and are familiar with the environment variables, we can start using Mongoose in our project. In the next section, we will explain how to migrate from local file storage to MongoDB.

Migrating a web application to MongoDB

We already added MongoDB to our project using Docker Compose and npm commands, but we have not started using it yet. In this section, we will migrate a web application to MongoDB.

Installing dependencies

We will install the following dependencies:

```
npm install mongoose@7.4 dotenv@16
```

Managing the secrets

We will create a `.env` file with the following content:

```
MONGODB_URI=mongodb://localhost:27017/whispering-database
PORT=3000
```

Then, we will load the environment variables from the `.env` file with the following code into `index.js`:

```
import { app } from './server.js'
import mongoose from 'mongoose'

const port = process.env.PORT

try {
  await mongoose.connect(process.env.MONGODB_URI);
  console.log('Connected to MongoDB')
  app.listen(port, () => {
    console.log(`Running in http://localhost:${port}`)
  })
} catch (error) {
  console.error(error)
}
```

We have included the `mongoose` package and have connected to MongoDB using the `MONGODB_URI` environment variable. We have also included the `PORT` environment variable to run the application in a different port.

> **Note**
>
> As you can see, the database must be running before we open the HTTP server connection. This is because we need to connect to the database to retrieve the information for our response to the HTTP requests.

Now, we need to update the npm scripts to use `dotenv`:

```
"scripts": {
    "start": "node --require dotenv/config index.js",
    "test": "jest --setupFiles dotenv/config",
    "test:coverage": "jest --coverage --setupFiles dotenv/config",
    "lint": "standard",
    "lint:fix": "standard --fix",
    "infra:start": "docker-compose up -d --build",
    "infra:stop": "docker-compose down"
}
```

Now, we can run the application with the following command:

```
npm run infra:start
npm run start
```

We should see the following output:

```
Connected to MongoDB
Running in http://localhost:3000
```

If the database is not running, we will see a similar error:

```
MongooseServerSelectionError: connect ECONNREFUSED ::1:27017, connect
ECONNREFUSED 127.0.0.1:27017
    at _handleConnectionErrors (node_modules/mongoose/lib/connection.
js:788:11)
    at NativeConnection.openUri (node_modules/mongoose/lib/connection.
js:763:11)
    at async file:///index.js:7:4 {
  reason: TopologyDescription {
    type: 'Unknown',
    servers: Map(1) { 'localhost:27017' => [ServerDescription] },
    stale: false,
```

```
      compatible: true,
      heartbeatFrequencyMS: 10000,
      localThresholdMS: 15,
      setName: null,
      maxElectionId: null,
      maxSetVersion: null,
      commonWireVersion: 0,
      logicalSessionTimeoutMinutes: null
    },
   code: undefined
}
```

Basically, it tells us that it cannot connect to the database; you can generate the same errors just by running the following:

```
npm run infra:stop
npm run start
```

In the next section we will start to work on the data layer migration.

Migrating the data layer

We want to refactor the store.js file to use MongoDB instead of a JSON file. Just to keep things simple, we will add the schema and model to the same file, but this can be changed later when we introduce authentication in the next chapter.

It is considered good practice to encapsulate the database-related code in specific files, with the idea of providing an interface that can later be used by other parts of our code to make changes in the data layer, without the need to understand how the data layer is implemented under the hood. This kind of abstraction is a very popular solution and will bring you a lot of support if you decide to migrate or combine other storage systems in the future. So, we will create a new file called database.js and explore together in the following paragraphs how it is structured and what is achieved in each statement. The file content is the following:

```
import mongoose from 'mongoose'
mongoose.set('toJSON', {
  virtuals: true,
  transform: (doc, converted) => {
    delete converted._id
    delete converted.__v
  }
})

const whisperSchema = new mongoose.Schema({
```

```
    message: String
})

const Whisper = mongoose.model('Whisper', whisperSchema)

export {
  Whisper
}
```

Creating the schema

The first step is to create the schema, which is the definition of the structure of the documents that we are going to store in the database. In our case, we only have one field called `message`, which is a string:

```
const whisperSchema = new mongoose.Schema({
  message: String
})
```

Creating the model

The second step is to create the model, which is a class that we use to interact with the database. In our case, we will use the `Whisper` model to interact with the `whispers` collection:

```
const Whisper = mongoose.model('Whisper', whisperSchema)
```

Transformers

One of the things that we have to do is to remove the `_id` and `__v` fields from the response. We can change this behavior globally so that we don't have to do it for every method, using the `toJSON` method:

```
mongoose.set('toJSON', {
  virtuals: true,
  transform: (doc, converted) => {
    delete converted._id;
    delete converted.__v;
  }
});
```

This means we start with the following data structure:

```
{
  "_id": "5dff03d3218b91425b9d6fab",
  "message": "I love MongoDB!",
  "__v": 0
}
```

Then, we move on to the following data structure:

```
{
  "id": "5dff03d3218b91425b9d6fab",
  "message": "I love MongoDB!"
}
```

Refactored methods

The key in this migration is to keep the same interface so that we don't have to change the behavior of the functions that we export. We will use the same data I/O, but we will use Mongoose to interact with MongoDB:

```
import {
  Whisper
} from './database.js'

const getAll = () => Whisper.find()
const getById = id => Whisper.findById({ _id: id })
const create = async (message) => {
  const whisper = new Whisper({ message })
  await whisper.save()
  return whisper
}
const updateById = async (id, message) => Whisper.findOneAndUpdate({
_id: id }, { message }, { new: false })
const deleteById = async (id) => Whisper.deleteOne({ _id: id })

export { getAll, getById, create, updateById, deleteById }
```

As you can see, we keep the same input and output in every method (getAll, getById, create, updateById, deleteById), so we don't have to change the behavior of the functions that we export.

This is the effect that we discussed in the previous chapter; we can change the implementation of the methods, but we don't have to change the interface. This is the power of abstraction.

So, even if you want to change the database in the future, you don't have to change the interface of the methods; you just have to change the implementation and the code still works. This is because the business logic is not coupled to the database interface.

Removing the old database file

Now, we can remove the db.json file because we are not using it anymore.

Improve the routes

In the previous chapter, we used numerical IDs, just to keep the code more simple, so now, we need to change the routes to use the MongoDB IDs, which are alphanumerical strings. We only need to remove the references to `parseInt` in the `server.js` file. The change is from `parseInt(req.params.id)` to `req.params.id`. You can even use *Find and Replace* to change all the references to `parseInt` in the file.

Running the application

At this point, you can just enjoy the migration by running the following:

```
npm run infra:start
npm run start
```

And if you go to `http://localhost:3000`, you can see the application working with MongoDB without any change in the interface.

Now, we are certain that the application is working as expected, but we shouldn't forget to properly test these changes. So, in the next section, we will refactor the tests to use MongoDB, and we will be able to move to the next chapter once all the tests are passing (green) as the refactor will be completed.

Testing our MongoDB integration layer

Yes, we have made the migration and everything seems to be running fine, but we need to ensure that the tests work as expected. Currently, the tests use the filesystem to store data, so we need to change the tests to make them use MongoDB.

Update the utilities

We will edit the `test/utils.js` file to use MongoDB instead of the filesystem. As we are now using MongoDB, we need to load the fixtures in the database to know the IDs. So now, the fixtures will keep the same structure, but they will be stored and collected in the database using `populateDb` and the new `getFixtures` function:

```
import mongoose from 'mongoose'
import {
  Whisper
} from '../database.js'

const ensureDbConnection = async () => {
    try {
        if (mongoose.connection.readyState !== 1) {
            await mongoose.connect(process.env.MONGODB_URI);
        }
```

```
    } catch (error) {
        console.error('Error connecting to the database:', error);
        throw error; // Re-throw the error for handling at a higher
    level
    }
}
const closeDbConnection = async () => {
    if (mongoose.connection.readyState === 1) {
        await mongoose.disconnect()
    }
}
const restoreDb = () => Whisper.deleteMany({})
const populateDb = () => Whisper.insertMany([{ message: 'test' }, {
message: 'hello world' }])
const getFixtures = async () => {
    const data = await Whisper.find()
    const whispers = JSON.parse(JSON.stringify(data))
    const inventedId = '64e0e5c75a4a3c715b7c1074'
    const existingId = data[0].id
    return { inventedId, existingId, whispers }
}
const normalize = (data) => JSON.parse(JSON.stringify(data))

export { restoreDb, populateDb, getFixtures, ensureDbConnection,
normalize, closeDbConnection }
```

Now, we can delete the `test/fixtures.js` file because we are not using it anymore.

Refactoring the test suite

So far, we have more tests than the ones that we really need. We can remove specific tests for the stores, as they are already covered by the integration tests, and we can remove the `test/store.test.js` file.

As part of the migration, we need to make some changes in how the tests are prepared to be executed. As a database is an external service, we need to control certain aspects before we execute the test. For example, we need a proper database connection working before we execute any test, as this can be a failure cause for the tests but is not related to the code that we are testing. Also, we need to be sure that the database has specific data stored in it so that our tests can be executed independently multiple times, without polluting the execution context between executions with the modifications that we make in the database. This can be achieved by adding certain steps before any specific test is executed, with methods such as `beforeAll`, `beforeEach`, `afterAll`, and `afterEach`, which are part of the Jest methods available to us. Now, let's update the tests to use the new functions. We will update the `test/server.test.js` file to use the new functions:

```
import supertest from 'supertest'
import { app } from '../server'
```

```
import { getById } from '../store.js'
import { restoreDb, populateDb, getFixtures,
ensureDbConnection, normalize, closeDbConnection } from './utils.js'

let whispers
let inventedId
let existingId

describe('Server', () => {
  beforeAll(ensureDbConnection)
  beforeEach(async () => {
    await restoreDb()
    await populateDb(whispers)
    const fixtures = await getFixtures()
    whispers = fixtures.whispers
    inventedId = fixtures.inventedId
    existingId = fixtures.existingId
  })
  afterAll(closeDbConnection)
  //... unchanged tests
})
```

In the next section, we will finish updating the test suite cases, as MongoDB introduced small differences that we need to take into account when querying data in the test context.

Some tests must change

Just to keep it simple, for the scope of the book, some tests have to change. All the tests that are use store will be refactored as follows.

When creating or updating whispers, we will check in the database that the whispers are stored correctly. In order to properly compare the data, we will use the normalize function. That way, we can compare the data without the _id and __v fields and in a normalized way, as we do when converting data to JSON while sending the HTTP response:

```
it('Should return a 201 when the whisper is created', async () => {
    const newWhisper = { message: 'This is a new whisper' }
    const response = await supertest(app)
    .post('/api/v1/whisper')
    .send({ message: newWhisper.message })
    expect(response.status).toBe(201)
    expect(response.body.message).toEqual(newWhisper.message)

    // Database changes
    const storedWhisper = await getById(response.body.id)
```

```
    expect(normalize(storedWhisper).message).toStrictEqual(newWhisper.
message)
})
it('Should return a 200 when the whisper is updated', async () => {
    const response = await supertest(app)
    .put(`/api/v1/whisper/${existingId}`)
    .send({ message: 'Whisper updated' })
    expect(response.status).toBe(200)

    // Database changes
    const storedWhisper = await getById(existingId)
    expect(normalize(storedWhisper)).toStrictEqual({ id: existingId,
message: 'Whisper updated' })
})
```

When deleting a whisper, we need to check that the whisper is not in the database anymore. Previously, we checked that the database returned `undefined` when not found; using MongoDB, we will get `null` instead, so we need to change the test as follows:

```
it('Should return a 200 when the whisper is deleted', async () => {
    const response = await supertest(app).delete(`/api/v1/
whisper/${existingId}`)
    expect(response.status).toBe(200)

    // Database changes
    const storedWhisper = await getById(existingId)
    expect(storedWhisper).toBe(null)
})
```

As we finished to refactor the tests, it is a great moment to review the testing coverage. In this section we will review this in detail.

Checking the coverage

Now, we can run the tests and check the coverage:

```
npm run infra:start
npm run test:coverage
```

The output should be similar:

```
---------------|----------|-----------|----------|----------|--------------
------
File           | % Stmts  | % Branch  | % Funcs  | % Lines  | Uncovered
Line #s
```

```
---------------|---------|----------|---------|---------|-------------
------
All files      |  97.43  |  85.71   |  94.44  |  97.18  |
app            |  96.66  |   100    |  91.66  |  96.42  |
  database.js  |   100   |   100    |   100   |   100   |
  server.js    |  95.34  |   100    |  83.33  |  95.34  | 11-12
  store.js     |   100   |   100    |   100   |   100   |
app/tests      |   100   |    50    |   100   |   100   |
  utils.js     |   100   |    50    |   100   |   100   | 7-12
---------------|---------|----------|---------|---------|-------------
------

Test Suites: 1 passed, 1 total
Tests:       13 passed, 13 total
Snapshots:   0 total
Time:        1.945 s, estimated 2 s
Ran all test suites.
```

Basically, we have the same coverage as before, but we have removed some tests, and the store.js file is covered up to 100%.

As we can see, there is a line that is not covered (*11–12*), in server.js. In the previous chapter, we added a new route to render the template in GET /about, but we forgot to add proper tests. So, let's add the following test:

```
describe('/about', () => {
    it('Should return a 200 with the total whispers in the platform',
async () => {
        const response = await supertest(app).get('/about')
        expect(response.status).toBe(200)
        expect(response.text).toContain(`Currently there are
${whispers.length} whispers available`)
    })
})
```

If you run the tests again, you will see that the line is covered now and the coverage has increased to 100%. We can also improve the scoring by removing from the coverage report the tests folder, which we can do by adding the following line to the jest.config.js file:

```
export default {
  modulePathIgnorePatterns: ['<rootDir>/node_test/'],
  "coveragePathIgnorePatterns": [
    "<rootDir>/tests/"
  ]
}
```

It is very important to keep a clear scope on what files you need to track or not for your coverage report; otherwise, the code coverage will become just a metric that won't guide you to focus on the most critical application parts. It is quite common to read articles about the frustration associated with a 100% coverage target, when, in most cases, we don't need to aim for that big number, and we should be clear on what parts of the code don't need to be tested.

No matter whether you work alone or in a team, having precise metrics will increase the developer experience for all the humans involved in a project. As you can see, the coverage is now 100%, as we ignored the files that we are not planning to test:

```
PASS   tests/server.test.js
  Server
    GET /about
      ✓ Should return a 200 with the total whispers in the platform
(61 ms)
    GET /api/v1/whisper
      ✓ Should return an empty array when there's no data (19 ms)
      ✓ Should return all the whispers (14 ms)
    GET /api/v1/whisper/:id
      ✓ Should return a 404 when the whisper doesn't exist (14 ms)
      ✓ Should return a whisper details (12 ms)
    POST /api/v1/whisper
      ✓ Should return a 400 when the body is empty (27 ms)
      ✓ Should return a 400 when the body is invalid (9 ms)
      ✓ Should return a 201 when the whisper is created (17 ms)
    PUT /api/v1/whisper/:id
      ✓ Should return a 400 when the body is empty (9 ms)
      ✓ Should return a 400 when the body is invalid (9 ms)
      ✓ Should return a 404 when the whisper doesn't exist (11 ms)
      ✓ Should return a 200 when the whisper is updated (18 ms)
    DELETE /api/v1/whisper/:id
      ✓ Should return a 404 when the whisper doesn't exist (10 ms)
      ✓ Should return a 200 when the whisper is deleted (13 ms)
```

File #s	% Stmts	% Branch	% Funcs	% Lines	Uncovered Line
All files	100	100	100	100	
database.js	100	100	100	100	
server.js	100	100	100	100	
store.js	100	100	100	100	

```
--------------|----------|-----------|----------|----------|--------------
-----
Test Suites: 1 passed, 1 total
Tests:       14 passed, 14 total
Snapshots:   0 total
Time:        2.024 s, estimated 3 s
Ran all test suites.
```

> **Information**
>
> If you are having issues running the project in this chapter while following the steps, or you tried an alternative approach, you can use the `step3` folder from the source code that you downloaded at the beginning of the chapter to compare and fix possible bugs more easily.

Now, that we have finished with the migration, it is time to do a recap in the next section.

Summary

In this chapter, we learned how MongoDB is different from other databases. We learned how to install MongoDB locally using containers, with Docker and Docker Compose.

Additionally, we explored how we can manage sensitive information in our application using environment variables and the `dotenv` package. We also learned how to use Mongoose to interact with MongoDB.

Finally, we migrated our application to use MongoDB instead of a JSON file. This gave us the opportunity to properly learn how to refactor and reorganize our previous code. This migration also made it easy to maintain and deploy the application, as data is stored and queried as an external source. This will help us to scale a lot in the future, as we can connect multiple replicas of our backend to the same database instance. We also learned how to test our application using MongoDB, and we used this testing approach to ensure that the migration was completed successfully.

In the next chapter, we will introduce authentication and authorization to our application. We will use JWT to authenticate users and use middleware to protect the routes that require authentication. Also, we will refactor code to use a database to store users and use `bcrypt` library to hash the passwords. Finally, multiple users will be able to use our application, which will include private whispers.

Further reading

- Fireship | MongoDB in 100 Seconds: `https://www.youtube.com/watch?v=-bt_y4Loofg`

- I Would Never Use an ORM, by Matteo Collina: `https://www.youtube.com/watch?v=qfRQ5zhYuJE`

- MongoDB in 5 Minutes with Eliot Horowitz: `https://www.youtube.com/watch?v=EE8ZTQxa0AM`

- MongoDB Explained in 10 Minutes | SQL vs NoSQL | Jumpstart: `https://www.youtube.com/watch?v=RGfFpQF0NpE`

13

User Authentication and Authorization with Passport.js

In this chapter, we will learn how authentication and authorization work in a modern web application. We will explore the cryptography behind many security mechanisms and will learn how to implement these concepts in our web applications using **JSON Web Tokens (JWT)**. We will also see how we can extend our authentication strategies with third-party providers such as Facebook or Spotify with Passport.js.

At the end of this chapter, we will implement authentication and authorization in our web application project iterating over the code that we generated in the previous chapter. We will also learn how to specifically test them.

To sum up, here are the main topics that we will explore in this chapter:

- How authentication and authorization work in a web application
- How to use JWT to authenticate users in our web application
- The cryptography basics that we need to know to understand modern authentication and authorization mechanisms
- How Passport.js works and how to use it to implement authentication with third-party providers such as Facebook or Spotify in our web application
- How to add authentication and authorization layers to any web project using JWT and Express

Technical requirements

In order to follow this chapter, the following are some recommendations:

You should be familiar with the code that we generated in the previous chapter, as this is an iteration of the code that we generated

- Node.js 20.11.0 installed on your machine
- A code editor such as Visual Studio Code
- Have Docker set up and running
- A modern web browser such as Chrome or Firefox

The code files for the chapter can be found at `https://github.com/PacktPublishing/NodeJS-for-Beginners`

Check out the code in action video for this chapter on `https://youtu.be/mdE5eXS5enM`

Understanding modern authentication and authorization

Authentication and **authorization** are two different concepts that are often confused. Authentication involves confirming the identity of a user, whereas authorization involves verifying the specific access privileges they possess. In this chapter, we will explore how to implement both concepts in our web application in the *Adding authentication and authorization to our web application* section.

Authentication

One of the big challenges of the HTTP protocol is that it is stateless. This means that the server does not keep any information about the client. Each request is independent, so we need to design and provide mechanisms that allow us to know who the user performing the request is. This is the main goal of the authentication process.

There are many ways to implement authentication in a web application. The most common way is to use a username and password, and there are many libraries that can help us to implement this mechanism as well as different approaches to follow.

We can delegate most of it to a third-party provider such as *Auth0* or we can implement it ourselves.

In this chapter, we will explore how to implement authentication in our web application using the *Passport.js library* and *JSON Web Tokens (JWT)*.

Authorization

We need to implement a clear way to determine whether a user is authorized to perform a certain action, such as creating a new post or deleting an old post. Even something as simple as accessing a certain page requires us to implement a way to determine whether the user is authorized to access it.

It is quite common that a lot of effort is put into the authentication part, but the authorization aspect gets forgotten about. Historically, web systems were less complex at the beginning of the internet and we didn't have a lot of roles assigned to each user, so we tended to focus more on who you are rather than whether you should be able to do certain actions. Today, it is quite common to build complex systems that end up having access control tables that define the relationships between the actions and the roles. As an example, we can take as a reference the Role-based Authorization Strategy plugin for Jenkins, described in *Figure 13.1*. Using this, we can easily understand and update relationships between the roles and the potential activities to be performed. For example, the **builder** role can cancel jobs but not configure them.

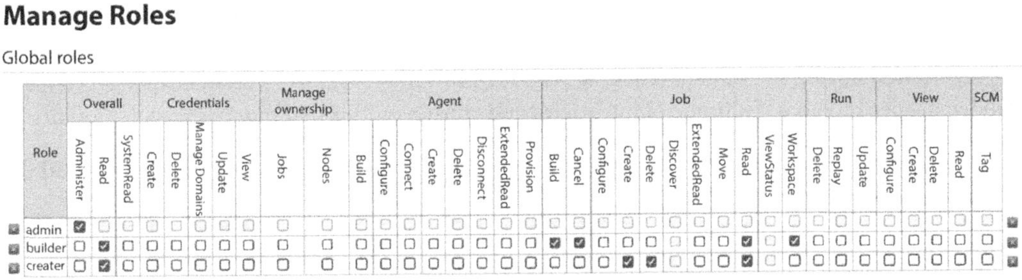

Manage Roles

Global roles

Figure 13.1 – Web browser screenshot from https://github.com/jenkinsci/
role-strategy-plugin, available under the MIT license

Failing to properly consider authorization is a very common mistake that can lead to severe security issues. For example, if we forget to implement the authorization part, we can end up with a web application that allows any user to access any page, or to perform any action. This is a very dangerous situation that can lead to security risks.

We will explore this topic in practical terms in the *Adding authentication and authorization to our web application* section of this chapter, seeing how to implement an appropriate authorization strategy in our web application.

Now that we have a clear understanding of the differences between authentication and authorization, let's explore how to implement them in our web application. In the next section, we will learn how we can use JWT to authenticate users in our web application.

JWT in a nutshell

One of the most popular ways to implement authentication in a web application is to use JWT.

So, let's see some definitions:

> *JSON Web Token is a proposed internet standard for creating data with optional signature and/or optional encryption whose payload holds JSON that asserts some number of claims. The tokens are signed either using a private secret or a public/ private key.*

(JSON Web Token, `https://en.wikipedia.org/wiki/JSON_Web_Token`)

> *JSON Web Tokens are an open, industry-standard RFC 7519 method for representing claims securely between two parties.*

(JWT, `https://jwt.io/`)

So, basically, a **JWT** is a string (*JSON*) that contains information (*claims*) and is signed using a secret key. This process ensures that the information within the JWT remains secure and tamper-proof, allowing for verification during subsequent requests. Although this may seem like a straightforward concept, delving deeper reveals a multitude of intricacies and considerations that must be understood first.

Let's list some of the most critical features that we expect to be supported to understand the underlying complexity:

- Anyone can send a request to our server, so we cannot trust any request by default.

- Anyone can try to manipulate the request, so we need to implement a mechanism that allows us to verify that the request has not been manipulated.

- We need to implement a mechanism that allows us to verify the request without the need to store any information on the server. That way we can scale our application without any issues and can even use the same JWT across multiple servers.

The process

In plain terms, the user will authenticate using a username and password, and then the server will return a JWT. The user will send the JWT in every request and the server will verify the JWT to authenticate the user.

The theory

The JWT is a string with information about the user (such as their name, role, etc.) and is signed using a secret key. So, the server can verify the JWT using the secret key and can then extract the information about the user. Any attempt to modify the JWT will invalidate the signature, so the server will reject the request.

So, in order to properly sign the tokens, first we need to understand the basics of cryptography.

Cryptography 101

To make the JWT work, we need to understand two things: hashing and signing.

Hashing

Hashing is a process that takes a string and returns a fixed-length string. This algorithm works as a one-way function, so we can hash a string, but we cannot get the original string from the hash.

Here is an example of hashing a string using the SHA256 algorithm in Node.js:

```
import crypto from 'crypto';

const hash = crypto.createHash('sha256');
hash.update('Hello World');
console.log(hash.digest('hex'));
// a591a6d40bf420404a011733cfb7b190d62c65bf0bcda32b57b277d9ad9f146e
```

We will use this algorithm to hash the password of the user later on in this chapter, in the *Adding authentication and authorization to our web application* section.

Signing

Signing is a process that takes a string and a secret key and returns a new string. This algorithm works as a two-way function, so we can sign a string and then we can verify the signature using the secret key.

Wide use

This pattern of using hashing and signing is very common across many different software fields. As an example, when a new Node.js version is released, the Node.js team will publish the hash of every binary file. This allows us to download the binary file and then verify the hash of the file using the hash that the Node.js team published. If the hashes are the same, then we can be sure that the file has not been modified.

The hash file is signed prior to publishing it, so we can verify the signature using the public key of the Node.js team members. If the signature is valid, then we can be sure that the hash file has not been modified.

As an example, the following link is the file shasum for Node v20.11.0 (https://nodejs.org/dist/v20.11.0/SHASUMS256.txt.asc). The following code block is the content of the file (redacted for space) to understand how it works:

```
-----BEGIN PGP SIGNED MESSAGE-----
Hash: SHA256
```

```
  f76a47616ceb47b9766cb7182ec6b53100192349de6a8aebb11f3abce045748f
  node-v20.11.0-aix-ppc64.tar.gz
  ...
  dce7cd4b62a721d783ce961e9f70416ac63cf9cdc87b01f6be46540201333b1e
  win-x86/node_pdb.zip
  -----BEGIN PGP SIGNATURE-----

  iQGzBAEBCA...aig9KO/s=
  =B/OP
  -----END PGP SIGNATURE-----
```

As you can see, the file contains two parts (the message and the signature) and uses **Pretty Good Privacy** (**PGP**). The signature is the result of signing the hash produced from `-----BEGIN PGP SIGNED MESSAGE-----` to `-----BEGIN PGP SIGNATURE-----`. This helps us to verify the authenticity of the file – basically, we can verify that a Node.js releaser has created this file and the content has not been manipulated, even if the server from which the file was downloaded was compromised.

The message itself contains the hash of every binary file, so we can download the `node-v20.11.0-aix-ppc64.tar.gz` file and check that the content of the file is the same as the hash published in the message, `f76a47616ceb47b9766cb7182ec6b53100192349de6a8aebb11f3abce045748f`. If the hash is the same, then we can be sure that the file has not been modified. This allows us to distribute information securely.

> **Important note**
>
> With JWT, we will use a similar pattern, but instead of PGP, we will use a different algorithm to sign the content. You can find the list of supported algorithms in RFC 7518 (`https://tools.ietf.org/html/rfc7518#section-3.1`).

JWT structure

JWT is a string that is composed of three parts separated by a dot. Each part is encoded in *base64*. The three parts are the following:

- **Header**: Contains information about the type of token and the algorithm used to sign the token
- **Payload**: Contains the claims (information) that we want to store in the token
- **Signature**: Contains the signature of the token that is used to verify the token

The signature is the result of signing the header and the payload using the secret key. The best part is that we can verify the signature using the secret key, so we can verify the token without needing to store any information on the server. Additionally, the information is encoded in base64, so anyone can decode it and read it, but we cannot modify it.

One important thing to mention is that you should never store sensitive information in the payload, as anyone can decode it and read it. This includes users' passwords and bank account details, among other sensitive information.

JWT.io

One of the best tools to work with JWT is the JWT Debugger (`https://jwt.io/`) (see *Figure 13.2*). This website allows us to encode and decode JWTs, as well as to verify the signature of the token. You can use it to play with or debug your JWTs.

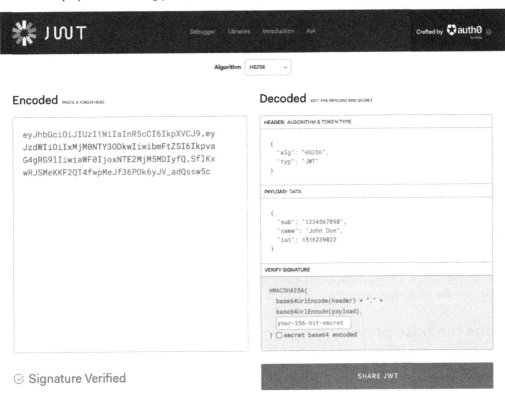

Figure 13.2 – Web browser screenshot showing how to digest and validate an encoded token

Feel free to play with it and explore how it works before moving to the next section of this chapter.

In the next section, we will learn how Passport.js works and how it can be used to implement authentication with third-party providers such as Facebook or Spotify in our web application.

Understanding Passport.js fundamentals

Passport.js is a fantastic library, widely used to implement authentication in Node.js applications. The official website of Passport.js defines the library as follows:

> *Passport is authentication middleware for Node.js. Extremely flexible and modular, Passport can be unobtrusively dropped in to any Express-based web application. A comprehensive set of strategies support authentication using a username and password, Facebook, Twitter, and more.*

(Passport.js, `http://www.passportjs.org/`)

In essence, Passport.js is a middleware (`https://expressjs.com/en/guide/using-middleware.html`) that we will include in our Express application to provide many different strategies to implement authentication. Having a selection of such strategies allows us to choose the one that best fits our needs. We can use the library to easily implement social login functionality (such as Facebook, Twitter, Spotify, GitHub, and much more in more than 500 strategies) and the typical username/password login.

In the next section, we will iterate the code from our web application to include authentication and authorization mechanisms using what we have learned in this chapter so far.

Adding authentication and authorization to our web application

In this section, we will add authentication and authorization to our web application. We will use the jsonwebtoken library to implement the authentication part and will use a custom middleware to implement the authorization part.

Clone the base project

The authentication and authorization additions are not very complex, but it is quite long to follow with ease, so for this chapter you can download the project from `https://github.com/PacktPublishing/NodeJS-for-Beginners/archive/refs/heads/main.zip` and access the `step4` folder. The implementation is ready to go, but I will comment on the most relevant changes that we made since the last chapter (`step3` folder) so you can easily follow what we've done.

Setup

Our first steps are to explore the folder, install the dependencies, configure the environment, and start the infrastructure. This can be performed by running the following commands:

1. Install the dependencies with npm i.

2. Update the secrets, adding the .env file in the root folder with the following content:

    ```
    MONGODB_URI=mongodb://localhost:27017/whispering-database
    PORT=3000
    SALT_ROUNDS=10
    JWT_SECRET=Tu1fo3mO0PcAvjq^q3wQ24BXNI8$9R
    Run npm run infra:stop && npm run infra:start.
    ```

3. Run npm run infra:stop && npm run infra:start.

Now, the infrastructure and configuration are ready, but before we start making more changes to the application, it is recommended to run some tests.

Run the tests

Next, we need to run some tests to ensure that the code is working as expected by typing npm run test in our terminal.

New tests added

We can see that we have a few new routes related to login/signup and specific tests for them. When we execute the tests, we will see that the test messages (descriptions) are clear and self-explanatory in terms of what the routes are expected to do and what we aim to do with the test, even if we are not yet familiar with the code:

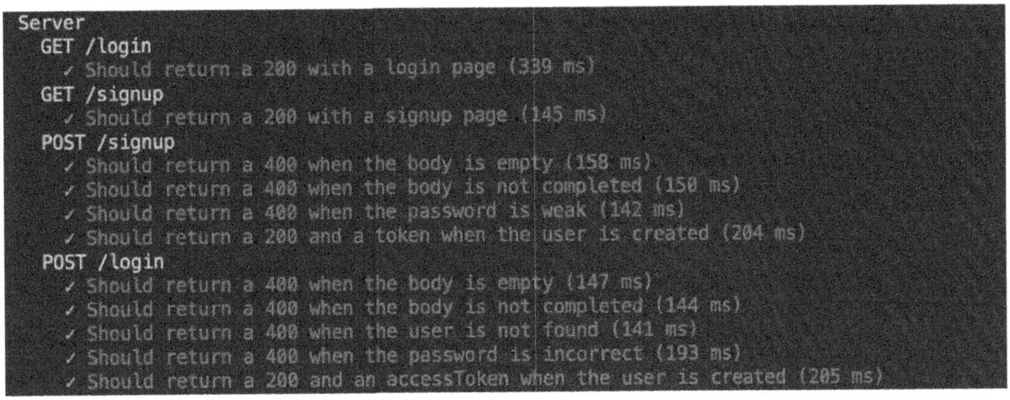

```
Server
  GET /login
    ✓ Should return a 200 with a login page (339 ms)
  GET /signup
    ✓ Should return a 200 with a signup page (145 ms)
  POST /signup
    ✓ Should return a 400 when the body is empty (158 ms)
    ✓ Should return a 400 when the body is not completed (150 ms)
    ✓ Should return a 400 when the password is weak (142 ms)
    ✓ Should return a 200 and a token when the user is created (204 ms)
  POST /login
    ✓ Should return a 400 when the body is empty (147 ms)
    ✓ Should return a 400 when the body is not completed (144 ms)
    ✓ Should return a 400 when the user is not found (141 ms)
    ✓ Should return a 400 when the password is incorrect (193 ms)
    ✓ Should return a 200 and an accessToken when the user is created (205 ms)
```

Figure 13.3 – Terminal screenshot that showcases how the routes are tested

We should recognize these tests as we worked on these routes in the previous chapters. But if we keep scrolling through the test output, we should see that new tests have been added as well.

Updated tests

The previous tests have been updated to include new test cases related to authentication for the routes that require authentication with JWT:

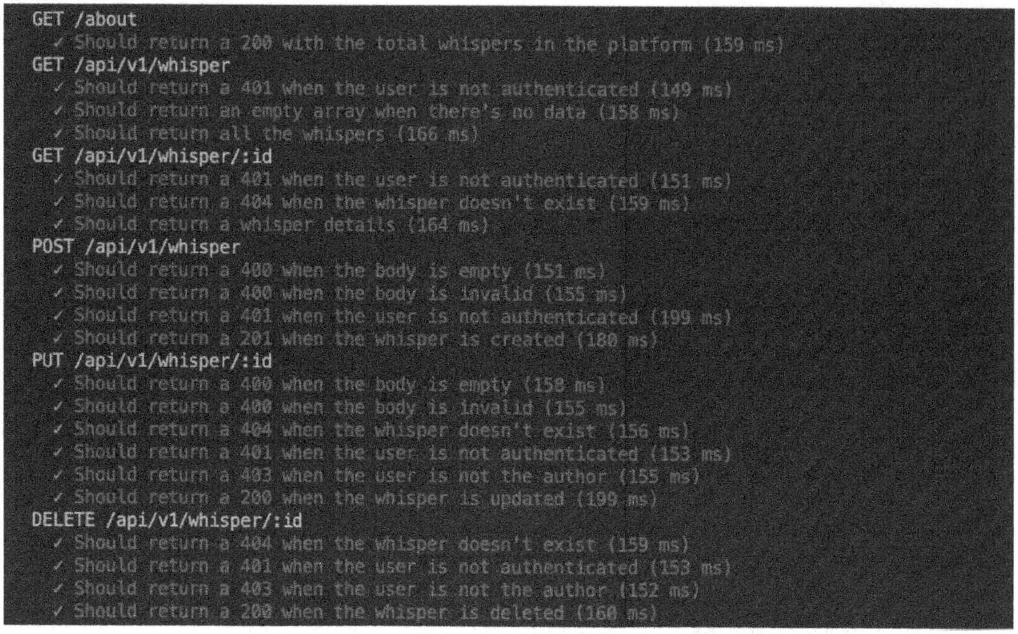

```
GET /about
    ✓ Should return a 200 with the total whispers in the platform (159 ms)
GET /api/v1/whisper
    ✓ Should return a 401 when the user is not authenticated (149 ms)
    ✓ Should return an empty array when there's no data (158 ms)
    ✓ Should return all the whispers (166 ms)
GET /api/v1/whisper/:id
    ✓ Should return a 401 when the user is not authenticated (151 ms)
    ✓ Should return a 404 when the whisper doesn't exist (159 ms)
    ✓ Should return a whisper details (164 ms)
POST /api/v1/whisper
    ✓ Should return a 400 when the body is empty (151 ms)
    ✓ Should return a 400 when the body is invalid (155 ms)
    ✓ Should return a 401 when the user is not authenticated (199 ms)
    ✓ Should return a 201 when the whisper is created (180 ms)
PUT /api/v1/whisper/:id
    ✓ Should return a 400 when the body is empty (158 ms)
    ✓ Should return a 400 when the body is invalid (155 ms)
    ✓ Should return a 404 when the whisper doesn't exist (156 ms)
    ✓ Should return a 401 when the user is not authenticated (153 ms)
    ✓ Should return a 403 when the user is not the author (155 ms)
    ✓ Should return a 200 when the whisper is updated (199 ms)
DELETE /api/v1/whisper/:id
    ✓ Should return a 404 when the whisper doesn't exist (159 ms)
    ✓ Should return a 401 when the user is not authenticated (153 ms)
    ✓ Should return a 403 when the user is not the author (152 ms)
    ✓ Should return a 200 when the whisper is deleted (160 ms)
```

Figure 13.4 – Terminal screenshot shows the tests passing and how easy
is to follow what is being tested with the descriptions

As you can see, the use cases in the tests cover more scenarios related to authentication and authorization, such as Should return 401 when the user is not authenticated and Should return a 403 when the user is not the author.

The UI changes

But overall, the most significant changes are related to the UI, as now we have new routes and views to login/register and so on. So we can start the application by running npm run start

Login

You can enter your credentials to log in at `http://localhost:3000/login`, upon which the backend API will return a JWT that you can use to authenticate for any CRUD operation.

Figure 13.5 – Web browser screenshot showing the login page where
the user can enter their username and password

Register

You can create a new account whenever you please at `http://localhost:3000/signup`. This operation will generate a new user in the database and the backend will return you a JWT that you can use to perform CRUD operations and authenticate yourself against the API.

Figure 13.6 – Web browser screenshot showing where the user can
create a new account or log in with existing credentials

> **Important note**
> The server has defined certain rules regarding username, email and password. So, as an example you can use the following values:

- Username: `nodejs`
- Email: `demo@demo.com`
- Password: `aA1#dt$tu`

CRUD operations

As remarked on in the previous section, it is important to understand how authorization works. So, here are the rules for our business logic:

- Any logged user can see all the whispers available on the Whispering platform
- You can modify or delete only the whispers that you have created

These clear rules will help us to build an authorization system that will cover all the scenarios, so, for example, you won't be able to delete a whisper created by another user. In some applications, this approach can be very complex, such as with Google Drive or Facebook. In those scenarios, it is quite useful to have a permission matrix in place and well documented. GitLab offers a great example (`https://docs.gitlab.com/ee/user/permissions.html`)

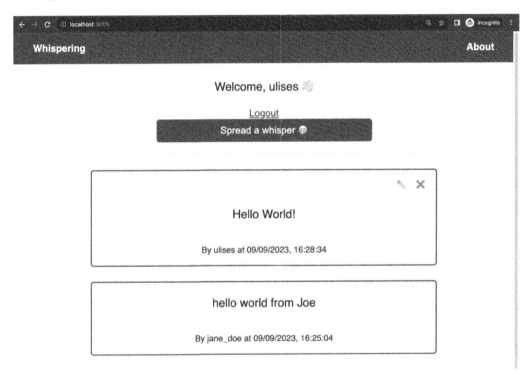

Figure 13.7 – Web browser screenshot showing the main page with all the
whispers and the buttons to interact with them from the UI

As you can see, we can modify only the whispers that we created but the option is not visually available for other whispers.

While the UI is a key factor in managing authorization, we need to ensure that the backend is also properly managing authorization on its part, so it won't allow the users to modify or delete whispers from other users. To ensure that the application is capable of preventing these scenarios (like modify other's users whispers) it is highly recommended to add specify test case. Check the test suite cases, as we have already included these scenarios that cover the `403 Forbidden` response.

Added dependencies

We have included the following dependencies:

- **Bcrypt** (`https://www.npmjs.com/package/bcrypt`): This is a library that will help us to store passwords safely in the database.

- **Jsonwebtoken** (`https://www.npmjs.com/package/jsonwebtoken`): This is a utility that helps us to generate and parse the JWTs.

- **Validator** (`https://www.npmjs.com/package/validator`): This is a library that we use to validate strings. Basically, we can use it to sanitize the inputs received from the users, including email addresses, URLs, phone numbers, and so on.

These dependencies will be used later in order to properly build our application. It is quite common in Node.js projects to rely on third-party libraries. The most important thing to remember is to be sure that we are using good-quality external dependencies without known vulnerabilities, as we learned in *Chapter 6*.

Changes in the frontend

We added a new file called `public/auth.js` to manage the form submissions while the user logs in or registers with the platform. After sending the requests, we will store the JWT in the local storage, so we can recover the JWT easily even if we refresh the page:

```
fetch('/login', {
    method: 'POST',
    headers: {
        'Content-Type': 'application/json'
    },
    body: JSON.stringify({
        username,
        password
    })
})
.then(response => {
    if (response.status !== 200) {
        throw new Error("Invalid credentials")
    }
    return response.json()
})
.then(({accessToken}) => {
    localStorage.setItem('accessToken', accessToken);
    window.location.href = '/';
})
```

With the previous changes, we now send the user and password to the /login route using the POST HTTP method. As a response, we expect JSON data that will contain the access token that we will store in the local storage in order to keep session persistence in case the user refreshes the page. Finally, we will redirect the user to the home page as the authentication has been completed successfully.

We also added the JWT to every request made against the API for any CRUD operation in public/ app.js:

```
const fetchAllWhispers = () => fetch('http://localhost:3000/api/v1/
whisper', {
    headers: {Authentication: `Bearer ${accessToken}`}
}).then((response) => response.json())
```

As you can see, every request includes the Authentication header with the Bearer TOKEN value, which is the expected way to authenticate against the backend. We also use the JWT to get the user's name and display it in the UI in the Whispers view.

Also, we disabled the edit/delete buttons from the Whisper view if the current user is not the user that created them:

```
`<article data-id="${whisper.id}">
    <div class="actions" ${controlEdition(whisper, user)}>
        <button data-action="edit">✏️</button>
        <button data-action="delete">✖️</button>
    </div>
</article>`
```

The controlEdition function can hide/show the actions depending on the author:

```
const controlEdition = (whisper, user) => {
    if(whisper.author.id === user.id) {
        return ''
    } else {
        return 'style="display:none;"'
    }
}
```

Now that we are clear on the changes made in the frontend part, it is time to jump to the backend part and review the changes needed in order to properly manage the users' authentication data in the databases. We'll start with the changes in the stores.

Added a new store for users

The most relevant changes were added to the `database.js` file, where a new schema was added for the users. We now include more advanced validations and transformations. The user has `username`, `email`, and `password` properties:

```
const userSchema = new mongoose.Schema({
  //...
  password: {
    type: String,
    required: [true, 'Password is required'],
    minlength: [8, 'Password must be at least 8 characters long'],
    validate: {
      validator: checkPasswordStrength
    }
  }
  //...
})
```

In the case of `password`, we include an additional validation with a new function that we added to the utilities file, `utils.js`. This new function uses a regular expression to validate the password strength (a minimum of eight characters, at least one letter, one number, and one special character):

```
export function checkPasswordStrength(password) {
  const strengthRegex = /^(?=.*[A-Za-z])(?=.*\d)(?=.*[@$!%*#?&])
[A-Za-z\d@$!%*#?&]{8,}$/
  return strengthRegex.test(password)
}
```

Now, the `whisperSchema` schema has a relation with `User`, as each whisper is owned by a specific author:

```
const whisperSchema = new mongoose.Schema({
  author: { type: mongoose.Schema.Types.ObjectId, ref: 'User' },
  message: String,
  updatedDate: {
    type: Date,
    default: Date.now
  },
  creationDate: {
    type: Date,
    default: Date.now
  }
})
```

We can see how this relationship takes place in `stores/whisper.js`, as we can populate the queries:

```
const getAll = () => Whisper.find().populate('author', 'username')
const getById = id => Whisper.findById({ _id: id }).populate('author',
'username')
const create = async (message, authorId ) => {
  const whisper = new Whisper({ message, author: authorId })
  await whisper.save()
  return whisper
}
```

Password management

As part of proper password management in the `database.js`, we will use the `bcrypt` library, specifically the `pre` middleware, to hash passwords before storing them in the database. The `pre` middleware is a function that is triggered before we perform a specific action such as a save. You can find great examples in the official documentation (`https://mongoosejs.com/docs/middleware.html#pre`):

```
userSchema.pre('save', async function (next) {
  const user = this
  if (user.isModified('password')) {
    const salt = await bcrypt.genSalt()
    user.password = await bcrypt.hash(user.password, salt)
  }
  next()
})
```

Also, in the same `database.js` file, we will add a new function to compare the saved password of the user with the password that the user is sending in the request:

```
userSchema.methods.comparePassword = async function
(candidatePassword) {
  const user = this
  return await bcrypt.compare(candidatePassword, user.password)
}
```

That way we can store and compare the password securely, never storing it in plain text.

JWT utilities

Our authentication is now done with **JSON Web Tokens** (**JWTs**), so we need to add some utilities to generate and parse the JWTs. We will use the `jsonwebtoken` library for this purpose.

In the `utils.js` file, we add one function to generate the JWT:

```
export function generateToken (data) {
    return jwt.sign({
        data: data
    }, process.env.JWT_SECRET, { expiresIn: '1h' })
}
```

We also add another function to parse the JWT; in our case, an Express middleware that will parse the JWT and add the user to the request:

```
export function requireAuthentication (req, res, next) {
    const token = req.headers.authentication
    if (!token) {
        res.status(401).json({ error: 'No token provided' })
        return
    }
    try {
        const accessToken = token.split(' ')[1]
        const decoded = jwt.verify(accessToken, process.env.JWT_SECRET)
        req.user = decoded.data
        next()
    } catch (err) {
        res.status(401).json({ error: 'Invalid token' })
    }
}
```

As you can see, we use the JWT_SECRET to sign and verify the JWTs. This environmental variable is stored in the .env file, so we can change it easily in any environment. Also, we set an expiration time of 1 hour for the JWTs, after which time the user will need to authenticate again. It is quite common to have short expiration times so that if the token did get compromised, the time in which it could be used to do harm is limited. This is a very popular secure measurement that can be combined with refresh tokens (https://auth0.com/learn/refresh-tokens) to have an even more solid implementation.

If the token has been modified or the secret is not the same, then the jwt.verify function will throw an error, so we can catch it and return an error to the user. The same will happen if the token is expired.

If the token is valid, then we will add the user to the request, so we can use it in the next middleware or in the route handler.

This completes the authentication part – we can now authenticate the users in our web application! It is important to note that we are not storing any information on the server so we can scale our application without any issues, but there are some drawbacks to this, as we will explore in *Chapter 15*.

Adding new routes

Now we have all the utilities to implement the authentication, so we can include the new routes. In our case, we will include the following routes:

- GET /login to render the login view to the user:

```
app.get('/login', (req, res) => {
  res.render('login')
})
```

- POST /login to process the login request, store the new user, and return the JWT:

```
app.post('/login', async (req, res) => {
  try {
    const { username, password } = req.body
    const foundUser = await user.getUserByCredentials(username,
password)
    const accessToken = generateToken({ username, id:
foundUser._id})
    res.json({ accessToken})
  } catch ( err ){
    res.status(400).json({ error: err.message })
  }
})
```

- GET /signup to render the signup view to the user:

```
app.get('/signup', (req, res) => {
  res.render('signup')
})
```

- POST /signup to process the signup request and return the JWT:

```
app.post('/signup', async (req, res) => {
  try {
    const { username, password, email } = req.body
    const newUser = await user.create(username, password, email)
    const accessToken = generateToken({ username, id: newUser._
id})
    res.json({ accessToken})
  } catch ( err ){
    res.status(400).json({ error: err.message })
  }
})
```

- Then, we also need to update the routes that require authentication to use the `require Authentication` middleware and modify the internal logic to ensure that the authorizations are properly managed. For example, users shouldn't be able to modify/delete whispers from other users:

```
app.put('/api/v1/whisper/:id', requireAuthentication, async
(req, res) => {
  const { message } = req.body
  const id = req.params.id
  if (!message) {
    res.sendStatus(400)
    return
  }
  const storedWhisper = await whisper.getById(id)
  if (!storedWhisper) {
    res.sendStatus(404)
    return
  }

  if(storedWhisper.author.id !== req.user.id) {
    res.sendStatus(403)
    return
  }
  await whisper.updateById(id, message)
  res.sendStatus(200)
})
```

As you can see, we use the `requireAuthentication` middleware to ensure that the user is authenticated, and then we check that the user is the author of the whisper that we are trying to modify. If the user is not the author, then we return a `403 Forbidden` error.

There are other scenarios that we also covered in the tests such as when the whisper is not found. In those cases is expected that we to return the proper HTTP error code in each case.

Improved testing utilities

We modified the testing utilities to include valid fixtures for the users, so we have predefined users that we can use to test the authentication functionality.

Also, we included sample whispers for the tests, so we can use them to test the authorization part.

And finally, we included some fixtures that include a valid JWT for each user, so we can use them to test the authorization part.

You can check the changes in detail in the `tests/utils.js` file.

Test case changes

Regarding the test cases, we updated them to include the new routes and to test the authorization part. You can check the changes in detail in the `tests/server.test.js` file.

In general, most of the routes now include specific test cases to test the authorization part, ensuring that the authorization is properly managed.

We added test cases for each route to test requests from users that are not authenticated:

```
it('Should return a 401 when the user is not authenticated', async ()
=> {
  const response = await supertest(app)
  .delete(`/api/v1/whisper/${existingId}`)

  expect(response.status).toBe(401)
  expect(response.body.error).toBe('No token provided')
})
```

Also, in some routes, we added test cases to test the authorization part, so we can ensure that the authorization is properly managed:

```
it('Should return a 403 when the user is not the author', async () =>
{
  const response = await supertest(app)
  .delete(`/api/v1/whisper/${existingId}`)
  .set('Authentication', `Bearer ${secondUser.token}`)

  expect(response.status).toBe(403)
})
```

Overall, many tests were modified to include the JWT with a specific Bearer token, in the form of `.set('Authentication', `Bearer ${firstUser.token}`)`.

Test coverage

If we run the tests with `npm run test:coverage`, we can see in detail how the changes affected the test coverage. If you check the `coverage/lcov-report/index.html` file, you can see the details of the coverage:

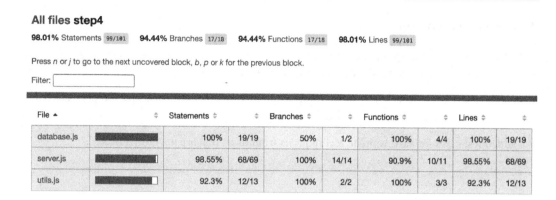

Figure 13.8 – Web browser screenshot with the test coverage report

Overall, the coverage is quite good (between 94-98%), but we can see that we have some lines that are not covered. We could improve the tests to cover them, but those are edge cases.

Summary

In this chapter, we had the opportunity to learn how authentication and authorization work in a web application. We implemented the authentication part using JWT and the authorization part using a custom middleware.

Additionally, we explored in detail how JWTs work and how to implement them in a Node.js application.

Finally, we added authentication and authorization functionalities to our web application, so we can now authenticate users and we can ensure that the users can only modify/delete the whispers that they created.

In the next chapter, we are going to learn in more detail how to properly manage errors in our web application and in any Node.js application or library.

Further reading

- *Session vs Token Authentication in 100 Seconds*: https://www.youtube.com/watch?v=UBUNrFtufWo

- *Authentication: It's Easier Than You Think*: https://www.youtube.com/watch?v=h6wBYWWdyYQ

- *JWT Handbook by Auth0*: https://auth0.com/resources/ebooks/jwt-handbook

- *Auth0 in 100 Seconds // And beyond with a Next.js Authentication Tutorial*: https://www.youtube.com/watch?v=yufqeJLP1rI

14

Error Handling in Node.js

Node.js applications require solid and consistent control over errors. Most applications are built using many dependencies or heavily rely on asynchronous operations (network, disk, and so on), which makes error management more complex.

In this chapter, we will learn about the different types of errors that we can encounter in a Node.js application and how to handle them properly. We will also learn how to throw custom errors and how to capture and resume the application from any kind of error, including the ones that occur in Express applications.

We will also learn how to manage a graceful shutdown when the service crashes, how to use exit codes according to the situation, and how to prevent zombie processes.

To sum up, here are the main topics that we will explore in this chapter:

- How to throw custom errors
- How to capture and recover from any kind of error
- How to manage application and user errors in Express
- How to manage a graceful shutdown when the service crashes
- How to prevent zombie processes
- How to use exit codes to indicate the reason why the application was shut down

Technical requirements

The code files for the chapter can be found at `https://github.com/PacktPublishing/NodeJS-for-Beginners`.

Check out the code in action video for this chapter on `https://youtu.be/VPXV1L1epIk`

Exploring the types of errors

As we learned in the first chapter, Node.js is a single-threaded application. This means that if an error occurs and we don't properly handle it, the application will crash. This is why it is important to handle errors properly.

There are two main types of errors in Node.js: **syntax** errors and **runtime** errors.

Syntax errors

Syntax errors are thrown when the code is parsed and it is not valid. These errors are thrown by the JavaScript engine, and they are usually easy to fix. Many IDEs and code editors can detect these errors and highlight them in the code editor, so you can fix them before running the application. In our case, we have been using StandardJS as a linter (which is a tool that helps us detect syntax errors and enforce a consistent code style) in previous chapters.

This is an example of a syntax error:

```
executeThisFunction()
```

The previous code will throw a `ReferenceError` error because the `executeThisFunction` function is not defined. This error can be easily fixed by defining the function:

```
executeThisFunction()

ReferenceError: executeThisFunction is not defined
    at file:///file.js:1:1
    at ModuleJob.run (node:internal/modules/esm/module_job:192:25)
    at async DefaultModuleLoader.import (node:internal/modules/esm/loader:228:24)
    at async loadESM (node:internal/process/esm_loader:40:7)
    at async handleMainPromise (node:internal/modules/run_main:66:12)
```

Runtime errors

Runtime errors are also known as **operational** errors. These errors are thrown when the application is running and are not related to the syntax of the code. These errors can be thrown by the application itself or by the dependencies that the application is using.

There are many ways to generate runtime errors, such as by accessing a property of an undefined object, calling a function that does not exist, trying to read a file that does not exist, trying to connect to a database that is not available, and trying to access a network resource that is not available.

As you can see, there are many ways to generate runtime errors. This is why it is important to handle them properly. If we don't handle them, the application will crash and it will stop working. So, while coding the application, it is very important to keep in mind the possible runtime errors that can be thrown and how to handle them.

Some errors can be recovered and others not, depending on the type of error. For example, if we have a REST API application and the database is not available, we could recover from this error by returning a 503 HTTP status code and a message to the client. You will be always in charge of deciding whether the error can be recovered or not and how to handle it.

Now that we know the types of errors that can be thrown in Node.js applications, let's see how to throw meaningful errors in the next section.

Throwing meaningful errors

When an error occurs, it is important that it is meaningful. This means that the error should contain enough information to understand what happened and, potentially, how to fix it.

The error object

The error object is an instance of the `Error` class. This class has a constructor that accepts a message as a parameter. This message will be used to describe the error. Here is an example:

```
const myError = new Error('This is an error message')
throw myError
```

Here is the output of the previous code:

```
file:///file.js:1
const myError = new Error('This is an error message')
                ^

Error: This is an error message
    at file:///file.js:1:17
    at ModuleJob.run (node:internal/modules/esm/module_job:192:25)
    at async DefaultModuleLoader.import (node:internal/modules/esm/
loader:228:24)
    at async loadESM (node:internal/process/esm_loader:40:7)
    at async handleMainPromise (node:internal/modules/run_main:66:12)

Node.js v20.11.0
```

As you can see, the error message is displayed in the output. This is the message that we passed to the constructor of the `Error` class. If you compare it with `ReferenceError: executeThisFunction is not defined`, we can see that the error message is not very descriptive and that we are using a generic error class.

Custom errors

You can create your own custom errors by extending the `Error` class. This is useful when you want to create your own `Error` classes and add more information to the error object. Here is an example:

```
class NotEnoughSleep extends Error {
  constructor (message) {
    super(message)
    this.requireSleep = true
    this.isRecoverable = true
  }
}

throw new NotEnoughSleep('Looks like you need more sleep')
```

If we run the previous code, we will get the following output:

```
file:///file.js:9
  throw new NotEnoughSleep('Looks like you need more sleep')

NotEnoughSleep [Error]: Looks like you need more sleep
    at file:///file.js:9:9
    at ModuleJob.run (node:internal/modules/esm/module_job:192:25)
    at async DefaultModuleLoader.import (node:internal/modules/esm/
loader:228:24)
    at async loadESM (node:internal/process/esm_loader:40:7)
    at async handleMainPromise (node:internal/modules/run_main:66:12)
{
  requireSleep: true,
  isRecoverable: true
}
```

As you can see, the error message `Looks like you need more sleep` is displayed in the output, as well as the class name, `NotEnoughSleep`. Additionally, we have added two properties to the error object: `requireSleep` and `isRecoverable`. These properties are created by us, and we can create as many as we need and be as specific as we want. These properties can be used to add more information to the error object, so we can handle the error properly using these properties in a `try/catch` block:

```
try {
  throw new NotEnoughSleep("Looks like you need more sleep");
```

```
} catch (error) {
  if (error.isRecoverable) {
    console.log("You are lucky, because you can recover from this
error");
  }
  if (error.requireSleep) {
    console.log("Please, go to sleep!");
  }
}
```

Here is the output of the previous code:

```
You are lucky, because you can recover from this error
Please, go to sleep!
```

As you can see, we have used the `isRecoverable` and `requireSleep` properties to handle the error. This is a very simple example, but you can add more properties to the error object to handle the error properly.

In the next section, we are going to learn how to capture and recover from any kind of error while using Express.

Managing errors in Express

In the previous chapters, we learned how to create a REST API application using Express and we saw how to handle errors in Express applications, but in this section, we are going to refresh the concepts and extend them.

Error-handling middleware

Express has a built-in error-handling middleware that can be used to handle errors in a centralized way. This middleware is executed when an error occurs in the application. This middleware is executed after all the other middleware and routes have been executed. It is executed only when an error occurs, so it is important to add it at the end of the middleware chain, like so:

```
import express from 'express'
const app = express()

// Other middlewares...
app.use((err, req, res, next) => {
  console.error(err.stack)
  res.status(500).send('Something broke!')
})

// Route handler...
```

Custom errors

If you are building a REST API application, you could add a property to the error object to indicate the HTTP status code that should be returned to the client. This way, you can handle the error properly in the error-handling middleware and return the proper HTTP status code to the client. Here is an example:

```
class NotFoundError extends Error {
  constructor (message) {
    super(message)
    this.statusCode = 404
  }
}

try {
  throw new NotFoundError('The resource was not found')
} catch (error) {
  console.log(error.statusCode)
  res.status(error.statusCode).send(error.message)
}
```

As you can see, we can use the `statusCode` property to return the proper HTTP status code to the client. This is a very simple example but you can add more properties to the error object to handle the error properly.

Now that we know how to handle errors, it is time to learn how to gracefully shut down the application when the application cannot recover from an error.

Gracefully shutting down the application

Throughout the book, we have learned how to handle errors using `try`/`catch` blocks, error-first callbacks, `catch` for promises, and also events to handle errors but, sometimes, we need to handle errors globally.

Node.js provides a way to handle errors globally and gracefully shut down the application when an error occurs: using `process.on()`. You can also use `process.exit()` to exit the application with a specific exit code. This is useful in CI/CD pipelines, to indicate whether or not the application was shut down because of an error, and also in productive environments.

Events

There are many events that can be used to handle errors globally:

- `uncaughtException`: This event is emitted when an uncaught exception occurs
- `unhandledRejection`: This event is emitted when an unhandled rejection occurs

- exit: This event is emitted when the Node.js process is about to exit

- SIGINT and SIGTERM: These events are emitted when the Node.js process receives these signals

Many other events can be used to handle errors globally but these are the most common ones. In the following example, we combine some scenarios to handle errors globally:

```
const events = ['uncaughtException','unhandledRejection', 'exit',
'SIGINT'];

events.forEach(event => {
  process.on(event, (error) => {
    console.log(`This is an ${event} that we track!`)
  })
})

setTimeout(() => {
  throw new Error('Exception!')
}, 10000)

setTimeout(() => {
  Promise.reject(new Error('Rejection!'))
}, 20000)
```

If you run the previous code, you will see that the application will be shut down after 20 seconds because of the unhandled rejection, but the uncaught exception was eventually caught and the process continues running. Also, if you press *Ctrl + C* at any time, the application will be shut down because of the SIGINT signal.

In the following example, we can see that the exit event is always triggered when we are closing the Node.js application. So, it is quite common to use this event to perform some actions before the application is shut down:

```
This is an uncaughtException that we track!
This is an unhandledRejection that we track!
This is an exit that we track!
```

Take into account that the exit event is not only triggered when an error occurs but also when the application is closed gracefully and does not support asynchronous operations.

In the next section, we will learn how to use exit codes to indicate the reason why the application was shut down. This is very useful in CI/CD pipelines to indicate whether the application was shut down because of an error or not.

Exit codes

Exit codes are used to indicate the reason that the application was shut down, as well as whether or not the application was shut down because of an error and whether the application was shut down gracefully or not.

If the exit code is 0, it means that the application was shut down gracefully. If the exit code is different from 0, it means that the application was shut down because of an error. By default, when there is nothing to do in the application, Node.js will exit with the exit code of 0.

By using `process.exit()`, we can indicate the exit code that we want to use. For example, if we want to indicate that the application was shut down because of an error, we can use `process.exit(1)`. If we want to indicate that the application was shut down gracefully, we can use `process.exit(0)`.

Some processes might finish correctly in terms of execution but use an error code. For example, when we run and complete application tests, if any test fails, the exit code will be different from 0. That way, the execution output will be an error that can prevent CI from continuing to execute the pipeline.

In the next section, we will learn how to prevent zombie processes while using the process library to handle errors globally.

Avoiding zombie processes

I love zombie movies but I don't like zombie processes. A zombie process is a process that is running in the background and is not doing anything. These kinds of processes eat resources from the host machine, and they can be a huge problem in certain scenarios such as low-capability devices.

Using `process.on()` can be dangerous because it can prevent the Node.js process from exiting. This is why it is important to use `process.exit()` to exit the application with a specific exit code when needed.

Let's see an example. If we don't use `process.exit()`, the application will not exit and it will be running forever, even if an error occurs while executing a function that is not defined:

```
process.on('uncaughtException', (error) => {
  console.log('We are not going to exit the application!')
})
setInterval(() => {
    executeThisFunction()
}, 1000)
```

This is shown in the following output:

```
We are not going to exit the application!
We are not going to exit the application!
We are not going to exit the application!
```

```
We are not going to exit the application!
We are not going to exit the application!
```

We can prevent that by adding `process.exit()` to exit the application with a specific exit code:

```
process.on("uncaughtException", (error) => {
  console.log("Now, exit the application!");
  process.exit(1);
});
setInterval(() => {
  executeThisFunction();
}, 1000);
```

The output will be as follows:

```
Now, exit the application!
```

As you can see, the application was shut down because we used `process.exit()` to exit the application with a specific exit code. If we don't use `process.exit()`, the application will be running forever, making it a zombie process.

Summary

In this chapter, we learned about the types of errors that can be thrown in Node.js applications. We saw how to throw custom errors and how to capture and recover from any kind of error.

Additionally, we reviewed how to manage application and user errors in Express. We also learned how to manage a graceful shutdown when the service crashed.

Finally, we learned how to prevent zombie processes.

In the next chapter, we are going to learn more about security, including how to protect our application by applying the best practices available and how to evaluate CVEs and security vulnerabilities.

Further reading

- *Express | Health Checks and Graceful Shutdown*: `https://expressjs.com/en/advanced/healthcheck-graceful-shutdown.html`

- *Express | Error Handling*: `https://expressjs.com/en/guide/error-handling.html`

- Node.js docs | *Error API*: `https://nodejs.org/dist/latest-v20.x/docs/api/errors.html`

- *Bash command line exit codes demystified*: `https://www.redhat.com/sysadmin/exit-codes-demystified`

15

Securing Web Applications

In this chapter, we are going to explore how to improve the security of our web applications. We will start by discussing the impact of a security incident on businesses and how to get started with security in our day-to-day work. Then we will explore key resources such as the OWASP Top 10, the **Common Weakness Enumeration** (**CWE**), and the **Common Vulnerabilities and Exposures** (**CVE**) to improve our understanding of security in modern web applications.

Then, we will explore the Node.js threat model and the official Node.js best practices to improve the security of our applications. We will apply this knowledge to create a checklist that we can use to improve the security of our existing applications.

Finally, we will explore how to take advantage of our security knowledge to become an ethical hacker and how to skill up while participating in community events and bug bounty programs.

To sum up, here are the main topics that we will explore in this chapter:

- The importance of security
- Where to start with security
- Improving the security of our applications
- Becoming an ethical hacker

Technical requirements

The code files for the chapter can be found at `https://github.com/PacktPublishing/NodeJS-for-Beginners`.

The importance of security

Historically, the security of applications was not considered a priority by developers. The main reason was that the security culture was not present in the developers' mindset as the main goal was to deliver features as soon as possible and, historically, the systems that we built were not critical for the business or exposed to the internet 24/7 as they are today.

"There are only two types of companies: those that have been hacked, and those that will be."

– Robert Mueller, FBI Director, 2012

Nowadays, we depend on a lot of third-party libraries and services that we don't control, and we don't know whether they are secure or not. We build very complex systems with many layers beyond our own business logic, and we need to be aware of the risks that we are taking and how to mitigate them.

At the end of the day, it is up to us as individuals to be aware of the risks, and the security of our applications is our responsibility. Quite often, we assume that security is someone else's responsibility but that is not true. Even in organizations with a security team, developers are the first line of defense and the ones that need to be aware of the risks and how to mitigate them.

Social engineering

I love Hollywood hacker movies that use super sophisticated tools to hack fictional systems, but the reality is that the most common attack vector is social engineering. It is easier to trick a human than to hack a system, which is why social engineering is the most common attack vector. There are many techniques (phishing, pretexting, baiting, and so on) and they evolve and get more sophisticated over time. All these types of attacks have psychological manipulation in common. This can include the use of authoritative roles (such as the attacker pretending to be a police officer), or the attacker using scarcity tactics (such as saying there are only five devices left at an ultra-cheap price in a special offer, which is a scam offer). These are just two examples but many more tactics use the weaknesses/desires that we all share as human beings.

"Social engineering bypasses all technologies, including firewalls."

– Kevin Mitnick

We all have received emails that claim to be from our bank or from a service that we use, asking us to click on a very suspicious link or to download a file. Most of these emails are phishing attacks that your email provider will detect and classify as spam. As technologists, we think that we are not going to fall for these kinds of attacks but the reality is that there are more and more sophisticated attacks that are targeting developers and that are very difficult to detect.

Let me introduce to you the **typosquatting** attack in the Node.js ecosystem. The attacker publishes a package with a very similar name to a popular package. Then, the attacker waits for someone to install the package by mistake. For example, you want to install the `lodash` package but you make a typo and instead install the `lodahs` package.

Two of the malicious activities that this can do are search for `.env` files in your project and send them to the attacker's server or install a backdoor in your application. There are many more activities, too.

We have seen this kind of attack in the past; for example, the popular `cross-env` package (`https://www.npmjs.com/package/cross-env`), which is used to set environment variables in a cross-platform way, has a malicious version called `crossenv` (`https://snyk.io/advisor/npm-package/crossenv`) that contains a malicious payload.

You can find more details about this kind of attack at `https://snyk.io/blog/typosquatting-attacks/`.

> **Information**
>
> Currently, npm has policies that prevent you from publishing packages with similar names to ones that have been previously published in order to prevent this kind of attack (`https://docs.npmjs.com/threats-and-mitigations#by-typosquatting--dependency-confusion`).

Risks in the supply chain

For many years, I was evangelizing about the importance of security in the supply chain. It is sometimes hard to understand the risks because the supply chain is not visible to us and the impact on our code is not as clear as a SQL injection or a memory leak.

In 2020, I wrote a blog post discussing how we can build a backdoor in a Node.js application using a malicious package from npm (`https://snyk.io/blog/what-is-a-backdoor/`). A backdoor is a piece of code that will allow us to take control of the application remotely. Basically, we have remote access to the operating system terminal to execute any command that we want with the privileges of the user who is running the application.

To make it more realistic, I created a malicious Express middleware that allows us to execute any command that we want in the operating system terminal. Then, I published the package in npm to make it available to the community. The package was called `browser-redirect` and the expected behavior was to redirect any user who was not using a Chromium-based browser to `https://browsehappy.com/`. To do that, you only need to use the package as a middleware in your Express application. The package performed the expected behavior but it also did more malicious things in the background, including adding specific headers to the HTTP response that helps find infected servers across the internet with tools such as Shodan (`https://www.shodan.io/`) and executing commands in the operating system terminal when certain conditions were met. This code didn't require any external library to perform any of the malicious activities, so the malicious payload was not easily recognizable when running scanning tools.

> **Information**
>
> You can find the blog post in the Snyk blog (`https://snyk.io/blog/what-is-a-backdoor/`) with a detailed explanation of the code execution, mitigation strategies, and much more.

The business impact

Any security incident has a direct impact on the business. We can lose our reputation and the trust of our customers. Also, the incident can directly affect our clients; for example, if we suffer a ransomware attack and we cannot provide the service to our customers or, even worse, if we lose the data of our customers, that can lead to legal problems and additional attacks directly targeting our customers.

Data breaches are so common that we don't even pay attention to them in the mass media. However, the impact on users can be very high. In recent years, we have seen many data breaches that have affected millions of users, providing access to information such as passwords, credit card details, payment logs, sexual orientation, criminal records, geolocation records, and so on. You can find a detailed ranking at `https://www.upguard.com/blog/biggest-data-breaches`.

In 2013, Troy Hunt (`https://www.troyhunt.com/about/`) created the website `https://haveibeenpwned.com/` where you can check whether your email address has been compromised in a data breach. You can also set up an alert to be notified if your email address appears in a new data breach.

Now that we have seen the importance of security in the business, let's see where we can start to learn more about security in the next section.

Where to start with security

Security is a vast topic, and it will require several books to cover all the aspects; even then, it will require more resources to keep it up to date. In this section, we will explore some resources to start learning but with a limited scope to the Node.js ecosystem and web application development.

We will learn about the OWASP Top 10, CVE, and CWE so we can have a clear compass to navigate through the security world as beginners.

OWASP Top 10 overview

Many possible attacks can affect our applications and we cannot cover all of them, so the task becomes overwhelming. To prioritize the most common attacks, the **Open Web Application Security Project** (**OWASP**) foundation created a list of the 10 most common attacks that affect web applications, and this is updated every few years. You can find the list at `https://owasp.org/www-project-top-ten`.

Let's see the list of the OWASP Top 10 for 2021:

- **A01:2021 Broken Access Control**
- **A02:2021 Cryptographic Failures**
- **A03:2021 Injection**
- **A04:2021 Insecure Design**
- **A05:2021 Security Misconfiguration**
- **A06:2021 Vulnerable and Outdated Components**
- **A07:2021 Identification and Authentication Failures**
- **A08:2021 Software and Data Integrity Failures**
- **A09:2021 Security Logging and Monitoring Failures**
- **A10:2021 Server Side Request Forgery (SSRF)**

I suggest you read the OWASP Top 10 carefully and try to find what the attacks have in common so you can understand the root cause of the attacks to help you define better strategies to mitigate them.

As an example, we can see that **A05 Security Misconfiguration** and **A06 - Vulnerable and Outdated Components** have a relationship with how we install and configure dependencies and how we keep them up to date. So, we can start to think about how to improve our CI/CD pipeline to automate the installation and updating of the dependencies and we can discuss whether we need a deeper understanding of the dependencies that we rely on. In a very specific case, this can be that we have an NGINX (reverse proxy) instance that is not properly configured and is outdated, and we need to put some effort into improving the configuration and updating the NGINX version regularly.

Another good way to understand the OWASP Top 10 is to compare the list over the years. For example, let's compare the OWASP Top 10 for 2017 with the OWASP Top 10 for 2021:

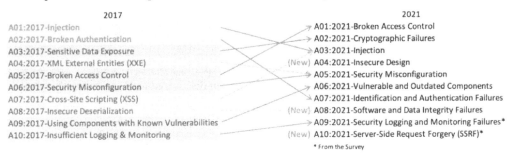

Figure 15.1 – Comparing OWASP TOP 10 from 2017 with 2021 (source: OWASP)

As you can see, there are some additions, deletions, and merges but, overall, the list is very similar with some changes in the order. This makes it easier to refresh your knowledge every few years when the list is updated.

CWE

The Owasp Top 10 includes references to the CWE, which is a community-developed list of common software and hardware weaknesses. You can find the list at `https://cwe.mitre.org/data/definitions/699.html`.

The CWE is a very extensive list and covers a lot of topics, so it is very difficult to read it all. However, it is a great resource to find more information about a specific topic. For example, let's look at **CWE-798: Use of Hard-coded Credentials** at `https://cwe.mitre.org/data/definitions/798.html`, which will show us a description, relationship with other CWEs, consequences, and much more.

CVE

The CVE is a list of publicly disclosed cybersecurity vulnerabilities. You can find the list at `https://cve.mitre.org/`. This list is different from the CWE as it is a list of vulnerabilities that have been discovered in specific software products and not a list of possible weaknesses.

In simple words, the CWE is a list of possible weaknesses, and the CVE is a list of vulnerabilities that have been discovered in the wild. We need to be very aware of the CVE that can potentially affect our applications and mitigate them as soon as possible. One common strategy is to subscribe to the security mailing list of the dependencies that we use in our applications so we can be notified when a new CVE is discovered, or use an automated tool such as Snyk (`https://snyk.io/`) that will notify us when a new CVE is discovered in our dependencies.

If we don't have a clear strategy to mitigate the CVE, we will feel overwhelmed very easily by the number of CVE that are discovered every day, especially in the Node.js ecosystem, where it is very common to have a lot of dependencies in our applications.

CVE in Node.js

If we visit `https://www.cvedetails.com/vulnerability-list/vendor_id-12113/Nodejs.html`, we can see the list of CVE that have been discovered in Node.js over the years.

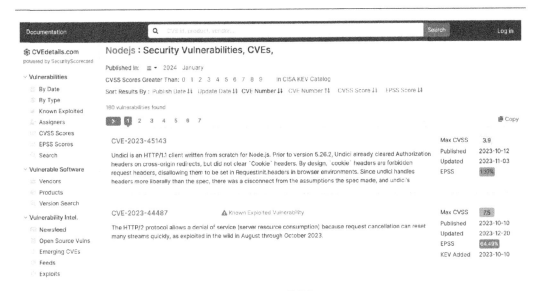

Figure 15.2 – CVE list

As you can see, we are going to pick the most recent one (**CVE-2023-45143**) and we are going to explore it in detail at `https://www.cvedetails.com/cve/CVE-2023-45143/`:

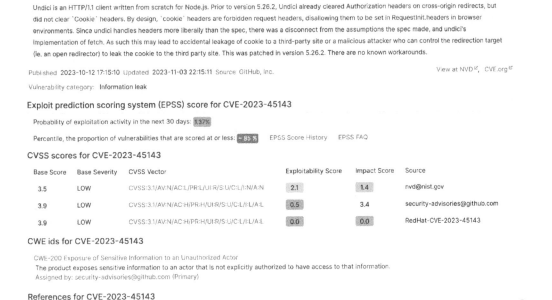

Figure 15.3 – CVE details

We should find a clear description of the vulnerability and references to the publication date. This will help us to determine whether we are affected by the vulnerability or not. Also, we can see the vulnerability category (in this case, **Information leak**) and the probability of exploitation activity in the next 30 days (in this case, **1.37%**). This will help us prioritize the mitigation of vulnerability, and the overall score will help us to determine the severity of the vulnerability.

With these things in mind, we can make a fast decision about the need for mitigation. Also, we can find a list of references that will help us to understand the vulnerability in more detail and also the CWEs that are related to the vulnerability.

It is up to us to decide how to mitigate the vulnerability. In some cases, we can just update the dependency to include the fix; in other cases, there is no fix available, and we need to find a workaround or remove the dependency. In other cases, we can just ignore the vulnerability as it is not relevant to our application because it has no impact.

As a recommendation, I suggest you perform the analysis with more colleagues so you can have different points of view and you can make a solid team decision.

> **Information**
>
> Node.js is doing a great job of keeping the CVE under control. You can find more information about each CVE in the Node.js blog. For example, **CVE-2023-45143** is described at `https://nodejs.org/en/blog/vulnerability/october-2023-security-releases`.

If you are developing modern frontend applications, you will probably use several libraries to build the application. Commonly, this becomes a great source of CVE because we have many transitive dependencies that we don't control. Also, it is not easy to upgrade the dependencies because we need to wait for the maintainers to update them and the compatibility with other dependencies. So, please evaluate carefully the dependencies that you use in your applications and divide them between the ones that are part of the running application and the ones that are part of the build process only. This will simplify the review process a lot.

Node.js threat model

Node.js has a threat model that is a great resource to understand how Node.js assesses the review of the vulnerabilities reported by the community. You can find the threat model at `https://github.com/nodejs/node/blob/main/SECURITY.md#the-nodejs-threat-model`, which we elaborated on in the Node.js Security Working Group (`https://github.com/nodejs/security-wg`).

One clear idea that we can extract from the threat model is that the Node.js project trusts many things by default, such as the dependencies that we use in our applications, our own code, or the infrastructure that we use to run our applications. This means that we are responsible for knowing what code is running in our applications (ours or from third parties) and ensuring that the infrastructure is secure.

The Node.js official recommendations

Aside from the threat model, in the Node.js Security Working Group, we have created a reference document that intends to extend the current threat model and provide extensive guidelines on how to secure a Node.js application. It includes a list of best practices that we recommend following to improve the security of your Node.js applications. We used a list of CWEs as the starting point with detailed mitigation strategies and recommendations:

- **Denial of Service of HTTP Server (CWE-400)**

- **DNS Rebinding (CWE-346)**

- **HTTP Request Smuggling (CWE-444)**

- **Information Exposure through Timing Attacks (CWE-208)**

- **Malicious Third-Party Modules (CWE-1357)**

- **Memory Access Violation (CWE-284)**

- **Monkey Patching (CWE-349)**

- **Prototype Pollution Attacks (CWE-1321)**

- **Uncontrolled Search Path Element (CWE-427)**

You can find the list at `https://nodejs.org/en/guides/security/`.

You can also find other popular community-built resources to get a better understanding of security in Node.js:

- *Node.js Best Practices* by Yoni Goldberg (`https://github.com/goldbergyoni/nodebestpractices`)

- *Awesome Node.js Security resources* by Liran Tal (`https://github.com/lirantal/awesome-nodejs-security`)

Now that we have a better understanding of security in Node.js, let's see how to improve the security of our web applications in more detail in the next section.

Improving the security of our applications

The tools and techniques that we are going to explore in this section are evolving very quickly, so I suggest you keep an eye on the Node.js Security Working Group (`https://github.com/nodejs/security-wg`) and the community to be aware of the latest trends. However, here is a solid checklist that you can use to improve the security of your applications:

- **Encrypt**: As we saw in *Chapter 13*, encryption is the backbone of security in the modern internet. We need to encrypt the data in transit and at rest. Also, we need to think about encrypting sensitive data in the database so we can reduce the risk of a data breach. As an example, in *Chapter 13*, we used the bcrypt library (https://www.npmjs.com/package/bcrypt) to encrypt the user's password in our project:

```
userSchema.pre('save', async function (next) {
  const user = this
  if (user.isModified('password')) {
    const salt = await bcrypt.genSalt()
    user.password = await bcrypt.hash(
user.password, salt
    )
  }
  next()
})
```

- **Sanitize the input**: When we receive data from a user or a third-party service, we need to sanitize the data to prevent injection attacks (SQL injections, Cross-site scripting (XSS), and so on) but this is not limited only to the user input. We also need to sanitize all the input that we receive from third parties or I/O operations such as reading a file, reading from a database, reading from a network socket, and so on. We can use libraries such as validator (https://www.npmjs.com/package/validator) or joi (https://www.npmjs.com/package/joi) to validate the data. For example, you can validate an email easily as follows:

```
import validator from 'validator';
validator.isEmail('foo@bar.com'); //=> true
validator.isEmail('<script>alert("XSS")</script>'); //=> false
```

- **Improve the default settings**: We tend to think that the default settings are secure but that is not always true. For example, the default settings of Express regarding HTTP headers are not as opinionated as we would think. We can use libraries such as helmet (https://helmetjs.github.io/) to increase the security of our applications. You can find a great guide on how to implement helmet at https://blog.ulisesgascon.com/how-to-use-helmet-in-express.

- **Keep logs**: The OWASP Top 10 (**A09:2021 – Security Logging and Monitoring Failures**) is very clear about the importance of keeping logs. We can use libraries such as pino (https://getpino.io/) to keep logs securely and we can use this information to audit the application and abuse from third parties. You can find a great guide on how to implement pino with Express in the official documentation (https://getpino.io/#/docs/web?id=pino-with-express).

- **Monitor**: We need to understand what is going on with the application once it is deployed and exposed to the internet. Monitoring the application will help us detect downtimes, performance issues, and much more. We can include alerts to understand whether we are having issues in real time. We can use New Relic (https://newrelic.com/), Datadog (https://www.

datadoghq.com/), or Sentry (https://sentry.io/welcome/). You can find a great guide on how to implement Sentry with Express in the official documentation (https://docs.sentry.io/platforms/node/guides/express/).

- **Track your dependencies**: You need to know your dependencies and keep them up to date. You can use Snyk (https://snyk.io/) or Socket (https://socket.dev/) to monitor the dependencies, be notified when a new CVE is discovered, and even automate the update of the dependencies.

- **Backup and recovery**: You need to have a backup for your critical information and to have a recovery plan in case of a disaster. Even if you don't suffer from a security incident, you could suffer from a natural disaster such as a fire or a flood in the data center where your information is stored. If you are depending on a cloud provider, you need to understand how multi-region replication works and how to recover the data in the case of a disaster.

- **Reduce the attack surface**: Sometimes, we code much more than is required by the business logic inside the core of our business. Each line of code that we write is a potential risk, so we can reduce the attack surface by using APIs in the areas that are security-critical. For example, we can use Auth0 (https://auth0.com/) to handle the authentication and authorization for us or Stripe (https://stripe.com/) to handle the payments. This will reduce the amount of code that we need to write and maintain, and sensitive information such as credit card numbers will be handled by a third party that is an expert in the area. Of course, we need to trust the third party and understand the cost of the service.

- **Enforce Two-factor authentication (2FA) in your services**: We need to enforce 2FA in all the services that we use to run our company activities (Slack, GSuite, and so on) and the infrastructure that we use to run our applications (Github, AWS, Azure, and so on). This will reduce the risk of a social engineering attack. Also, it would be great if we could implement 2FA in our own applications to mitigate the risk of a stolen password from a user.

- **Review the secrets**: Leaking secrets is a very common mistake that we can make. We can use tools such as GitGuardian (https://www.gitguardian.com/) to scan our repositories and be notified if we have leaked secrets.

- **Implement good practices**: There are many good practices that we can follow as a team to improve the security of our applications. For example, use a control version, use pull requests to review the changes, use a CI/CD tool to automate the review of the code, and so on.

- **Automation**: Once you have a CI/CD tool in place, you can automate many tasks, even those related to infrastructure. For example, you can use Terraform (https://www.terraform.io/) to automate the creation of the infrastructure and to reduce human errors.

- **Keep learning**: Security is no different from any other technical topic; it is evolving very fast and we need to keep learning.

- **Use a secure protocol**: We need to use secure protocols such as HTTPS to protect the communication between the client and the server.

Put it into practice

Now that we have a checklist and a better understanding of security in Node.js, I suggest you go through the application that we built in the previous chapters and review the application to find possible improvements to make it more secure.

Here are some ideas to get started:

- Review the dependencies and check whether there are any known vulnerabilities
- Use a linter to enforce the code style
- Use a static code analysis tool to find possible bugs, such as SonarQube or CodeQL
- Add key libraries to improve security, such as `helmet` or `validator`
- Add a control version system and use a CI/CD tool to automate the review of the code, such as Github Actions
- Add a control version system to review the changes in pull requests

In the next section, we will explore how we can take advantage of our security knowledge to become an ethical hacker.

Becoming an ethical hacker

When we think about hackers, we tend to think about cyber criminals who are trying to steal our data or take control of our systems. In reality, it is not that simple. Let's read the definition of a hacker from the paper *How Hackers Think: A Study of Cybersecurity Experts and Their Mental Models* (`https://papers.ssrn.com/sol3/papers.cfm?abstract_id=2326634`).

> *"Regardless of what type of hacker a person is, identifying system weaknesses requires logical reasoning and the ability to systematically think through possible actions, alternatives, and potential conclusions. This combination of reasoning and systematic thinking implies the use of mental models. Hacking is a cognitive activity that requires exceptional technical and reasoning abilities."*

So, basically, we are talking about a person with high technical skills who is doing things by thinking out of the box. The problem is not the activity itself but the intention behind the activity.

Today, we define an ethical hacker as a hacker who does things with good intentions. For example, when you are doing a penetration test on your own application to find possible vulnerabilities, you are doing ethical hacking. Sometimes, you end up discovering vulnerabilities in other applications/libraries/services that you don't own. In those cases, we can face two different scenarios: doing a **coordinated vulnerability disclosure** (previously known as a **responsible disclosure**) or trying a **bug bounty program**.

Coordinated vulnerability disclosure (CVD)

When you discover a vulnerability in a third-party application/library/service, you can contact the owner of the application/library/service and explain the vulnerability and how to mitigate it. While the process seems simple, it is not always easy.

First of all, an unknown vulnerability can affect many users, companies, and services. So, you need to be very careful about how you communicate the vulnerability and to whom. Also, this will require a validation process to ensure that the vulnerability is real and that it is not a false positive. Then, it is expected that a patch will be developed and made available to the affected services before the public disclosure is done.

To make the process easier, many companies and open source projects have a security policy that explains how to report a vulnerability and what to expect from the process. For example, you can find the Node.js security policy at `https://nodejs.org/en/security/`:

> *"Normally your report will be acknowledged within 5 days, and you'll receive a more detailed response to your report within 10 days indicating the next steps in handling your submission. These timelines may extend when our triage volunteers are away on holiday, particularly at the end of the year.*
>
> *After the initial reply to your report, the security team will endeavor to keep you informed of the progress being made towards a fix and full announcement, and may ask for additional information or guidance surrounding the reported issue."*

Other companies, such as Google, have a dedicated website to report vulnerabilities in their products (`https://www.google.com/about/appsecurity/`).

Bounty programs

Some companies and open source projects have a bounty program that will reward you for finding vulnerabilities in their applications/libraries/services. Actually, the scenario is very similar to CVD but, in this case, you have clear rules regarding engagement and boundaries.

Let's see the Node.js bounty program at `https://hackerone.com/nodejs` to get a better understanding of the process. We also have a hacktivity page (`https://hackerone.com/nodejs/hacktivity`) where we can see the reports that have been submitted and the status of the reports with plenty of details, including the rewards.

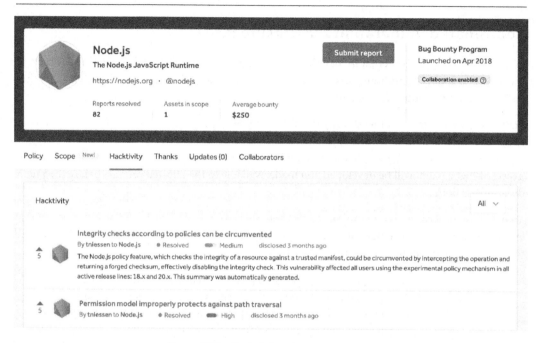

Figure 15.4 – Node.js bug bounty program

As you can see in the figure, there is a list of disclosure information that leads, in many cases, to security patches. Feel free to explore them and see how the communication was made and how the process worked in each case. You can learn a lot from these disclosed reports.

Getting the skills

Building software is different from breaking software. The are many skills that you need to learn and some tools to get familiar with. One great overview of the skills that you need to learn is `https://roadmap.sh/`, which has a section dedicated to cybersecurity (`https://roadmap.sh/cyber-security`).

In order to get more practical skills, you can use the *Hack the Box* platform (`https://www.hackthebox.eu/`), which will allow you to practice your skills in a safe environment. The challenges in *Hack the Box* are used as a learning tool by many hackers and security professionals in the community, so you can find a lot of write-ups on the internet that will help you to solve the challenges when you get stuck.

Summary

In this chapter, we explored the importance of security in modern web applications and the impact that a security incident can have on the business. Then, we learned how to get started with security in our day-to-day work by using OWASP, CWE, CVE, the Node.js threat model, and the official Node.js best practices.

Additionally, we learned how we can raise the security of our applications by using a simple checklist and how to apply it in our application.

Finally, we learned how to take advantage of our security knowledge to become an ethical hacker.

In the next chapter, we are going to learn how to deploy our application to the internet and local devices in a different way.

Further reading

- *CVE-2020-19909 is everything that is wrong with CVEs*: https://daniel.haxx.se/blog/2023/08/26/cve-2020-19909-is-everything-that-is-wrong-with-cves/

- *Auditing package dependencies for security vulnerabilities*: https://docs.npmjs.com/auditing-package-dependencies-for-security-vulnerabilities

- *OWASP NPM Security best practices*: https://cheatsheetseries.owasp.org/cheatsheets/NPM_Security_Cheat_Sheet.html#npm-security-best-practices

- *DEFCON – The Full Documentary*: https://www.youtube.com/watch?v=3ctQOmjQyYg

- *State of Open Source Security 2023*: https://snyk.io/reports/open-source-security/

- *Threats and Mitigations*: https://docs.npmjs.com/threats-and-mitigations#by-typosquatting--dependency-confusion

Part 5: Mastering Node.js Deployment and Portability

In *Part 5*, we will deploy our application to the public internet. We will learn how to decide the best approach based on our requirements, then we will use virtual machines in DigitalOcean to deploy the application using PM2, and we will also learn how to dockerize our application for better portability.

We will use GitHub to store our application code, and we will learn how to create a continuous deployment pipeline for our projects.

Our last step in the journey will be to use Cloudflare to manage our domain and the SSL certificates and we will explore the Twelve-Factor App principles.

This part has the following chapters:

- *Chapter 16, Deploying Node.js Applications*
- *Chapter 17, Dockerizing a Node.js Application*

16

Deploying Node.js Applications

In this chapter, we will learn how to deploy our application to the public internet. We will learn how important it is to have a clear definition of the requirements and how to choose the best solution for our needs. We will push the application code to the GitHub repository in order to use GitHub Actions for continuous integration.

Finally, We will deploy the application in DigitalOcean and we will use PM2 to keep the application running. We will configure and use MongoDB Atlas to host the database in the cloud.

To sum up, here are the main topics that we will explore in this chapter:

- How to define the requirements and how to choose the best solution for our needs
- How to push the application code to the GitHub repository
- How to use MongoDB Atlas to host the database as an external resource
- How to use DigitalOcean Droplet to host the application
- How to use PM2 to keep the application running

Technical requirements

You will need to create accounts with the following providers in order to follow the examples in this chapter:

- DigitalOcean: `https://www.digitalocean.com/`
- MongoDB Atlas: `https://www.mongodb.com/docs/atlas/tutorial/create-atlas-account/`
- GitHub: `https://github.com/signup`

The code files for the chapter can be found at `https://github.com/PacktPublishing/NodeJS-for-Beginners`.

Check out the code in action video for this chapter on `https://youtu.be/cWkqR2xJJ0k`

> **Note**
>
> We will use DigitalOcean to host the application, but you can use any other provider or even your own laptop (as an alternative). If you don't have a DigitalOcean account, you can create one here: `https://www.digitalocean.com/`.

Defining the requirements

We have the application working on our computer, but we need to deploy it to the public internet. So, we need to define the requirements in order to choose the best solution for our needs.

First of all, we need to consider the following technical questions:

- *What is the target environment (bare metal, VMs, containers, cloud solutions...)?* As our application uses Node.js and standard NPM libraries, we can deploy it easily directly in bare metal machines or VMs. Other solutions are also possible but require some work to be done in terms of configuration.

- *What is the target platform (AWS, Azure, GCP, DigitalOcean, Heroku...)?* In our case, we don't expect much traffic or many users at all. Also, we are not working in a team and don't have any specific requirements, such as a Service-Level Agreement (SLA). We can safely choose to use the most simple provider in terms of the onboarding process that also has competitive pricing. In our case, we will use DigitalOcean.

- *What is the target operating system (Linux, Windows, macOS...)?* Node.js is capable of running on common and exotic operating systems. Our application does not have any special dependencies on an operating system so we can easily choose Linux as it is the most popular OS for servers and also has the most extensive offering of the providers.

- *What is the target architecture (x86, ARM...)?* In this case, our application is pure JavaScript. Node.js supports both architectures (x86 and ARM), so we can easily choose x86 because it is a more common architecture for servers, often with lower prices.

- *What is the target Node.js version (18, 20, 21...)?* We have a clear dependency on Node.js 20.11.0, as we used this version while developing the application, but we can be sure that the application should work on any Node.js 20 LTS version.

- *What is the target database (MongoDB, MySQL, PostgreSQL, Redis...)?* We depend on MongoDB, so we need to consider that as a dependency for our infrastructure decisions. Aside from this, there are no more external dependencies or services that we depend on. Managing a database is not simple, so in this case, we can safely choose any managed service. MongoDB provides MongoDB Atlas (`https://www.mongodb.com/atlas/database`) as their cloud solution for MongoDB in the cloud. Also, the free tier should cover our needs.

So, as a summary, we will deploy the application that we have been building in the previous chapters. We will deploy a Node.js application with Express. The only external dependency is MongoDB. We will use a Linux machine with x86 architecture and the Node.js 20.x version. Also, we will use MongoDB Atlas to host the database so we don't need to worry a lot about the operational aspects of the database.

Also, we need to consider the following things that are relevant to the team and the project, especially if we are working in a professional environment, if we plan to deploy an application for a long time, or expect to scale soon:

- What is the budget?
- How many deployments are we expecting?
- What is the team size?
- What is the team's experience and knowledge?

It is not the same to deploy a Node.js application for a pet project as for a big company with aggressive **Service-Level Agreements (SLAs)** and an infrastructure team with a lot of experience.

In our case, I will assume that this is the first time that you are deploying a Node.js application. Also, I will assume a limited budget, experience, and time to invest in maintaining the infrastructure, so we will try the cheapest option possible. Certainly, we won't have a lot of deployments and we won't have a lot of traffic. So, we don't need to worry about scalability, performance, or high availability.

Overall, we have two main options that we will explore in this chapter and the next one:

- Deploying the application on a bare metal machine or VM
- Deploying the application in a cloud solution

You can deploy the application on a bare-metal machine, which can be an old laptop, a **single-board computer (SBC)** such as a Raspberry Pi, or a virtual machine on your own computer. In this scenario, you can choose to enable remote access to the machine or not. But in any case, this is a good option to learn and test the application.

Another option is to face the public internet and deploy the application in a cloud solution. There are many providers with a big product offering out there. So, in order to keep this simple, I will focus on a single provider for the compute resources (DigitalOcean) and a single provider for the database (MongoDB Atlas).

In the next section, we will create the GitHub repository, and we will push the code to the repository.

Using a GitHub repository

We will use GitHub to host the code and deploy the application. We will use GitHub Actions to run the tests and to check the code quality. We will then use GitHub to pull the code from the repository and deploy the application.

Creating a GitHub repository

You can create a new repository using this guide: `https://docs.github.com/en/repositories/creating-and-managing-repositories/quickstart-for-repositories`

In my case, I created a repository called `nodejs-for-beginners`, as you can see in the screenshot:

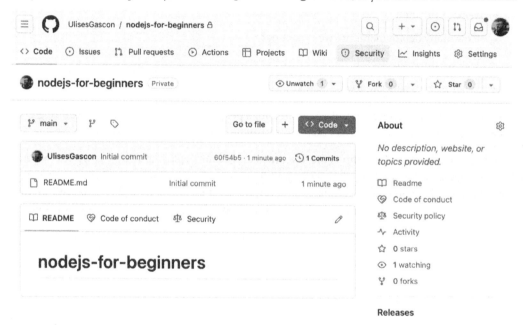

Figure 16.1– Web Browser Screenshot of the repository created

Now that we have a repository ready, it is time to start using it by adding our code to it.

Pushing the code to the repository

You will need to download the project from `https://github.com/PacktPublishing/NodeJS-for-Beginners/archive/refs/heads/main.zip` and access the `step4` folder, and then you will need to push the code to the repository. You need to be sure that the `package.json` file is present in the root folder of the repository.

Here are two guides that can help you to push the code to the repository:

- How to clone a repository: `https://docs.github.com/en/repositories/creating-and-managing-repositories/cloning-a-repository`

- How to push code: `https://docs.github.com/en/get-started/using-git/pushing-commits-to-a-remote-repository`

> **Note**
>
> In order to simplify the process, we are going to use only the `main` branch. But in the real world, most teams use multiple branches to manage their code so they can use great features such as pull requests, code reviews, and so on. That is out of the scope of this book.

Once this is done, the repository should look like this:

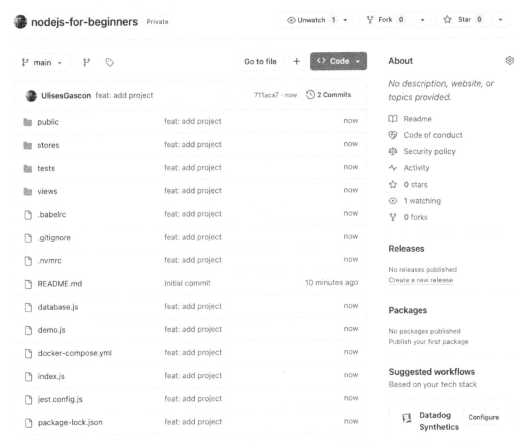

Figure 16.2 – Web browser screenshot of the repository with the files and folders added

> **Note**
>
> If you are having issues running the project in this chapter while following the steps, or you tried an alternative approach, you can use the `step5` folder from the source code that you downloaded at the beginning of the chapter to compare and fix possible bugs more easily.

In the next section, we will implement continuous integration with GitHub Actions. This is a great way to ensure that the application is working as expected.

Continuous integration with GitHub Actions

We can understand continuous integration as a way to do automatic checks on the code. This will help us to reduce human errors and will help us to mechanize the process of checking the project's quality.

This is an optional step that is not required in order to deploy the application, but if you want to get a better understanding of professional development environments, you can follow along.

So, the first step is to define what we expect from the automation and then we can implement it. In our case, we want to install the dependencies, run the linter, and run the tests. And we want to do this every time that we push code to the repository.

In order to implement this, we will create the `.github/workflows/ci.yml` file with the following content:

```
name: Continous Integration
on: [push]
jobs:
  check:
    runs-on: ubuntu-latest
    steps:
      - uses: actions/checkout@v3
      - name: Install dependencies
        run: npm install
      - name: Check code style
        run: npm run lint
      - name: Generate a random JWT secret
        id: generate-secret
        run: echo "::set-output name=JWT_SECRET::$(openssl rand
-base64 30)"
        shell: bash
      - name: Prepare environment
        run: npm run infra:start
      - name: Run tests
        run: npm test
        env:
          MONGODB_URI: mongodb://localhost:27017/whispering-database
          PORT: 3000
          SALT_ROUNDS: 10
          JWT_SECRET: ${{ steps.generate-secret.outputs.JWT_SECRET }}
```

This YAML file defines a workflow called **Continous Integration** that will be triggered every time we push code to the repository. This workflow will run in a virtual machine with Ubuntu and it will run the following steps:

1. Check the code from the repository.

2. Install the dependencies by running the npm install command.

3. Run the linter by running the npm run lint command.

4. Generate a random JWT secret. We generate a random string with 30 characters that will be used as a JWT secret later on.

5. Prepare the environment by running the npm run infra:start command.

6. Run the tests with the MONGODB_URI, PORT, SALT_ROUNDS, and JWT_SECRET environment variables, and we will use the JWT secret generated in the previous step.

Once we push the code to the repository, we can check the status of the workflow in the **Actions** tab:

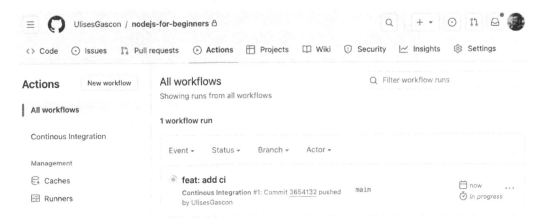

Figure 16.3 – Web browser screenshot showing the GitHub actions

If we click on the workflow, we can see the details of it:

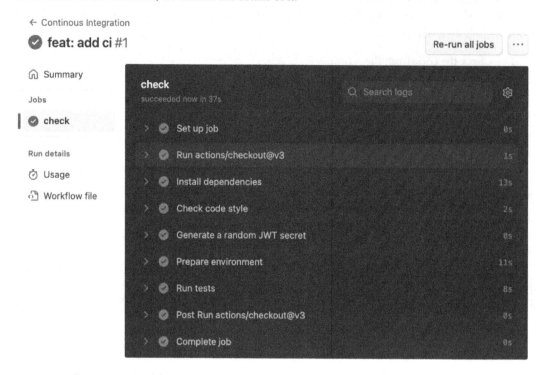

Figure 16.4 – Web browser screenshot showing the GitHub Action execution details

As we can see, all the checks are passing, so we can be confident that the application is working as expected.

We can click on the **Run tests** step to see the details of the tests:

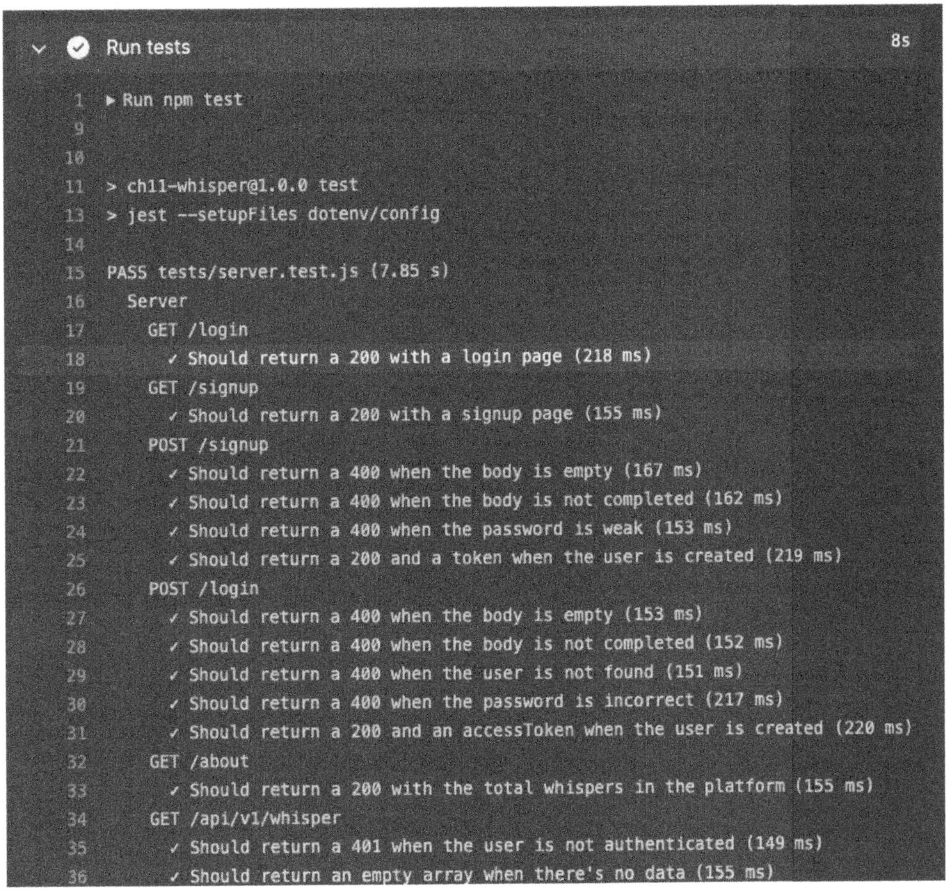

Figure 16.5 – Web browser screenshot showing the tests execution step in detail

As you can see, the tests are passing, the same way as on our local machine. Ultimately, the continuous integration machine is just a remote machine that will follow the steps that we define, and it is not very different from our own environment in that respect.

Now, that we have the continuous integration in place, we can start thinking about preparing the MongoDB instance using Atlas in the next section.

Using MongoDB Atlas

We will use MongoDB Atlas to host the database. We will create a free tier cluster and we will use the connection string to connect to the database.

Here are some guides that will help you:

- How to create a free tier cluster: `https://docs.atlas.mongodb.com/tutorial/create-new-cluster/`

- How to connect to the database: `https://www.mongodb.com/docs/atlas/driver-connection/`

In my case, I created a free tier cluster called `nodejs-for-beginners`, as you can see in the following screenshot:

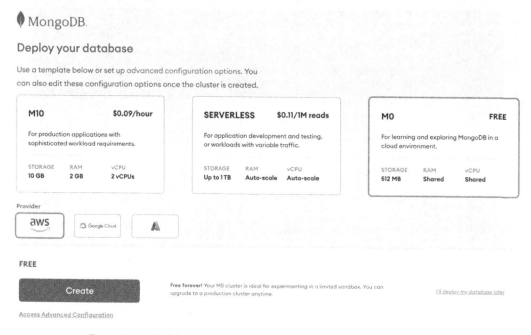

Figure 16.6 – Web browser screenshot showing the cluster creation details

At the end of the process, you will have a connection string like this (but with your own credentials):

```
mongodb+srv://<username>:<password>@<cluster-url>/
test?retryWrites=true&w=majority
```

You can use that connection string to connect to the database from the application. You only need to replace the value of the MONGODB_URI environment variable with the new connection string in the .env file.

It is important to notice that the username and password need to be URI encoded, so the special characters are converted. This can easily be done with the `encodeURIComponent` function (`https://developer.mozilla.org/en-US/docs/Web/JavaScript/Reference/Global_Objects/encodeURIComponent`). Here is a conversion example:

```
encodeURIComponent('P@ssword') // P%40ssword
```

If you run the test or run the application locally, you will see that the application is using the new database and the data is persisted in the cloud, as expected.

In the following screenshot, you can see the data in the database:

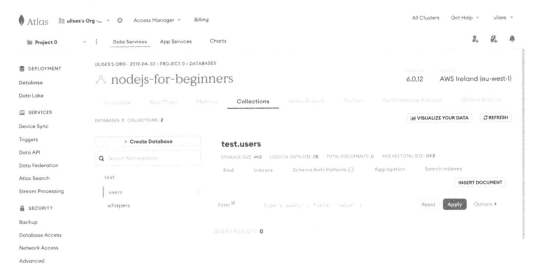

Figure 16.7 – Web browser screenshot showing the project details

> **Note**
>
> Once you are ready with the database, you can restore the `.env` file to the original state to avoid polluting the database with test data in future executions.

Now, that we have the external database ready, we can start thinking about deploying the application. In the next section, we will prepare the application using PM2.

Deploying Node.js applications with PM2

This is a very *exciting* moment! We are about to make our application available on the public internet. In this case, we will use a DigitalOcean Droplet to host the application. A Droplet is a virtual machine with Ubuntu 23.10 and 0.5 GB of RAM that will host the application. We will use PM2 to keep the application running and to restart it if it crashes.

If you don't want to use DigitalOcean, as an alternative, you can use an old computer that has at least 4 GB RAM, Ubuntu (or another Linux distro), and have SSH communication enabled (no need to install Node.js or deploy a website at this point). An old laptop is a great option or even a Raspberry PI (3, 4, or 5) (`https://www.raspberrypi.com/`) with Raspbian (`https://www.raspberrypi.com/software/`) will do the job. Here, you can find two tutorials that will help you with the setup:

- `https://www.xda-developers.com/turn-old-laptop-into-home-server/`
- `https://www.youtube.com/watch?v=iSAF8D8rp0o`

If the setup was done properly, you can skip the next section and jump directly to the *Preparing the machine* section.

Creating a DigitalOcean Droplet

We will use DigitalOcean to host the application. We will use the most basic, cheap Droplet possible, currently with 512 MB RAM and 1 virtual CPU.

> **Note**
>
> We will use the SSH key to access the machine, so please follow this guide if you don't know how to do it:
>
> `https://docs.digitalocean.com/products/droplets/how-to/add-ssh-keys/`

In my case, I created a Droplet called `nodejs-for-beginners`, as you can see in the following screenshot:

Figure 16.8 – Web browser screenshot showing the droplet details

As you can see, the droplet is available at the IP address 144.126.217.34 and we will use that IP address to access the machine using SSH or HTTP when the application is running.

Connecting to the machine

There are many ways to access the machine with SSH. The most common is to use the terminal directly. But in this case, we will use VSCode to connect to the machine. You can follow the guide at https://code.visualstudio.com/docs/remote/ssh to learn how to do it as it is more convenient than directly connect from your terminal to the machine.

In both cases, we need to use the same credentials. The username is root and the password is replaced by your SSH key that was added to your Droplet.

Now that we are able to connect to the machine, it is time to start setting up the environment.

Preparing the machine

Once you are connected to the machine, you can run the following commands in the terminal in order to create the working directory and access the new directory created:

```
mkdir nodejs-for-beginners
cd nodejs-for-beginners
```

Then we will install Node.js 20.11.0 using nvm:

```
apt update
wget -qO- https://raw.githubusercontent.com/creationix/nvm/v0.39.3/
install.sh | bash
source ~/.profile
nvm --version
nvm install 20.11.0
```

The output should be something like this:

```
Downloading and installing node v20.11.0...
Downloading https://nodejs.org/dist/v20.11.0/node-v20.11.0-linux-x64.
tar.xz...
################################################################################
############################ 100.0%
Computing checksum with sha256sum
Checksums matched!
Now using node v20.11.0 (npm v10.2.4)
Creating default alias: default -> 20.11.0 (-> v20.11.0)
```

The next step is to install PM2 globally on the machine:

```
npm install pm2 -g
```

You can check the version of PM2 with the following:

```
pm2 --version
```

The output should be something like this:

```
[PM2] PM2 Successfully daemonized
5.2.2
```

Now, we have the machine ready to work with our code. Our next step will be to bring the application code to our machine.

Cloning the repository

If you are using a private repository, you will need to add the SSH key to the machine. You can follow the guide at https://docs.github.com/en/github/authenticating-to-github/connecting-to-github-with-ssh, but you can prevent this step if you make the repository public.

Then we will clone the repository:

```
git clone https://github.com/YOUR-USER/YOUR-REPO.git
```

We can check that the code is present in the folder by checking the directory in VSCode or by running the following command:

```
ls -la
```

This command will list all files, including hidden ones, in the current directory, and show detailed information about these files. The output should be something like this:

```
README.md       docker-compose.yml   node_modules       public      tests
coverage        index.js             package-lock.json   server.js   utils.js
database.js     jest.config.js       package.json        stores      views
```

We can confirm that the code has been downloaded, so our next step will be to install the dependencies.

Installing the dependencies

After cloning the repository, we will install the dependencies:

```
npm install
```

This might take a while as the machine is not very powerful, but it should finish without errors. If you have errors or the process is much longer than expected, you can try to increase the size of the Droplet, but this will increase the price per hour.

Preparing the environment

We will create a .env file as we did in the previous chapters, but we will use the connection string of the MongoDB Atlas cluster that we created in the previous section.

Once this is ready, the application is ready to run, but we will use PM2 to keep the application running and restart it if it crashes.

Managing the application with PM2

We decided to use PM2 as the process manager for our application, so you won't start the application directly using node command like node index.js. We will let PM2 handle the application lifecycle.

We will start the application with PM2:

```
pm2 start index.js
```

We can check the status of the application with the following:

```
pm2 status
```

We can check the logs of the application with this:

```
pm2 logs
```

We can stop the application with this:

```
pm2 stop index.js
```

Now, we can start the application again with PM2 and check whether the application is available through the internet.

Accessing the application

Now, we can access the application using the IP address of the Droplet. In my case, the IP address is 144.126.217.34 and the application is running in port 3000, so I can access the application using the following URL: http://144.126.217.34:3000.

> **Note**
>
> If you are using a different host, such as a machine in your local network, this might be different, as it will depend on your local network configuration and/or firewalls. But if your network is correctly set up, then you should be able to access the website by using the IP address of the machine in your local network, for example, 192.168.1.44.

We can see the application running as expected:

Photo by Brooke Cagle from Unsplash

Figure 16.9 – Web browser screenshot showing the project running using the droplet IP

Yes! The application is running as expected. We'll explore another way to run our application in the next chapter, but this time we will use Docker.

Summary

In this chapter, we learned how to deploy our application to the public internet. We learned how important it is to have a clear definition of the requirements and how to choose the best solution for our needs. We created accounts with the providers that we used in this chapter and we pushed the application code to the GitHub repository to have proper source control in place.

Finally, we used MongoDB Atlas to host the database as an external resource and we used a DigitalOcean Droplet to host the application. We learned how to use PM2 to keep the application running.

Further reading

- How To Set Up a Node.js Application for Production on Ubuntu 22.04: `https://www.digitalocean.com/community/tutorials/how-to-set-up-a-node-js-application-for-production-on-ubuntu-22-04`

- Express Production best practices: `https://expressjs.com/en/advanced/best-practice-performance.html`

17

Dockerizing a Node.js Application

In this chapter, we will learn how to deploy our application to the public internet using Docker. We will explore how we can use GitHub Actions to ensure that our Docker images are working well in the **continuous integration** (**CI**) pipeline.

We will learn how to Dockerize the application and publish the image to Docker Hub for better portability so we can download our images in different environments.

Finally, we will discuss how to do a proper domain setup and how to add a **Secure Sockets Layer** (**SSL**) certificate to the application using Cloudflare. We will also explore the Twelve-Factor App principles.

To sum up, here are the main topics that we will explore in this chapter:

- How to use GitHub Actions for CI
- How to use DigitalOcean Droplet to host the Docker application
- How to use Docker to build the application and publish the image to Docker Hub
- How to do a proper domain setup and add an SSL certificate to the application using Cloudflare
- What are the Twelve-Factor App principles and how can they help you grow?

Technical requirements

To start working on this chapter, we need to continue with the code that we uploaded to GitHub in the previous chapter. If you haven't completed the previous chapter you can download the project from `https://github.com/PacktPublishing/NodeJS-for-Beginners/archive/refs/heads/main.zip` and access the `step5` folder as a reference.

You will need to create accounts with the following providers in order to follow the examples in this chapter:

- Docker Hub: `https://hub.docker.com/signup`

- Cloudflare: `https://www.cloudflare.com/` (optional)

The code files for the chapter can be found at `https://github.com/PacktPublishing/NodeJS-for-Beginners`.

Checkout the code in action video for this chapter on `https://youtu.be/VWBuF_Q3KPY`

Containers and cloud-native solutions with Docker

While using a VM is a good option, it is not the best option for many applications. Currently, containers are the most popular way to deploy applications. Containers are lightweight, portable, and easy to use. In this section, we will learn how to deploy a Node.js application using Docker.

We covered the basics of Docker in previous chapters and we have been using Docker and Docker Compose to run the MongoDB database. We now need to learn how to create a Docker image for our application and how to deploy it.

Docker lifecycle

We need to have a clear understanding of the Docker lifecycle to use it properly. Let's start with a brief introduction. In the following figure, we can see the Docker lifecycle:

Figure 17.1 – Docker lifecycle diagram

We need to start with a `Dockerfile`, which is a file that contains the instructions to build the image. Then, we can build the image with the `docker build` command. We can then run the container with the `docker run` command.

If we want to share the image with other people, we can push the image to a registry with the `docker push` command. Then, other people can pull the image from the registry with the `docker pull` command. This last step is quite similar to `npm publish` but, instead of sharing the code, we are sharing the image.

Now that we are clear on the theory, let's Dockerize our application in the next section.

Dockerizing the application

In your local machine, using Docker Desktop 1.18, you can run docker init in the project root folder (where package.json is located) to create a Dockerfile (see https://docs.docker.com/engine/reference/commandline/init/). So, we can create the files automatically with an interactive process:

```
Let's get started!

? What application platform does your project use? Node
? What version of Node do you want to use? 20.11.0
? Which package manager do you want to use? npm
? What command do you want to use to start the app? npm start
? What port does your server listen on? 3000

CREATED: .dockerignore
CREATED: Dockerfile
CREATED: compose.yaml


✔  Your Docker files are ready!
```

This tool will create the following files: .dockerignore, dockerfile, and compose.yaml. We will use dockerfile to build the image and we will use compose.yaml to run the container.

The Dockerfile will look like this:

```
# syntax=docker/dockerfile:1
ARG NODE_VERSION=20.11.0
FROM node:${NODE_VERSION}-alpine
ENV NODE_ENV production
WORKDIR /usr/src/app
RUN --mount=type=bind,source=package.json,target=package.json \
    --mount=type=bind,source=package-lock.json,target=package-lock.
json \
    --mount=type=cache,target=/root/.npm \
    npm ci --omit=dev
USER node
COPY . .
EXPOSE 3000
CMD npm start
```

This is a `Dockerfile` that sets up a Node.js environment inside a Docker container. It starts by specifying the Node.js version to use (`20.11.0`) and uses the Alpine version of the Node.js image for a smaller footprint. It sets the `NODE_ENV` environment variable to `production`. It then sets the working directory inside the container to `/usr/src/app`. The `RUN` command mounts the `package.json` and `package-lock.json` files from the host to the container and also sets up a cache for npm modules. It then runs `npm ci --omit=dev` to install the `production` dependencies only. It changes the user to `node` for security reasons, copies all files from the current directory on the host to the current directory in the container, exposes port `3000` for the application to be accessible, and finally, sets the command to start the application to `npm start`.

For our current application, we can remove the `compose.yaml` file as we don't need it. It is important to review the content in the `.dockerignore` file as it excludes some files from the build process when we execute the `COPY . .` command in the Dockerfile.

We have all the files needed to properly use Docker to manage our application, so in the next section, we will cover that in detail.

Managing the application with Docker

In the previous chapter, we used PM2 to manage the application. This time, we will use Docker. We can build the image with the following:

```
docker build -t nodejs-for-beginners .
```

Then, we can run the container with the following command, which will expose port `3000` and will use specific environment variables:

```
docker run \
-e MONGODB_URI='mongodb+srv://<username>:<password>@<cluster-url>/
test?retryWrites=true&w=majority' \
-e PORT='3000' \
-e SALT_ROUNDS='10' \
-e JWT_SECRET='Tu1fo0mO0PcAvjq^q3wQ24BXNI8$9R' \
-p 3000:3000 \
nodejs-for-beginners
```

You will need to replace `mongodb+srv://<username>:<password>@<cluster-url>/test?retryWrites=true&w=majority` with the connection string of your MongoDB Atlas cluster.

If you open the browser and access `http://localhost:3000`, you will see the application running as expected.

Now that we know that the Dockerized application is working fine, we can add a step in the CI to ensure that the Docker image is properly generated.

Adding docker build to the CI

We can add the `docker build` step to the CI process to ensure that the image is built correctly. We can add the following step to the CI process in `.github/workflows/ci.yml`:

```
- name: Build Docker image
  run: docker build -t nodejs-for-beginners .
```

Once you commit these changes, you can check the status of the workflow in the **Actions** tab. You will see that the workflow is passing, including the new `Build Docker image` step:

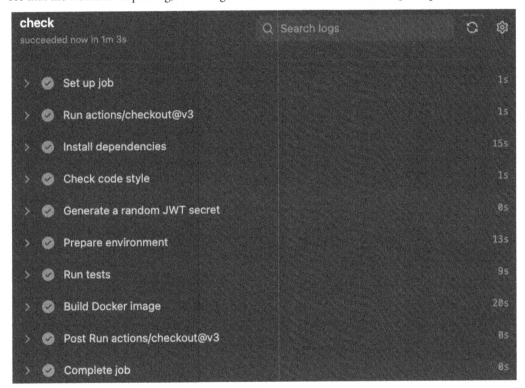

Figure 17.2 – Checking the workflow status

As you can see in *Figure 17.2*, we successfully built the Docker image. In the next section, we will learn how to make this image public.

Pushing the image to Docker Hub

You need to create a new repository in Docker Hub: `https://hub.docker.com/repositories/new`. In my case, I created a private repository called `nodejs-for-beginners`, as you can see in the following figure:

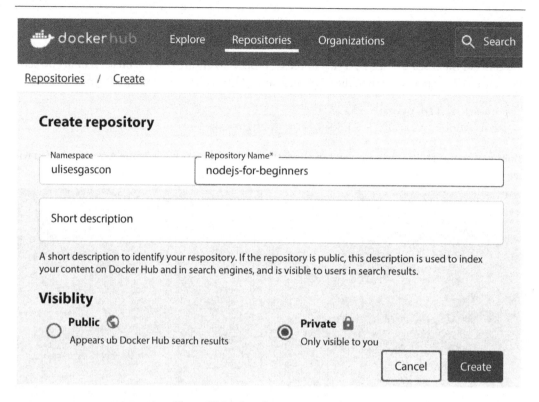

Figure 17.3 – Creating a new repository

I recommend you create a **Public** image but if you want to create a **Private** image, then you will need to log in to Docker Hub using the Docker CLI in your target machine (DigitalOcean Droplet or an alternative).

Then, from your local machine, you need to log in to Docker Hub using the following command:

```
docker login
```

You can then build the image with the name of the repository with the following command:

```
docker build -t YOUR-USER/YOUR-PROJECT:latest .
```

You will need to replace `YOUR-USER/YOUR-PROJECT` with your user and project name. In my case, I used `ulisesgascon/nodejs-for-beginners`.

This command will print a lot of logs but, at the end, you should not see any errors.

Then, you need to push the image to Docker Hub with the following command:

```
docker push YOUR-USER/YOUR-PROJECT
```

The output should be something like this, using the default `latest` tag:

```
The push refers to repository [docker.io/ulisesgascon/nodejs-for-
beginners]
204442a0fb02: Pushed
c797ca72cc32: Pushed
c2f374546252: Pushed
9841711cc266: Mounted from library/node
b748d0576055: Mounted from library/node
f866f7afbf16: Mounted from library/node
4693057ce236: Mounted from library/node
latest: digest: sha256:b82d23e398cf03165e89b8d1661125eda0f7b930e21
eef8c62281acd427e2d06 size: 1787
```

If you go to the Docker Hub repository, you will see that the image has been pushed and is ready to be used in other machines with the `docker pull YOUR-USER/YOUR-PROJECT:latest` command.

As you can see in the following figure, the image is available in the Docker Hub repository:

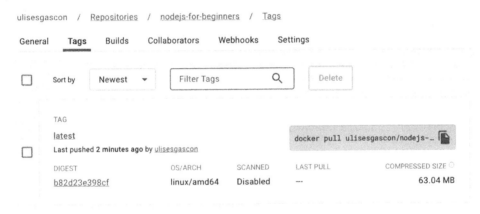

Figure 17.4 – The image in the Docker Hub repository

Publishing the image with GitHub Actions

As an alternative way to push the image to Docker Hub, we can publish the image directly with GitHub Actions. This is a great way to automate the process, avoiding the need to install Docker on our local machine and ensuring that the image is built correctly.

I invite you to achieve this by yourself as the last challenge of this book. Here are some hints to help you:

- GitHub guide to publishing Docker images: `https://docs.github.com/en/actions/guides/publishing-docker-images`

- A pipeline reference from the `simple-api` project: `https://github.com/UlisesGascon/simple-api/blob/main/.github/workflows/release.yml#L58`

In the next section, we will learn how to use Docker to run the project in the DigitalOcean Droplet.

Running the containers

In the previous chapter, we used PM2 to manage the lifecycle of our application. This time, we will do it differently: we will use Docker directly.

Our first step will be to install Docker on our target machine using SSH. Follow the installation guide (`https://docs.docker.com/engine/install/ubuntu/`) and then run `docker run hello-world`. The command will run without generating any error, this was a simple test to check whether the Docker engine was properly set up and running.

Please check that you stopped the PM2 application before we move to the next step as only one service can control port `3000`. Then, our last step will be to run the container but, this time, we won't need to build the container as we are pulling directly the image from Docker Hub:

```
docker run \
-e MONGODB_URI='mongodb+srv://<username>:<password>@<cluster-url>/
test?retryWrites=true&w=majority' \
-e PORT='3000' \
-e SALT_ROUNDS='10' \
-e JWT_SECRET='Tulfo0mO0PcAvjq^q3wQ24BXNI8$9R' \
-p 3000:3000 \
YOUR-USER/YOUR-PROJECT
```

You will need to replace `mongodb+srv://<username>:<password>@<cluster-url>/test?retryWrites=true&w=majority` with the connection string of your MongoDB Atlas cluster, and `YOUR-USER/YOUR-PROJECT` with your user and project name. In my case, I used `ulisesgascon/nodejs-for-beginners`.

We can see the application running as expected using the same IP address and port as when running PM2:

Photo by Brooke Cagle from Unsplash

Figure 17.5 – Application running using the Droplet external IP

In the next section, we will learn how to use Cloudflare to handle domains and certificates so your users won't need to remember your server's IP address to access it. If you are using a local machine, then your setup will be different as you probably won't have a static IP address so I suggest you follow this tutorial: `https://www.youtube.com/watch?v=DCxt9SAnkyc`. That way, your project will be accessible from the internet using ngrok (`https://ngrok.com/`). This will generate a connection tunnel to your machine and will expose your service as `https://xxxxsxx.ngrok.io` without worrying about network setup. Take into account that self-hosting applications that are open to internet traffic require a solid knowledge of security (`https://www.youtube.com/watch?v=URWlY3Qr918`), especially if you plan to use this approach for a long time.

> **Note**
>
> If you are having issues running the project in this chapter while following the steps, or you tried an alternative approach, you can use the `step6` folder from the source code that you downloaded at the beginning of the chapter to compare and fix possible bugs more easily.

In the next section, we will discuss how to do a proper domain setup and how to add an SSL certificate to the application.

Using Cloudflare

The application is running in the DigitalOcean Droplet but is accessible only by IP address and port. So, we need to do a proper domain setup and add an SSL certificate to the application. Acquiring a domain has a financial cost associated with it. Depending on the domain register, this cost may vary, and some domains are more expensive than others. SSL, together with **Transport Layer Security** (**TLS**), acts as a mechanism that we can add to our web project that will allow encryption between the clients and the server. In plain English, this will be the difference between accessing your website using http://myproject.com or https://myproject.com.

Many browsers today will prevent access to websites that are not using `https://`. We can use Cloudflare to enable both (`http` and `https`) and it is free for the basic features, so these are the steps to follow:

1. Add a new domain in Cloudflare: `https://www.youtube.com/watch?v=7hY3gp_-9EU`.

2. Add a new DNS record in Cloudflare: `https://www.youtube.com/watch?v=PYSIt3fEEoI`. In our case, we will add an A record with the domain name or subdomain and the IP address of the Droplet.

    You need to wait for the DNS propagation; this can take a while.

3. When the DNS propagation is finished, you can access the application using the domain name. In my case, I can access the application using the domain name `https://demo.ulisesgascon.com`. In the following figure, you can see the domain set up in Cloudflare:

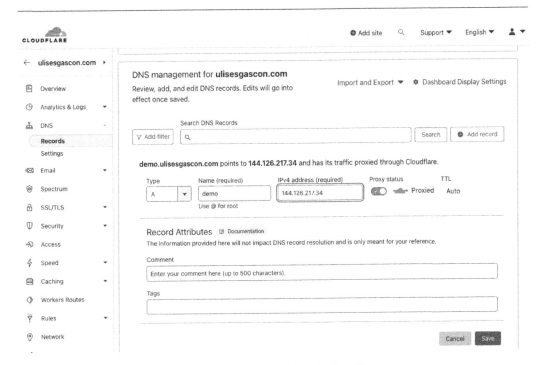

Figure 17.6 – Domain settings in Cloudflare

If you don't want to specify the port in the URL, you can run the application in port 443 (the default for `https`) or 80 (the default for `http`) instead of port 3000.

Now that we have finished with the domain setup, we can think of more advanced topics. In the next section, we will explore the Twelve-Factor App principles.

Next level – Twelve-Factor App principles

A great way to continue learning is to follow the Twelve-Factor App principles. This is a methodology to build modern, scalable, maintainable, and portable applications, and it is structured in 12 principles. The following are the 12 principles along with their definitions, taken from `https://12factor.net`:

- *Codebase*: One codebase tracked in revision control, many deploys
- *Dependencies*: Explicitly declare and isolate dependencies
- *Config*: Store config in the environment
- *Backing services*: Treat backing services as attached resources
- *Build, release, run*: Strictly separate build and run stages
- *Processes*: Execute the app as one or more stateless processes

- *Port binding*: Export services via port binding

- *Concurrency*: Scale out via the process model

- *Disposability*: Maximize robustness with fast startup and graceful shutdown

- *Dev/prod parity*: Keep development, staging, and production as similar as possible

- *Logs*: Treat logs as event streams

- *Admin processes*: Run admin/management tasks as one-off processes

There are many principles that we already covered in this book, such as configuration management, but there are some that we haven't covered yet. As an example, we don't have a staging environment and we haven't covered the admin processes. We built and deployed a simple app that is not designed to be used by real users or to handle real traffic, but if you want to build and deploy actual projects, it is highly recommended to follow these principles.

Overall, this is a great way to continue learning and getting a deeper understanding of the topic while improving the application that we just built together in this book.

In the next section, we will review the steps to clean up the resources that we used in this chapter just in case you don't need them anymore.

Cleaning up

Once we are done with the application, we can clean up the resources that we used in this chapter as we won't need them in the near future. Most of the resources are free but I highly recommend deleting the resources that you don't need anymore, especially if you are paying for any of those.

These are the resources that you can delete:

- DigitalOcean Droplet(s) created in this chapter

- MongoDB Atlas cluster

- Docker Hub repository

- Cloudflare domain

- GitHub repository (although I recommend you keep it as you can use it as a reference in the future)

> **Information**
> You can get additional hard drive space in your local environment by deleting the Docker images that you don't need anymore or the `node_modules` folders that you created while following along with the book.

This cleaning-up process was the last step for us in this journey. Before you move to the final section, I recommend you organize the notes you have taken during this journey and properly store them so you can access them in the future. In the next section, we will summarize this chapter.

Summary

In this chapter, we learned how to deploy our application to the public internet using Docker and how to use GitHub Actions for CI with our Docker images.

We learned how to use Docker to build the application and how to publish the image to Docker Hub, and we discussed how to do a proper domain setup and how to add an SSL certificate to the application using Cloudflare. We looked at the Twelve-Factor App principles and we reviewed the steps to clean up the resources that we used in this chapter.

Congratulations, you made it! This is the end of the journey. I hope that you enjoyed it and that you learned a lot. I hope that you will continue learning and improving your skills and that you will continue building amazing applications with Node.js. I will be very happy to hear from you and to know what you think about the book. You can reach me on X/Twitter (`https://twitter.com/kom_256`) or LinkedIn (`https://www.linkedin.com/in/ulisesgascon/`).

Further reading

- Twelve-Factor App principles: `https://12factor.net/`

- So what is Cloudflare?: `https://www.cloudflare.com/learning/what-is-cloudflare/`

- *What 19th century railroad wars can teach us about building a future-ready cloud*: `https://cloud.google.com/blog/transform/what-19th-century-railroad-wars-can-teach-us-about-cloud-containers`

Index

F

G

packtpub.com

Subscribe to our online digital library for full access to over 7,000 books and videos, as well as industry leading tools to help you plan your personal development and advance your career. For more information, please visit our website.

Why subscribe?

- Spend less time learning and more time coding with practical eBooks and Videos from over 4,000 industry professionals

- Improve your learning with Skill Plans built especially for you

- Get a free eBook or video every month

- Fully searchable for easy access to vital information

- Copy and paste, print, and bookmark content

Did you know that Packt offers eBook versions of every book published, with PDF and ePub files available? You can upgrade to the eBook version at packtpub.com and as a print book customer, you are entitled to a discount on the eBook copy. Get in touch with us at customercare@packtpub.com for more details.

At www.packtpub.com, you can also read a collection of free technical articles, sign up for a range of free newsletters, and receive exclusive discounts and offers on Packt books and eBooks.

Other Books You May Enjoy

If you enjoyed this book, you may be interested in these other books by Packt:

Node.js Web Development

David Herron

ISBN: 978-1-83898-757-2

- Install and use Node.js 14 and Express 4.17 for both web development and deployment
- Implement RESTful web services using the Restify framework
- Develop, test, and deploy microservices using Docker, Docker Swarm, and Node.js, on AWS EC2 using Terraform
- Get up to speed with using data storage engines such as MySQL, SQLite3, and MongoDB
- Test your web applications using unit testing with Mocha, and headless browser testing with Puppeteer
- Implement HTTPS using Let's Encrypt and enhance application security with Helmet

Node Cookbook

Bethany Griggs

ISBN: 978-1-83855-875-8

- Understand the Node.js asynchronous programming model
- Create simple Node.js applications using modules and web frameworks
- Develop simple web applications using web frameworks such as Fastify and Express
- Discover tips for testing, optimizing, and securing your web applications
- Create and deploy Node.js microservices
- Debug and diagnose issues in your Node.js applications

Packt is searching for authors like you

If you're interested in becoming an author for Packt, please visit `authors.packtpub.com` and apply today. We have worked with thousands of developers and tech professionals, just like you, to help them share their insight with the global tech community. You can make a general application, apply for a specific hot topic that we are recruiting an author for, or submit your own idea.

Share your thoughts

Now you've finished *Node.js for Beginners*, we'd love to hear your thoughts! Scan the QR code below to go straight to the Amazon review page for this book and share your feedback or leave a review on the site that you purchased it from.

`https://packt.link/r/1803245174`

Your review is important to us and the tech community and will help us make sure we're delivering excellent quality content.

Download a free PDF copy of this book

Thanks for purchasing this book!

Do you like to read on the go but are unable to carry your print books everywhere?

Is your eBook purchase not compatible with the device of your choice?

Don't worry, now with every Packt book you get a DRM-free PDF version of that book at no cost.

Read anywhere, any place, on any device. Search, copy, and paste code from your favorite technical books directly into your application.

The perks don't stop there, you can get exclusive access to discounts, newsletters, and great free content in your inbox daily

Follow these simple steps to get the benefits:

1. Scan the QR code or visit the link below

https://packt.link/free-ebook/9781803245171

2. Submit your proof of purchase
3. That's it! We'll send your free PDF and other benefits to your email directly

Made in United States
North Haven, CT
24 August 2024